Praise for Smart 2 Smarter

"Shows us all what it really means to be SMARTER! Great coaching for a changing world! A wonderful resource for coaches—and their clients."

—Marshall Goldsmith, world-renowned executive coach and *New York Times* best-selling author of *MOJO* and *What Got You Here Won't Get You There*

SMARTER Coaching Clients

"Cynthia served as an executive coach. She was great to work with and provided insights on how I could change in ways that would have a positive impact on my career. Within six months after finishing my work with Cynthia, I was promoted to a VP position."

—Tom Capetta, VP, Pharmaceuticals

"Cynthia is deeply committed to making sure her client's needs are met. I partnered with her to solve some team issues that we had in a business unit. She offered great assessments, insights and solutions. She delivered quality work that really made a difference with the team. This will always stand out to me as a success!"

—Jodi Lanis, VP Human Resources, Consulting

"The guidance, instruction and knowledge that Cynthia shared and employed were new, inventive, versatile and sensible. My management peers and staff immediately noted the changes. I recommend Cynthia Kivland to anyone who is willing to do the work to achieve results. I applaud her talents, and bow my Thanks."

—Rosa Miller, IT Director

Graduates who provided feedback on the book and the SMARTER process
(from the Board Certified Social Emotional Intelligence Coach Course, formerly known as EQ Career Strategist™) For more information, visit www.smart2smarter.com.

"The EQ Career Strategist™ course was insightful and powerful. I felt renewed and learned strategies to help clients become 'whole.' When you understand your strengths and limitations and learn how to manage them, you are able to establish boundaries, gain courage, find your inner peace, and engage in stronger relationships.

—Dr. Renee Green, CEQS, Passionate Coaching and Career Services

"The EQ Career Strategist™ Certification program hits the bull's eye when it comes to what individual contributors, team members and business leaders need to demonstrate for optimal effectiveness in the workplace. The program utilizes the most coveted EQ text and coaching tools. You will acquire an advanced understanding and application of emotional intelligence to not just merely survive, but to THRIVE, as you encounter relational roadblocks, bumps and hiccups along your career journey."

—Michelle Hauser-Wallace, CEQS, Corporate Recruiter

"Love the structured approach! [This] course has impacted me immensely and I feel so much more knowledgeable."

—Kim Batson, CLTMC, CCMC, CPBS, CEQS, CJST, CTC
and Career, Leadership & Personal Branding Coach

"The incredible amount of insight, practical skills and encyclopedic mind of Cynthia in this important course and generous sharing of resources made this class exceptional."

—Gail Fox, Assistant Director, Career and Leadership
Development, University of Wisconsin, Whitewater

"I had the pleasure of participating in the four-week EQ Career Strategist™ Certification course facilitated by Cynthia Kivland. The information that Cynthia covered during the course was comprehensive, and the resources/coaching tools she so kindly shared were amazing. In fact, the course far exceeded my expectations and I am extremely grateful [that] Cynthia shared both her wisdom and generosity

[and] the powerful coaching tools she granted us access to. I can certainly see how EQ and other coaching tools we covered during the course will support my clients in accelerating their levels of success in the job market and the workplace. Thank you once again, Cynthia and Leadership Coach Academy, for offering such an interesting and comprehensive course."

> —Annemarie Cross, Career Management Specialist, EQ Career Strategist, author of *10 Key Steps To Ace that Interview!* and featured expert on Career Success Radio, http://careersuccessradio.com

"*Smart 2 Smarter* is a terrific social and emotional intelligence resource for coaches, learning and development professionals, leaders and staff worldwide. The SMARTER Skills Model provides a conceptual framework that is rooted in solid theories. It contains stories that drive home key points, self-evaluations to heighten one's awareness, and numerous developmental activities to enhance oneself at work."

> —Nancy Branton, MA, PCC, CEO of Workplace Coach Institute, http://www.workplacecoachinstitute.com

smart*2*SMARTER

Seven Smarter Emotions
Every Employer Wants and
Every Employee Needs

Cynthia Kivland

Join the Smart 2 Smarter Community
to *LIVE and WORK SMARTER!*

Smart 2 Smarter is available as an eBook, and as a download for Kindle from Amazon.com and other retailers. For academic course or corporate adoption and speaking engagements, contact Cynthia Kivland at Cynthia@Smart2Smarter.com.

Cover and Book Design: Shawn Sargent (www.shawnsargent.com)
 & David Penna (www.davidpennastudios.com)
Managing Editor, Copy Editor, Creative and Design Editor: Shawn Sargent
Layout and Production: Shawn Sargent

If your behaviors, relationships and words
inspire you and others to dream more,
learn more, do more, give more and become
more, then you are living SMARTER!

–Cynthia Kivland, 2010

I dedicate this book to my husband Mike, my children, Kelly, Chelsey and Michael, my mother Anne Guzi, and my two grandchildren, Sabine Kivland Stackhouse and Michael Louis Kivland, each of whose support is abundant and who continue to be a wonderful source of learning, and provide a constant reality check on how to use the intelligence of your emotions to nurture powerful, loving, social connections.

I am also dedicating 5% of *Smart 2 Smarter* proceeds in support of Haiti:  Chelsey Kivland, a Fulbright Hays Program scholar, survived the Haiti earthquake in January 2010. Chelsey, along with her sister Kelly, brother Michael, and a cadre of SMARTER colleagues, are rebuilding a school in the town of Bel Air, Port-au-Prince. In support of their quest, 5% of all of the proceeds from the sale of this book will be donated to rebuild the school and the lives of Haitian children.

Since 2007, Konbit pou Rebati Bèlè (KOREBEL), which means "Team to Rebuild Bel Air," has run a primary school and community cafeteria in Bel Air, one of the poorest and most historic neighborhoods of central Port-au-Prince, Haiti. Until the earthquake on January 12, they provided quality education to 400 students and low-cost meals to the community. The KOREBEL school and cafeteria collapsed in the earthquake, halting the school year and the futures of countless children. Now KOREBEL is holding classes for 200 students in makeshift tents with limited supplies.

With your help, we hope to construct sturdy, temporary classrooms—designed by Terreform ONE [Open Network Ecology], an ecological design group for Urban Infrastructure, Building, Planning and Art, based in Brooklyn, NY.
Retrieved from http://korebel.org

Please visit www.korebel.org for more information.

Acknowledgments

This work of non-fiction is based on my research of *smart* people, my passion for bringing humanity into the workplace and into one's life, and my twenty-five years of experience as a Board Certified Coach, Master Career Counselor, emotional intelligence trainer and Certified Leadership and Talent Management Coach.

The following individuals have made significant contributions to this book

- Daniel Goleman, author of the bestselling book that brought EQ to the world's attention and *Mindfulness @ Work* (http://danielgoleman.info)
- Joshua Freedman, renowned emotional intelligence expert and COO, Six Seconds (http://jmfreedman.com)
- Marshall Goldsmith, world-renowned executive coach and author on coaching individuals to be their personal best (www.marshallsmithlibrary.com)
- Graduates of Board Certified Social Emotional Intelligence Coach (www.smart2smarter.com)
- Gerry, Alexia, Robert, Bo and Philip, my colleagues in the PEI moderator training, Liautaud Institute, EQ (www.liautaudinstitute.com)
- Shawn Sargent, editorial manager, creative and copy editor, production artist, cover and interior co-designer (www.shawnsargent.com)
- David Penna, cover and interior co-designer, website designer (www.davidpennastudios.com/design.html)

A special shout out to all my SMARTER clients and students who have contributed to the research and provided feedback on content and case studies—I thank you. It is your stories and triumphs that bring both significance and reality to my words.

Table of Contents

smart*2*SMARTER

In the Beginning

The Four Research Questions

Leaders, individuals and scholars have often asked, "So, what prompted you to write this book?" Over the last 25 years of working as a trainer, coach and consultant, I have had the privilege of working with very smart graduates, millennials, boomers, leaders and their teams. My clients have spanned a range of professions, including scientists, programmers, professors, CEOs, CFOs, presidents, financial analysts and engineers. Each of these individuals had "designer college degrees" and were deemed well accomplished by their peers. They were employed in good jobs, but were unhappy—each stating they had "lost their groove." I also work with smart people who have derailed their careers, often leaders and those who work alongside them. These smart people do not intentionally set out to derail their careers, but do so as a result of unhealthy behaviors and habits that take their career off track.

Whether these smart people derailed their careers due to unhealthy habits or were unhappy and employed, I began to witness a series of behaviors, excuses and stories that had nothing to do with intellect, age, gender or level within the organization. What these behaviors, habits and excuses did indicate was the inability to make emotional or social connections that ignite the passion—or "groove"—in oneself and in others.

Thus, I began to acquire knowledge, research and best practices on how emotional and social intelligence impacts one's career success and significance. Along with several colleagues, I developed training and coaching programs for career clients, leaders and teams on the benefits of emotional and social intelligence.

As part of these programs, I began to ask four questions:

1. What are two characteristics of a smart person you know?
2. What defines a smart person in your organization or culture?
3. What derails a smart person in your workplace?
4. If you were to give a career tip to a smart person, what would it be?

The responses I received from a sampling of over 1,000 individuals, between January 2007 and January 2010, in various industries, employment levels and cultures, prompted me to write this book on the *SMARTER skills every smart person needs and every employer wants!*

In the following pages, I have summarized quotes and trends of these key four questions.

1. What are two characteristics of a smart person you know?

Most respondents stated that it was difficult to identify one smart person. Whether the smart person was from academia, government, corporate or technical and scientific environments, several common themes began to emerge.

A respondent from Poland stated, "The way I understand being smart is having high intellectual skills, the ability to discern issues, and an insightful mind as well as substantial work knowledge. It also connotes certain quickness of reasoning, and the ability to arrive at the conclusions faster than average. Smart people I know seek answers. They want to expand their knowledge, are fast learners and are able to look at issues from various angles. Smart is the opposite of acting slow, rigid, superficial or one-sided. On a cultural note, what smart seems to connotate in America goes beyond the Polish translation of smart. What smart means in America is a compound meaning of two words in Polish—*smart* and *wise*."

Another international respondent stated that smart is "intellectually bright and able to connect and communicate well. Smart people make common-sense judgments, are able to think in innovative ways, and can often predict well what is going to happen next (visionary)."

Other respondents distinguished *intellectually smart* from smart: Intellectually smart people are generally extraordinarily good at one discipline only. The smartest people I know are well-read in multiple disciplines, and they surround themselves with an impartial sounding board. Smart people do their job well, produce what is necessary, yet earn the respect and favor of their peers, those they report to and their community. They have the courage to say what needs to be said, and demonstrate respect for the concerns and challenges of others.

The smartest people typically have outstanding communication skills, especially listening skills. They have the ability to take in a lot of information, immediately sort through it and pick out the key or important pieces of information. —VP level

The smartest person I know happens to be a member of Mensa; he is really good at picking up concepts and ideas in both the abstract and physical reality (e.g., how this machine or that computer program works); [he] can speak with authority on a variety of topics (well-informed); his mind works fast; [he is] very articulate in speaking and writing, and he also happens to make reasoned, good choices; he's pretty good at life (which may be more a function of wisdom and not innate intelligence...). —Millennial respondent

Smart people recognize that work gets done by and through other people. Relationships are key. They gather information and listen to learn what the other person needs, thinks or feels. Then they know how to respond, and how to develop the relationship. —Technical leader

Quiet but assertive confidence, thirst for knowledge and learning, listens, is aware of own weaknesses and builds contacts around them to compliment areas of improvement; has a genuine balanced approach to work and home, communicates clearly and believes in its strength; is pleasant to everyone. —Female HR leader

Core theme characteristics of smart people

- Inquisitive and intellectually curious
- Great listener rather than talker
- Not the dominant person in a discussion
- Thinks ahead several steps
- Not reactionary, has flexibility
- Has wisdom based on reflection and experience
- Learns from own failures and mistakes, as well as the failures and mistakes of others
- Intuitive about consequences and trends
- Highly analytical, thinks strategically
- Ability to cultivate powerful, authentic relationships
- Can articulate complex ideas or patterns
- Honest desire to understand and develop others

- Constantly reading or learning
- Generosity
- Authenticity

2. *What defines a smart person in your organization or culture?*

The second question sought to discover how one's workplace or organization defines a smart person. Respondents were from government, education, counseling, financial, human resources, technical and healthcare work environments. The majority of responses do not mention high IQ or grade-point average, but instead mention other skills that relate to social and emotional skills.

One healthcare worker stated that a smart person in their organization is "insightful, knowledgeable and has a horizontal mind. They display qualities clustered under the term 'wise.' He or she displays empathy and understanding for difference in opinions. He or she truly values high self-awareness. Such a person will withhold judgment until uncovering the hidden issues, and seeks to confront one's biases."

Another respondent stated, "Smart people in my organization have a *politically smart* half of the brain. They do not get bent out of shape in conflict. They are good at moving things along to reach a company's overall goals and objectives. They do not necessarily have high IQs, but know how to read people. They understand that when individuals are not in sync, even the best ideas have dim futures. Smart, [in] my organization, means the person slows down to listen. Fast is not always smart. Respect, [in] my organization, is more valued than smart."

Many respondents stated that a smart person is an individual who understands the "big picture" and is able to lead the organization, regardless of the immediate impact on them or their teams. Another common theme was that a smart person has the drive to continually develop themselves. They are the CEO of their career. They inspire and motivate others to act, produce and think beyond their comfort zone. They are not afraid to make themselves redundant in defining better ways to do things. They are not intimidated by more experienced or educated people.

Other respondents emphasized a results orientation. They described a smart person in their organization as someone who works hard and is dedicated to the mission of the organization; a person that can accomplish any given task with little guidance. They appear natural at doing the work. They enlarge the scope of the position and are respected by others in the organization. A smart person in a financial firm was described as one that has excellent command of the technical material, or is a very shrewd political operator—they can predict the immediate future while also overseeing large or multiple projects.

A respondent in an international organization defined character traits of smart people that are respected and rewarded in his global organization, such as the ability to recognize opportunities, exhibit emotional intelligence, communicate candidly, show willingness to hear feedback and learn from it, and appreciate the courage of others to offer it. Additional character strengths include the openness, desire and interest to understand oneself and one's personal strengths, and to capitalize on those strengths for the benefit (career and leisure time) of self and others.

Character strengths also included *interpersonal smartness*. A smart person in another global organization had the ability to cultivate the relationships that allowed them to produce results, and had sensitivity to red flags that identified lack of integrity, authenticity or emotional intelligence of associates, which allowed major breakdowns to be avoided.

A summary of core themes of how organizations define smart people

- Forward-thinking
- Anticipates market changes
- Adaptable
- Listens
- Sees patterns or themes, and makes connections
- Interpersonal skills
- Emotionally intelligent
- Good memory for people, issues or information
- Driven and persistent (sees a job through to the end)
- Researches and learns

3. What derails a smart person in your workplace?

The third question sought to gain insight about what derails a smart person's career. The responses are from multiple work environments and employee levels. A majority of respondents used their boss as a reference point for their smart person.

Some career derailers had to do with overcomplicating events or tasks. This overcomplication creates a climate of emotional overwhelm. Examples of this are: Creating a vision without action to support the vision, or underestimating how long a change will take. One respondent stated that when in overwhelm, they get overemotional about their "vision" and lose objectivity, which then pushes their hot buttons and everyone's around them.

Another theme was an exaggeration of strengths. Each person's strengths can be a derailer when overused or not balanced. One respondent stated, "Weaknesses are [not always] the issue—it's often overused strengths that get people in trouble. Smart people in my organization derail if they do not know when their strengths are on steroids."

A lack of passion or challenge was also cited as a career derailer. A human resource director stated that derailing factors would include a lack of stimulation at work. The brain is a muscle, and counting widgets may not be the best exercise. Ego may also come into play as a smart person is relegated to dealing with tasks, problems or people that are perceived to be beneath them and their abilities. "One would think that with great abilities comes great expectations for success, and when that doesn't occur frequently enough, disappointment may follow," said a respondent. What can also derail smart people are tasks where they cannot incorporate their broad thinking skills or apply perspective taking.

Overconfidence in one's ability to be the best at everything can often result in an entitlement mentality—another career derailer. This creates a toxic environment where others perceive the smart person as arrogant and a corporate bully. Communication derailers include an inability to read social cues. The smart person believes that others don't understand what they are saying, or can't appreciate their depth of knowledge. This leads to a perception that these smart people lack sensitivity to others' needs when communicating. One respondent stated, "Smart people who derail their careers are just plain annoying—they don't know how to socially interact with others."

A respondent from a technical firm described a career derailer as a person who cannot complete a project on time. "Often during a project, more information becomes available, and the project gets delayed due to information paralysis." This very smart person gets stuck in making the project perfect, focusing too much on the small stuff, which eventually derails the project.

In a healthcare firm, the biggest career derailer was listed as being arrogant toward co-workers and exhibiting very little patience with them. Another derailer cited was that really smart people get bored. If the organization is not committed to keeping these people engaged, they can wander off, sometimes abandoning what could have been a continuing rise within that organization. Or they become complacent with what they do, and often don't move onto something more challenging, even if they are encouraged to by the organization. They have difficulties with interpersonal situations because they expect others to understand what they know or want as quickly as they do. This can lead to inappropriate comments, emotional outbursts and blaming the organization or others.

Finally, a core derailer was a belief that a person is the smartest, and therefore cannot possibly learn anything from anyone. This is the blind belief that one's ideas are so good that there's no need to convince anyone, play politics or use interpersonal skills to get an idea across. This was summarized as the unwillingness to recognize and learn from areas of blindness, and especially the inability to cultivate relationships needed to accomplish what is important to that person or the institution.

A summary of core themes of career derailers

- Overconfidence and arrogance
- Inability to listen to, or learn from, others
- Lack of, or underdeveloped, people skills
- No ability, or underdeveloped ability, to delegate
- Belief that no one can do the job as well as they can
- Need to always be right
- Stubbornness
- Emotional and social stagnation

4. If you were to give a career tip to a smart person, what would it be?

The final question addressed how a smart person can become SMARTER. Most respondents agreed that *intellectually smart* people would benefit from projects or committees where they can sharpen their interpersonal skills. Another core theme was to be CEO of your career; choose a career that engages you, especially the core aspects of you, and that involves you to the degree that you often feel *in flow*—"in the groove" (see page 33 for more information on being *in flow*).

A healthcare respondent shared the career tip of learning how to respond to those aspects of a job that are less compatible with your individual style and preference. This included taking inventory of your strengths and style. Learn how to adjust your style to other people to have more influencing power in your organization. Remember that things change, and whatever might be frustrating you now could change in the blink of an eye.

A respondent from the technology arena stated that it is important for smart people to realize that no job can meet all of their expectations. Smart people need to learn how to be crystal clear on their non-negotiable values and decide what they cannot live without (as opposed to what they can live with or tolerate).

Another respondent shared the career tip that just because you are smart doesn't mean that your career will spiral upward in a consistent way. According to Marshall Goldsmith's bestselling book, *What Got You Here Won't Get You There: How Successful People Become Even More Successful!*, it takes more than being smart to sustain a career of success and significance. If you are not the expert, then bring someone aboard who is. No matter how good you are at something, you always have to take a look at the market to see where it is and where it's headed. Being complacent in a job without looking at your future is a professional death sentence.

More than 70% of respondents provided the career tip of asking for feedback. Ask, *What else can I pay attention to?* and *How can I be of help to you?* The eye cannot see itself—we need perspective and input from others. Invest in learning how to have candid, direct, frank and caring conversations. Say what needs to be said, and learn how to do it as diplomatically as possible. Also, realize that the skill in cultivating relationships is fundamental to accomplishment, and it becomes increasingly more important as you advance in your career. A truly intelligent person can learn even from the lesser parts of all of us. Be open to suggestions—*you don't know everything about everything.*

Another career tip would be to make an honest assessment of yourself so that you understand your strengths and weaknesses. Then work to put yourself on a career path that favors your strengths, and learn to appreciate how those, coupled with the opposite "smarts," can benefit you.

Finally, career tips were shared that distinguished intellectual and other kinds of smartness. There is more to success in business than inherent intelligence, and there are more important "smarts" than "book smarts." Be prepared to play the game, and know that at least at one point in your career you will be underemployed, even given your abilities and your experiences—that's just life.

Career tips for smart people include

- Use common sense
- Be humble and listen
- Follow your heart, not your head
- Network and remain open to all opportunities

- Ask questions to ensure comprehension (don't assume others understand you)
- Do not ignore people or the political factor
- Embrace learning from others

Summary

As I reviewed the responses gathered over the three years, it became clear that a new definition of *smart* had emerged. Also, the literature on emotional and social intelligence was becoming more salient as must-read career books. Furthermore, my coaching, consulting and training experience provided me "on the ground" research and validation that to be and contribute your personal best required more than just being smart. And it certainly did not mean being the smartest person in the room.

What has emerged is the desire and ability to be SMARTER, to view SMARTER as a process, without an end-point. To be SMARTER involves intellectual, social and emotional intelligence, with the latter two driving one's career success or derailment.

The remainder of this book will focus on the *seven SMARTER skills* most employers want—and the skills *everyone needs to be their personal best*. I suggest you read a chapter, complete the exercises, reflect and then act. If you are a smart person, I ask you to be patient. Expect setbacks. Ask for feedback. Be humble. **Be SMARTER!**

After every chapter is a list of resources that align with each of the **SMARTER** skills: **S**trengths, **M**astery, **A**ttraction, **R**esilience, **T**olerance, **E**volution and **R**eciprocity. Use the worksheets in the book and online to be your personal best.

Join the *Smart2Smarter Community* and receive free access to additional tools, articles and assessments to *develop the skills every employer wants and every smart person needs*.

Go to www.smart2smarter.com and click on *Join the Smart2Smarter Community* to be your personal best!

Join to *LIVE* SMARTER!

Introduction
Chapter 1

Smart Is Not Enough to Stay Employed

According to renowned psychologist Daniel Goleman, author of *Emotional Intelligence, Working with Emotional Intelligence*, and *Leadership That Gets Results*, "At best, intelligence (IQ) contributes 20% to the factors that determine career success, which leaves 80% to other factors." These other factors are the *must-have employability skills* wanted by most employers in all industries and at all levels. These must-have skills are not based on how smart you are (IQ). They are based on how you manage your emotions (EQ) and social skills (SQ) to either optimize or derail your career, and often the career of those with whom you work!

Employers want employees who do more than show up to work. They want employees who show up with their head and their heart to contribute their personal best. This requires a new kind of *smart*. It requires social and emotional intelligence to positively impact your own or others' (peers, bosses, direct reports or customers) thoughts and actions to achieve improved performance or business results.

Emotions and SMARTER Employability

Emotional intelligence is the name of a discipline that focuses on human behavior. Some experts call it "EI" and some call it "EQ." For this book, we will call it EQ.

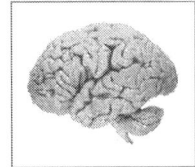

Research in the field began as a backlash to IQ. Historically, we tend to be awed by individuals with high intelligence. However, we all know people who are not "IQ smart" but have high career success and fulfillment. At the same time, we also know people who have high IQs who were not productive or good at working with others, and who had poor relationships and often a career that derailed. Obviously there is something more to career success than IQ!

EQ is *not*, as Goleman is misquoted as saying, "eight times more important to your success and happiness than your IQ." He said it could be. Other things being equal (expertise, education, skills and experience), most employers would choose the candidate with the best EQ skills.

Staying Engaged and Employed Requires SMARTER Skills

To stay engaged and employed in a global economy requires looking at your career with a view of improvement and adaptation. Consider these 21st century career realities:

- 7 out of 10 Americans say that they would change jobs tomorrow if wishing could make it so
- The average twenty-something entering the job market will experience nine to thirteen job shifts in their career
- A generation ago, statistics stated that a person would have an average of three to five career shifts within a working lifetime; today, the expectation is five to seven
- A career shift is a complete redefinition of your vocational self—from financial analyst to teacher, for example
- The average job in America now lasts 3.6 years

These projected median figures mean that 50% of you can expect more job changes. In a global, ever-changing career world, how do you not just survive, but thrive? I propose that what will distinguish those who remain employable during career and economic shifts are individuals who:

- Contribute the best of their head (knowledge)
- Use the positive energy of their heart (emotion)
- Learn from mistakes and successes (learning)
- Inspire others to contribute their personal best and, if necessary, provide the hard truths (leadership)

The SMARTER Skills Employers Want

Employers, whether in the United States, Mexico, India or Europe, state that they have no problem finding new graduates or mature workers who are competent in their chosen disciplines. However, these same employers have difficulty finding workers with the SMARTER skills they want and need. *What are these SMARTER skills?* They are the skills listed below, where the gap is the biggest between the employers' needs and the candidate's perceived availability.

- **Personal initiative** without excessive external rewards
- **Focused commitment** to the task, the person and the deadline
- **Desire, skills and experience** to contribute to team goals
- **Oral communication,** bilingual preferred
- **Business writing and report communication,** not internet jargon
- **Leadership and followership,** a willingness and ability to lead and be led
- **Ability to solve problems,** not needing someone to fix your "issues"

What Does the Hedgehog Have to Do With SMARTER Skills?

In *Good to Great: Why Some Companies Make the Leap...and Others Don't,* Jim Collins introduced "The Hedgehog Concept." The hedgehog survives and thrives because it knows one thing really well: How to roll up in a ball with needle-sharp defenses. When examining companies that went *from good to great,* Collins found that the great companies are hedgehogs. "Hedgehogs see what is essential, and ignore the rest," stated Collins.

We all need to become masters of hedge-hogging by *doing great work with and for others* that provides an economic and social value.

We need to continuously ask and answer

- What am I deeply passionate about?
- What can I be the best at in the world?
- What am I *not* the best at? Can I let go of that?
- What drives my career motivation engine?
- What stalls my career motivation engine?

Does the Hedgehog Need a Heart?

Absolutely! It is the heart that ignites the passion to contribute your personal best. It is the heart that encourages or discourages others to take your lead. How many of you have been told, *Do not bring your emotions to work*? To be employable (contributing your personal best) in a global economy requires just that—bringing your emotions to work. And it is hard not to anyway. Building on Goleman's social and emotional intelligence framework is to really know and articulate the business of you—*You, Inc.*—(Focus on Me), demonstrate initiative and buoyancy to manage career and economic shifts (Personal Impact), learn about and appreciate diversity (Focus on Others), and demonstrate entrepreneurism, support and guidance to bring out the personal best in others (Social Impact) (see *Focus and Impact* chart on next page for more information).

It is your emotions that either optimize or derail your personal best.
It is your emotions that encourage you to embrace
and understand cultural diversity.
It is your emotions that inspire others to be their personal best.

Where do you start?

So, you are a parent raising a very smart kid, or a teacher trying not to leave a child behind, or a new graduate or manager with a team of very smart people. What we now know is that getting the "A" or mastering a skill does not guarantee career and business success. And it definitely does not guarantee career significance. We need to teach, model and coach others and ourselves to develop SMARTER skills and behaviors. This requires not settling for being smart, but reaching for being SMARTER!

Career Success vs. Career Significance

Setting goals for *career success is driven by being the best **in** the world* while setting goals to achieve *career significance is driven by being the best **for** the world*. It is the difference between defining yourself as what you do and defining yourself by how you live.

Being SMARTER means you must be able to effectively self-evaluate yourself with objectivity, to be able to step outside of yourself and really look at who you are through your behavior. This enables you to make powerful and personal choices about how you will contribute your personal best.   *−Kivland, 2006*

The SMARTER Skills That Matter

SELF Strengths and efficacy

MASTERY Emotions, thoughts and actions

ATTRACTION Energy and optimism

RESILIENCE Adapt, reinvent and renew

TOLERANCE Accept, acknowledge and appreciate

EVOLVE Innovate, initiate and improve

RECIPROCITY Teach and be taught, lead and be led, receive and give

SMARTER Skills Require Focus and Impact!

	Success	Significance
Focus How well I know and appreciate my own and others' uniqueness	Focus on Me **S**elf: Strengths and Efficacy	Focus on Others **T**olerance: Accept, Acknowledge and Appreciate
Impact How I optimize or derail my own and others' career success and significance	Impact to Me **M**astery: Emotions, Thoughts and Actions **A**ttraction: Energy and Optimism **R**esilience: Adapt, Reinvent and Renew	Impact to Others **E**volve: Greatness or Sabotage (Innovate, Initiate and Improve) **R**eciprocity: Teach and Be Taught, Lead and Be Led, Receive and Give

Still Not Convinced That SMARTER Skills Matter to Your Career?

Let's look at how SMARTER skills align with 21st century economic, social, career and lifestyle realities:

- **Competition is global and local** All employees are competing with other employees halfway across the world or an aisle away. It will be *tolerance* and *reciprocity* that distinguish those who can build relationships, whether across the globe or down the hall.

- **Customers are more fickle** How well you know and treat your customers is directly related to SMARTER skills. All relationships are a reflection of the one you have with yourself. It is that simple! It will be *acceptance* and *appreciation* that will make this happen.

- **Job security is a myth** The old work paradigm reached its peak two generations ago and was based on trading loyalty for security. The new paradigm is one of trading performance commitment for meaningful work and contribution. *Self-knowledge* and *resilience* are required in the new paradigm.

- **Career success vs. career significance** It is the difference between defining yourself as what you do and defining yourself by how you live. Significant goal-driven behavior is motivated by your principles and values—core components of *attraction* and *reciprocity*.

- **Life balance is on everyone's wish list** I have counseled over 1,000 clients on achieving career fulfillment, and I cannot remember one client that did not want more life/work balance. In a 24/7, just-in-time, drive-through economy, it will be how well you *master* your *energy*, remain vulnerable and build *reciprocal* relationships that will help you and the companies you work for set healthy life/work boundaries.

- **Everyone's job involves high tech (IQ), high touch (EQ) and now high Concept** According to Daniel Pink, author of *A Whole New Mind: Why Right-Brainers Will Rule the Future,* there is a new set of abilities necessary to stay employed and engaged. These new skills are described as right-brain driven, and they rely on *empathy* and *reciprocity*.

Still Not Convinced?
Take These Seven SMARTER Steps to Increase Your Employability

1. **Find passion in what you do** It is important to choose a profession that gets you excited. Passion gives us energy like no other feeling. You speak about your work with enthusiasm. When people hear you talk about your work, they pick up on your enthusiasm and energy. Once you discover that profession, discover on a more specific level what you are doing that excites you. (**SMARTER skill: Strengths**)

2. **Find excellence in what you do** What is it that you do well? These may be specific skills or more general attributes. You can be very good with technical tasks, or handling difficult customers. When you have identified your excellence, tell the world. You will also be able to see how your excellence can transcend to other jobs. (**SMARTER skill: Efficacy**)

3. **Become a lifelong learner** Constantly improving and diversifying your skills is critical to lifetime success and employment. This may mean working with a coach or a mentor. Every quarter, review your skills with an eye toward the future. Identify two new skills to acquire, then take classes, find a master, surf the internet or read books. **(SMARTER skill: Evolve)**

4. **Be flexible** Instead of whining every time there is a change, look for how you can take advantage of a new need or opportunity to make yourself valuable. **(SMARTER skill: Resilience)**

5. **Focus on productivity** Look for ways to save money, time and resources to align with current and future business goals. When you actively look for ways to improve productivity and efficiency, you are seen as a value-added commodity. See yourself as an intrapreneur, always thinking in ways that are new and improved. **(SMARTER skill: Evolve)**

6. **Be a team player** Seek opportunities to help your co-workers, boss or customers shine. Express genuine appreciation to someone each week who has contributed to your career success or fulfillment. **(SMARTER skill: Reciprocity)**

7. **Market yourself to both internal and external customers** You are the CEO of *You, Inc.*, and you have a reputation to create and maintain. Let people know about your career successes. Customers, people within your company, colleagues or friends need to feel your enthusiasm for what you are doing. Be authentic—not self-promoting. **(SMARTER skill: Attraction)**

Join the Smart 2 Smarter Community *to access the following activities and additional* **INTRODUCTION** *resources and assessments online at* www.Smart2Smarter.com

How Do You Define Career Success and Significance? book and website

The SMARTER Emotional and Social Intelligence Assessment book and website

SMARTER Focus and Impact book and website

Daniel Goleman's EQ Strengths website

SWOT Analysis website

Activity   How Do You Define Career Success and Significance?

Definitions

Career Success vs. Career Significance Setting goals for *career success is driven by being the best in the world*, while setting goals to achieve *career significance is driven by being the best for the world.*

Reflect...	Then Ask...
Look at your life as it is right now	
What is most important to you?	What do others see as important to you?
What are you noticeably good at doing?	What do others see you noticeably good at doing?
What is your number one asset?	What do others see as your number one asset?
How do you want others to describe your success in the world of work? Of life?	How do others describe your success in the world of work? Of life?
How do you want others to describe your significance in the world of work? Of life?	How do others see your significance in the world of work? Of life?

Activity   The SMARTER Emotional and Social Intelligence Assessment

This self-evaluation will measure your perception of the seven areas of emotional and social intelligence within *The SMARTER Career Model* (see page 14). **In the space provided next to each of the following statements, circle the number that best describes your agreement with the item, using the scale below.** After each series of five questions, calculate the total and write it in the shaded area after each section.

1 = Mostly Disagree	3 = Slightly Disagree 5 = Moderately Agree
2 = Moderately Disagree	4 = Slightly Agree 6 = Mostly Agree

1.	I use negative *and* positive emotions as a source of wisdom about how to navigate my life.	1 2 3 4 5 6
2.	I know the BestFit components required for my career success and significance (see Strengths: My BestFit Life, Chapter 4).	1 2 3 4 5 6
3.	I have confidence that my strengths will positively impact my own and others' career and life.	1 2 3 4 5 6
4.	I know how to manage my own and others' expectations of my success.	1 2 3 4 5 6
5.	People who know their emotional, cognitive and social strengths are better pilots of their lives.	1 2 3 4 5 6
	Strengths Total	
6.	I face my negative feelings and work through the issue at hand.	1 2 3 4 5 6
7.	I am in charge of how I feel about myself.	1 2 3 4 5 6
8.	After something has upset me, I find it easy to regain my composure.	1 2 3 4 5 6
9.	I challenge my life stories and create new ones based on present reality.	1 2 3 4 5 6
10.	I know when I react from a position of strength or weakness after a crucial event.	1 2 3 4 5 6
	Mastery Total	
11.	When challenged, I am good at attracting what I need to flow with life's demands.	1 2 3 4 5 6
12.	I see life as half-full and not half-empty.	1 2 3 4 5 6
13.	I am often able to improve the moods of others.	1 2 3 4 5 6
14.	I am adept at reading people's feelings by their facial expressions.	1 2 3 4 5 6
15.	I know how to minimize the distractions in my life.	1 2 3 4 5 6
	Attraction Total	

16.	I do not recycle and dwell on negative emotions that reinforce the blame or victim role.	1 2 3 4 5 6
17.	I am able to motivate myself to try again in the face of setbacks.	1 2 3 4 5 6
18.	When challenged, I know how to move from a survive mode of fight or flight to a thrive mode of hope and solutions.	1 2 3 4 5 6
19.	I easily enter into a thrive-and-flow state, a state characterized by calmness, alertness and focus.	1 2 3 4 5 6
20.	I see setbacks as challenges to learn from, and I move on to try new approaches.	1 2 3 4 5 6
Resilience Total		
21.	I am effective at listening to other people's problems.	1 2 3 4 5 6
22.	I am sensitive to the emotional needs of others and respond appropriately.	1 2 3 4 5 6
23.	I know what to get rid of in my life to be more tolerant.	1 2 3 4 5 6
24.	I am aware of subtle social signals that indicate what others need.	1 2 3 4 5 6
25.	I demonstrate empathy toward others and myself.	1 2 3 4 5 6
Tolerance Total		
26.	I am able to formulate and execute a life and career plan.	1 2 3 4 5 6
27.	I know how to influence others by responding appropriately to their emotions, motivations and desires.	1 2 3 4 5 6
28.	I use positive energy to create positive outcomes in my own and others' lives.	1 2 3 4 5 6
29.	I can easily set negative feelings aside when called upon to perform.	1 2 3 4 5 6
30.	I seek creative and rational solutions to life's challenges.	1 2 3 4 5 6
Evolution Total		
31.	I have a calming and inspiring influence on other people, and often improve the moods of others.	1 2 3 4 5 6
32.	I easily receive advice, wisdom and leadership from others.	1 2 3 4 5 6
33.	People view me as an effective model for bringing out the best in others.	1 2 3 4 5 6
34.	I am a good person to come to for advice about handling relationships.	1 2 3 4 5 6
35.	I help others use their motivations to achieve their personal goals.	1 2 3 4 5 6
Reciprocity Total		
All Total		

Interpreting Your Scores

Compare your scores with the chart below to assess your current standing on the various social and emotional competencies relative to a cross-industry sampling of managers and professionals. Each of the SMARTER competencies are important to perform well in all careers, whether at home, on site, in the virtual community or in another country. Most importantly, *these SMARTER competencies are needed to have a life filled with career success and significance.* This book will provide you with the knowledge, tools and actions to create a development plan to bring out the personal best in yourself and others!

SMARTER Competency	Needs Substantial Development	Needs Some Development	Definite Strength
Strengths Knowing how to use your strengths and emotions to make decisions that bring out your own and others' personal best. **Strengths and Efficacy**	15 or below	16 - 24	25 or above
Mastery Mastering your emotional impulses to thrive and not just survive. **Emotions, Thoughts, Stories and Actions**	15 or below	16 - 24	25 or above
Attraction Attract what needs to be present to be your personal best, and eliminate or manage distractions. **Energy and Optimism**	15 or below	16 - 24	25 or above
Resilience Persist in the face of setbacks and build reserves to pursue your goals. **Adapt, Reinvent and Renew**	15 or below	16 - 24	25 or above
Tolerance Accept other people's emotions and behaviors without judgment, and eliminate tolerations that restrict evolving. **Accept, Acknowledge and Appreciate**	15 or below	16 - 24	25 or above
Evolution Seek opportunities to achieve success and significance. **Innovate, Initiate and Improve**	15 or below	16 - 24	25 or above
Reciprocity Willingness, readiness and ability to Teach and Be Taught, Lead and Be Led, Receive and Give	15 or below	16 - 24	25 or above
Total	90 or below	91 - 120	121 or above

Iceberg

> What is opportunity, and when does it knock? It never knocks. You can wait a whole lifetime, listening, hoping, and you will hear no knocking. You are opportunity, and you must knock on the door leading to your destiny. You prepare yourself to recognize opportunity, to pursue and seize opportunity as you develop the strength of your personality, and build a self-image with which you are able to live–with your self-respect alive and growing. *–Maxwell Maltz*

Are SMARTER skills part of your personality, either something you have or don't have? The answer is both yes and no. The good news is that SMARTER skills can be learned with practice and reinforcement. However, as individuals of habit, we default to behaviors that say, *This is the way I do things*. Personality inventories, such as the *Myers-Briggs Type Indicator*© or *Occupational Personality Questionnaire*© have shown that each of us develops a stable and comfortable default personality style. This default style influences how we approach our work, life and school experiences, and how we interact with others. It does not change much after our mid 20s; however, to stay employable, SMARTER workers know they must manage and adapt their style to the situation, person, culture or social context.

Combining head and heart is the link to SMARTER skills. As stated in the introduction, Daniel Goleman's premise is that "sensitivity to emotional states (one's own and others') and effective relationship skills are the critical competencies in today's global, self-reliant work environment." Simply put, IQ and expertise are no longer considered the best predictors of performance or leadership effectiveness.

Consider, once again, the traditional formula for career success: Possessing cognitive intelligence, an analytical, detached decision style, and getting results, often through people. Most importantly, within that formula, you did not show emotional sensitivity, you were not transparent (which kept others from knowing what you really thought), and you did not focus on understanding others first to build rapport. However, the skills employers actually want are the ability to encourage others, bring them together and inspire them to do their personal best.

Focus and Impact

SMARTER is the ability to intentionally understand and manage yourself and social interactions skillfully. The key word in the above sentence is *intentionally*. Being SMARTER is *intentionally focusing* on what matters most, and being aware of the *impact you are having* on yourself and others. It is a heightened awareness to intentionally manage the default personality settings without excuses.

SMARTER skills evolve over a lifetime of hard work. Developing and sustaining SMARTER skills requires a constant—and often uncomfortable—commitment to personal and social skill development. You cannot simply read a book or attend a self-development course. Developing SMARTER skills requires being willing and able to ask for and accept feedback on your behavior—the good, the bad and the ugly.

SMARTER Skills and the Iceberg

The development of SMARTER skills is similar to the creation of an iceberg. It takes years for an iceberg to develop. Weather shifts, glaciers, pressure, favorable and unfavorable conditions, and unpredictable climatic events shape the iceberg, above and below the water's surface. What keeps you, and possibly others,  up at night cannot be seen (just like most people cannot see the iceberg below the water's surface). However, what can be seen in the light of day is our behavior.

It takes years to shape your character and your SMARTER skills. SMARTER skills are the interplay between your experience, emotions, beliefs and behavior, just like the iceberg is the interplay between environmental conditions influenced by humankind or climatic events. This was found in the Somerville study, a 40-year longitudinal investigation of 450 boys who grew up in Somerville, Massachusetts. The study demonstrated that IQ had little relation to how well the boys did in their adult lives. Two-thirds of the boys were from welfare families, and one-third had

IQs below 90. What made the biggest difference? It was the experiences and people who shaped their "iceberg" that facilitated their SMARTER skills of how to handle frustration, control emotional impulses and rebound from setbacks.

Are You Raising a Scientist? If you are raising your child to be a scientist, an IQ of 120 or higher is needed simply to get into graduate school. What future employers find attractive has less to do with IQ differences and more to do with SMARTER skills. It is more important to be able to persist in the face of difficulty and to get along well with colleagues and subordinates than it is to have an extra 10 or 15 points of IQ.

Another example of this is a study of 80 Ph.D.'s in science who underwent a battery of personality tests, IQ tests and interviews at Berkeley in the 1950s. Forty years later, these scientists were tracked down and estimates were made of their success based on resumes, evaluations by experts in their own field and sources like American Men and Women of Science. It turned out that the SMARTER skills of *social reciprocity, empathy* and *tolerance* were four times more important than IQ in determining professional success and prestige.

Your Life Is a Story and You Are the Director!

In the book, *The No Complaining Rule: Positive Ways to Deal with Negativity at Work*, Jon Gordon proposes the question to readers: "If my life was made into a movie, I would characterize it as a: A) Drama, B) Love Story, C) Comedy, or D) Inspirational Tale." Everyone plays a part in your story. What role do you play? Are you the Victim? The Hero? A Fighter? A Lover? The Star? An Underdog? Or a Winner? What roles do others play?

We often do not live our lives based on reality, but rather by our iceberg story of reality. Your iceberg story is influenced by scripts you tell yourself that define your life. But you have a choice! Don't believe this story if it is not working for you or for others. Stop tuning in. Change the dial. Hit the pause button.

Start to tune into a different story from a position of emotional maturity and SMARTER choices. You are the director of your story. What perspectives, camera angles, colors, thoughts, characters, beliefs and actions will change your life story?

Use this book to direct the story of your life.

Your Life Story and Optimism

"Learned optimism," a concept developed by Dr. Martin Seligman, one of America's most influential psychologists, refers to the causal attributions people make when confronted with failure or setbacks. Dr. Seligman found that optimists make specific, temporary, external causal attributions while pessimists make global, permanent, internal attributions. In a study of learned optimism, he tested 500 members of the freshman class at the University of Pennsylvania. He found that their scores on a test of optimism were a better predictor of actual grades during their freshman year than SAT scores or high school grades.

The facilitator of SMARTER skills is *optimism*. It's like oil in the engine; it makes everything work better and run more smoothly.

In another research study at MetLife, Dr. Seligman and his colleagues found that new salesmen who were optimists sold 37 percent more insurance in their first two years than did their pessimist counterparts. When the company hired a special group of individuals who scored high on optimism, but failed the normal skill-based screening, they outsold the pessimists by 21 percent in their first year, and 57 percent in their second.

The importance of optimism displayed through customer service and after-sales care and support becomes more and more critical to the success of any company. Customers form relationships with people; therefore, measuring and developing SMARTER skills is critical to a company's vitality.

SMARTER Skills From the Playground to the Boardroom

Whether you are in the boardroom or on the playground, strengthening SMARTER skills is critical to employability and likeability. The emotional climate of a group, when guided constructively, will enhance the individual's and the group's performance. The most important element in a social group's success is the interplay of SMARTER skills. For example, Robert Rosenthal, a Harvard University expert on empathy, has shown that when teachers treat their subjects warmly, test scores are higher. Furthermore, a single player who is low in SMARTER skills, on the playground or in the boardroom, can lower the sum total of curiosity and initiative to drive performance results. Robert Sternberg and Wendy Williams of Yale University have studied this "group IQ." What they found is that a social group often performs SMARTER than its members' collective intelligences *and* can also rapidly

Most people prefer to be around others who are pleasant, flexible and optimistic.

work dumber by tolerating domineering egos or bullying that derails performance, and by not allowing people to share talents or display empathy.

Conclusion *SMARTER Skills Are Always Evolving*

What we do know is that SMARTER skills evolve over time. Some of us may have a jump start because of a personality trait, such as empathy. However, each of us has an iceberg story that shapes our SMARTER evolution. What we also know is that optimism sparks the development of SMARTER skills that ignite and elevate a group's performance. The rest of this book will provide an overview of each SMARTER skill, and includes practice assignments to help you strengthen your SMARTER skills, whether on the playground or in the boardroom.

Join the Smart2Smarter Community *to access*
the following activities and additional
ICEBERG *resources and assessments online*
at www.Smart2Smarter.com

Every Iceberg Has a Story...What Is Under Your Surface? book and website
Practice SMARTER Affirmations book

Activity   Every Iceberg Has a Story...What Is Under Your Surface?

To understand what has shaped your iceberg, it is important to tap your emotional and visual mind. First, imagine a picture or symbol of what you want to work on, such as *procrastination*. This picture will set off a chain of pictures that will flow freely, helping you to understand what has shaped your iceberg and, more importantly, which SMARTER skills will change your behavior and, as a result, change your life path.

Imagine a picture of _____ (the behavior you want to improve). Then...	
1. Draw a circle in the middle of a white sheet of paper. Put in, or draw in the circle, a picture of the behavior on which you are working.	2. Next, stare at the picture. As your mind wanders, a series of thoughts or key words emerge related to the picture in the circle.
3. Starting at the edge of the circle, draw a line and *print* key words or messages about your picture. Continue drawing lines from the circle's edge until there are no more key words coming to you.	4. One at a time, look at each of the lines with your key words. Staring at each line, key words will emerge again. Draw a line again, this time from your primary key word line, writing the key word about which you feel the strongest. Continue drawing lines until you have no more words coming to you.
5. Now stop and analyze the flow of words. Then write your story using the key words you have written concerning the subject on which you were working.	6. What part of this story are you ready to give up? What parts elevate your personal best and what parts derail your personal best?

Sample circle activity drawing

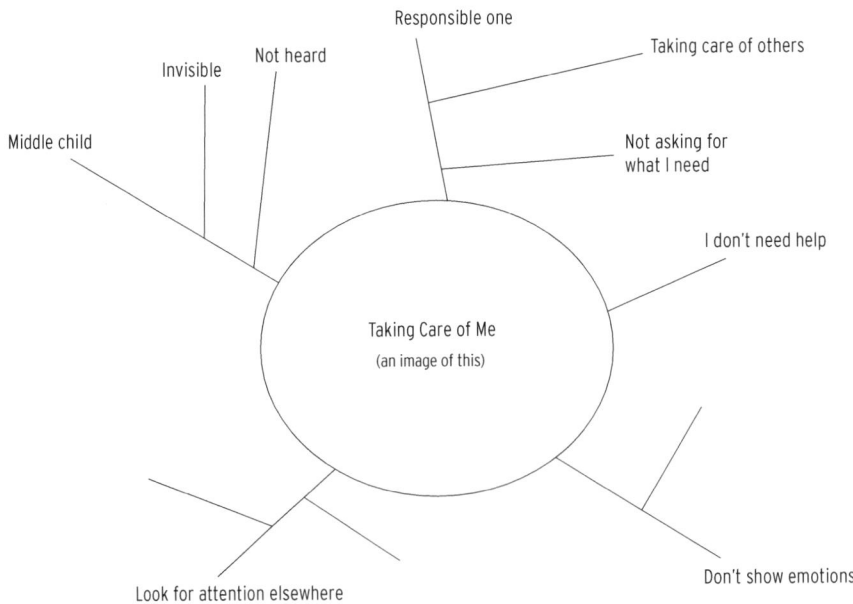

Activity Practice SMARTER Affirmations

Choose a statement below that will begin to "chip away" at your iceberg story. Put the statement on an index card and place it where you will see it daily.

Nobody is coming to my rescue.
> I am responsible for my personal and career life. I choose who will share parts of that life with me.

Leadership of others starts with self-knowledge.
> How can I be expected to know and lead others if I do not know myself?

Negative self-talk develops negative behavior and habits.
> I must learn to recognize negative self-talk and eliminate it, and do the same with negative criticism of others.

A goal written down is a dream with a deadline.
> Work and life goals are only wishes if not in writing and time dated. Life and career fulfillment is continuous and, at times, uncomfortable. Create time and space to step out of your comfort zone to evolve.

Accept that we all need each other.
> We need the help of others to survive and thrive. Guide others to achieve what they want first before achieving what you want.

Continually add value to yourself.
> Never cease to evolve.

SMARTER ICEBERG

Join the Smart 2 Smarter Community
and learn to *CONNECT* SMARTER!

Personal Best

Chapter 3
Focus on Me

Know Your Iceberg

Your iceberg stories tell the history of what brings out your personal best. Ask yourself, *Who, what, where and how optimizes my personal best?* Then ask, *What hijacks or derails my personal best?* This leads you to question what's still under the surface that is traveling with you from the past and is derailing you from being your best today. This excess baggage can be past messages, emotional habits, or beliefs that create barriers to feeling and being your personal best. For example, some of my clients have organized their lives so tightly to avoid the experience of feeling fully. Maybe in the past, as a child, they acted on their intuition or a creative impulse, such as writing on the wall with a crayon. Suppose the first words they heard about that were, *How could you do that?* Now suppose this same child was greeted with and heard praise for acting on their intuition and creativity. *Which child would you guess develops the SMARTER skills to stay employable in a global economy?*

> If you want to be successful, it's just this simple: Know what you're doing. Love what you're doing. And believe in what you're doing.
> —*Will Rogers*

Self-awareness is the cornerstone of becoming a SMARTER person. *If you don't understand yourself, you don't understand anyone.* Self-awareness starts with understanding your natural passions and how best to develop these passions into marketable skills in a global economy. Next is to heighten your awareness of what needs to be present to contribute your personal best.

Steven Covey, author of *The Seven Habits of Highly Successful People: Powerful Lessons in Personal Change*, says there is a "spiritual renaissance taking place in the business world today." While leaders are searching for ways to ignite commitment and performance, for most people this means finding true meaning or career significance in what they do. The rapidly changing job environment causes us to ask questions such as, *What is the true meaning or purpose in my work?* The following four personal questions are worth asking:

1. What is my purpose here?

2. How can I bring more meaning to my work?

3. Is this job what I am really meant to do?

4. Is there a place for me to fulfill my significance in this workplace?

Companies are learning how to foster loyalty and commitment from a new generation of workers that wants more from work than just money. When a person is emotionally, physically and spiritually overwhelmed from work, it calls into question one's inner sense of significance, caring, and vitality that makes work feel significant. When a person has not found, or has lost, their career significance, their work becomes routine, boring and without passion. For some, this leads to irritability and difficult interpersonal relations. For others, it leads to burnout and depression. For a small few, there can be violence, disruption of work, and personal or other sabotage.

Basic Human Needs

Human beings need to feel a sense of belonging, having a role to fulfill, and making a meaningful contribution. For many, these needs come through work. For most, work is as much about spirit or soul (significance) as it is about salary. Even when the salary is seen as the biggest carrot, it is often because the money goes toward a higher purpose such as raising a family and providing a life for others.

Abraham Maslow, the renowned organizational psychologist, defined the human "hierarchy of needs" on five main levels: Physical, Security, Relationships, Self-Esteem and Self-Actualization. As one's basic security needs are met (i.e., food, clothing and shelter), one progresses on to fulfill the other needs. This could be applied to the workplace as well. Once one's salary provides the basic survival needs, one searches to fulfill satisfying relationships, acquire self-esteem and realize one's full potential.

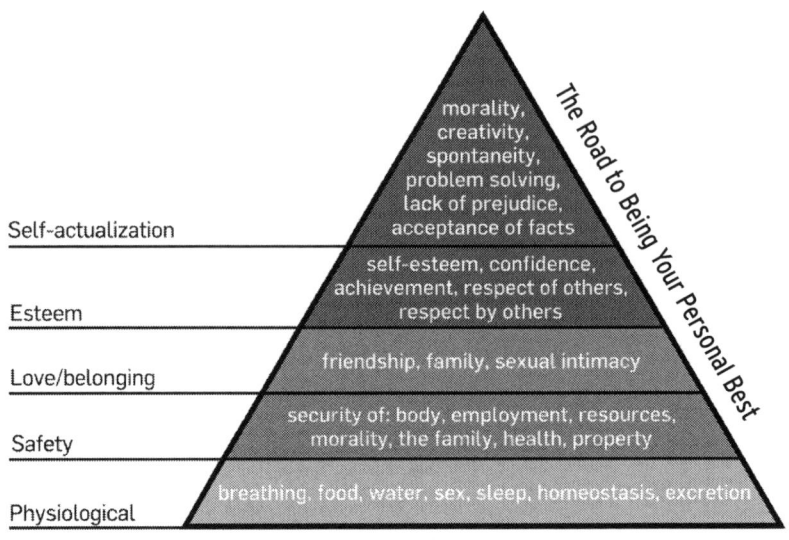

Maslow's Hierarchy of Needs

A *Fortune* magazine survey indicated that eight out of ten people would continue working even if they became rich enough that they did not need the money. Why? Most replied that they needed to have a sense of service, to help themselves and others grow and to perfect their skills. Many said that they would modify or change the nature of their work to conform more toward their spiritual, social or artistic values. Research from the Gallup Organization reveals that less than one third of the U.S. workforce feel truly engaged in their work. The other two-thirds are either just showing up, or are actively disengaged.

Significance Fuels Success

For corporations, big or small, the degree that each worker can find significance in their work will be reflected in the quality—or lack—of commitment and excitement that is present in the workforce, and ultimately in the competitiveness of the business. In most workplaces, there is a longing to find true meaning, joy or enthusiasm.

Many people are seeking a fuller life at work, one that is consistent with the larger focus of their lives. It is becoming more common to hear workplace discussions of meaning, purpose, spirit and passion. These ideas are now seen as a vital component of workplace satisfaction, which in turn affects performance and productivity.

> There is a change in vocabulary that is gradually taking hold. Words like "values" and "meaning" are becoming as bold and common in the corporate lexicon as "bottom-line" and "return on investment." Corporations are realizing that who you are and what you stand for are as important as what you produce.

The Language of Significance

Of the things that you can do to awaken a sense of significance at work, using language is powerful. It does not merely describe reality, but also shapes it. Language becomes the filter through which we perceive the world. When we talk about finding significance at work, we are addressing fundamental and essential human questions about true purpose. Corporations need to *stop* using words such as "empowerment," "commitment," "teamwork" and "quality," and *start* using words such as "soul," "spirit," "courage," "personal values" and "higher purpose."

How can leaders tap into employees' deeper level of engagement? Using language that incorporates community, meaning, service, contribution, joy, passion and soul is powerful and meaningful to most individuals.

Awakening Your Significance at Work

There are things you can do to awaken a sense of meaning at work. If you are an executive or leader looking for ways to rekindle engagement and enthusiasm, here are some questions for awakening meaning in yourself and others.

Ask three questions daily

1. **What ignites my passion in today's work?** This first question serves to reclaim attention from the pull of the urgent, and redirect it to what is truly important and significant.

2. **How can I bring true value to this moment?** The second question serves to disengage from emotional entanglements to view issues with a fresh inner perspective. This leads to constructive action.

3. **What signature strength do I want to highlight, and what story do I want others to tell about me after this assignment?** This third question serves

to bring more value and meaning to a project. Whenever an assignment begins to weigh heavily and becomes a work pressure, this question can redirect and reenergize. Meeting outer responsibilities while fulfilling inner goals becomes one process.

If I do this, then:

- I will be one step closer to…
- I will free up time for…
- It will enable us to move toward…

Significance at an Organizational Level

In the same way that the three above questions can provide personal energy to everyday work life, an organization might ask itself these questions:

1. What brings meaning and community to our company?
2. How can this meeting or project be an expression of our highest aims?
3. What would be of service right now?
4. How can this conversation be more open, clear or authentic?
5. What is our larger responsibility as a team or organization?

It is clear that there is a definite thirst for deeper ways of working. Eric Klein and John Izzo have used one question extensively in their book, *Awakening Corporate Soul.* They asked people to describe what elements were present when they had experienced meaningful moments in their work, moments when they felt energized and committed, when performance and satisfaction were at their peak "at 150-percent levels."

> Our emotions need to be as educated as our intellect. It is important to know how to feel, how to respond, and how to let life in so that it can touch you.   *–Jim Rohn*

Four paths to fulfilling your potential were identified by this question, which the authors describe as "paths toward finding 150-percent levels." I refer to this potential as your Personal Best Zone!

1. The **path of self**, whereby the person finds a personal passion in his or her work, is in touch with core values, and actively brings this into the daily work

2. The **path of contribution**, whereby the person becomes engaged in the worthy goals of his or her daily efforts

3. The **path of craft**, whereby the person develops an intense enjoyment in the moment-to-moment action of his or her work

4. The **path of community**, whereby the person finds that connection to others goes deeper than the job description, and he or she connects to bring out the best of each other

Know Your Personal Best Zone

Albert Einstein was quoted as using only 10% of his potential. He understood that human beings had far more potential than they actively used. So, what is interfering with tapping into the other 90% of your potential to contribute your personal best? Is it a lack of positive performance outcomes, a lack of passion or significant work, or a little of both? When passion aligns with performance outcomes, you are engaged to contribute your personal best. Let's look at the passion and performance definitions below:

Passion-Performance Development Cycle	
High	
P E R F O R M A N C E	Conforming High Performance Declining Passion	Performing High Passion High Performance
	Storming Declining Performance Declining Passion	Norming High Passion Inclining Performance
Low	PASSION High

Passion

Passion is the emotional energy, motivation and enthusiasm about how you want to contribute in the world of work. It is doing and learning whatever is important and necessary to make this contribution. It is an attitude of *I love to do this*, and is something from much deeper inside of us—a "fire in the belly," if you will. While this may sound idyllic, we are often in a *state of flow* when using our natural talents and preferences and meeting our interpersonal needs. This state may not be at our foremost awareness at the time, but when we walk away from completing the task, meeting a challenge or interacting with another person, we feel good about the moment, refreshed and engaged in a more meaningful way—we are at our personal best.

It is important that you travel a career path that you can get excited about.

Passion gives us energy. Once you are clear on a career path in which you are emotionally passionate, the next step is to be crystal clear on what needs to be present to ignite this passion. Which people, tasks, rewards and environments are present that fuel your passion?

Performance

Performance is converting career passion into tasks, assignments or activities that meet or exceed agreed-upon individual, team or business goals. To sustain high performance, one needs skills, knowledge, resources, people and rewards to transform passion into performance.

Outcome

An outcome reminds us that it is not enough to have passion to perform our work, but to know how our contributions align with professional, business or personal outcomes.

The Personal Best Zone = *Flow*

The Personal Best Zone is a space that artists, athletes, leaders and my clients talk about when they perform at their personal best without conscious thought or effort. The Personal Best Zone (also called *flow*) was identified in long distance running because it seemed that, upon reaching a certain point, the running took place without effort. Researchers believe that what propels one to enter the Personal Best Zone is first an internal trigger (emotions) that aligns with positive external circumstances (perceived achievable goals). When in the Personal Best Zone, the heart aligns with the rational brain to propel a focused, and seemingly effortless, peak performance.

This *flow* just seems to happen on its own. It is a state of being that is easily experienced when your career passions are aligned with performance and life values. You are *in flow* when you are being simple, natural, authentic and free of energy holding you back (*hyper*activity)—when you are *in flow*, you don't care whether or not others perceive you as being great. *Flow is a state of being, not a condition of achievement.*

A personal best hijacking occurs when the emotions swamp the rational (performance) brain. You have this experience when you are frustrated, overwhelmed, stressed or tired, and therefore are unable to contribute your personal best. Your emotions, and the thoughts that accompany them, overtake your rational brain and derail your performance.

The Personal Best Zone is a dynamic process that requires regular **Discovery** (self-assessment), focused **Commitment** (written and supported development plan) and **Forward Action** (learning and feedback) to align passions with performance tasks to achieve career significance and success.

Example

Flow is an ecstatic state of mind where whatever you are doing seems to happen on its own. *Going with the flow* is a process of cooperating with whatever is going on. It may seem like play rather than work.

What interferes with *flow* is limiting beliefs, self-sabotage, assumptions, environmental blocks and conflicting intentions. *Blocks to flow* are mostly internal, not circumstantial.

Coaching Toward *FLOW*

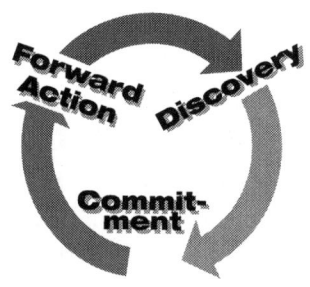

Discovery

Individuals often are clear about their limitations, but are not as clear about what needs to be present to be their potential and perform their personal best. Most individuals want to be successful and feel significant in their career. *Discovery* is a process of gathering self-knowledge and asking for feedback from your work and life community about *You, Inc.* Discovery helps to answer these questions:

- How well do your natural interests and motivators fit with performance tasks?
- How well do you know what optimizes your own talents, skills, interests and values?
- Does your environment, whether at work or at home, encourage development and alignment of your career passion with current and emerging professional goals?

What evidence do you have for your response to the above three questions?

Commitment

Commitment is an alliance established between you and your manager, peer, friend or coach, with a focus on sharpening your career significance and career outcomes. This alliance reviews Discovery data, analyzes development options, identifies and writes SMARTER development goals, and creates a practice plan with clear success and progress markers.

Commitment includes a clear definition of the business or career value received when development goals are achieved, along with any speed bumps that may slow down goal attainment. Finally, during the Commitment stage, a support network is named and contacted to keep you on track and committed to the development schedule.

Forward Action

During *Forward Action*, the commitment plan is activated and monitored. The role of your support network is to provide resources, feedback and redirection. During Forward Action, positive energy fuels, supports and reinforces development activities and performance milestones. As a SMARTER person, your role and responsibility is to ask for support when you find yourself off course—and ask for acknowledgement when you hit the mark.

Where Are You on the Passion-Performance Development Cycle?

The first step is to know your natural passion and strengths. As Peter Drucker puts it, "It's much easier to move from competence to excellence than it is to move from mediocrity to competence." In other words, focus first on your passion and strengths rather than wasting energy trying to become competent at something you are not passionate about.

Assess Your Personal Best

Learn what needs to be present to optimize your passions into high performance and career significance by taking the *Personal Best Zone Assessment*. This tool provides activities and a development plan to align your passions with performance tasks to achieve business outcomes.

Visit www.Smart2Smarter.com and click on PERSONAL BEST to take the *Personal Best Zone Assessment*

Join the Smart2Smarter Community *to access the following activities and additional PERSONAL BEST resources and assessments online at* www.Smart2Smarter.com

Ten Steps to Ignite Your Passion to Be Your Personal Best! book and website
Being, Doing and Having book and website
Awaken Your Significance at Work website
Personal Best Zone Assessment website

Activity   Ten Steps to Ignite Your Passion to Be Your Personal Best!

First, make several copies of this worksheet. Choose one step to use as an affirmation to ignite your *passion-performance moment*. Cut and paste it in a location where you see it everyday for at least a week. Repeat the process for no less than six steps over the next six weeks. Of course, you can continue the process for all 10 steps.

Steps	
1. The fun of finishing	It is that sense of knowing that something has an ending, and that you will get there. You get a clear sense of this when you're knitting, for instance. You work away while reading a pattern and, while you're enjoying yourself, something begins to take shape. Before you know it, a sweater or hat is made and your work is done!
2. The fun of focus	This is when you concentrate so fully on what you are doing, and are so immersed in it, that you aren't thinking about what you have to do next, or that you have more important things to do.
3. Trust in the process	Artists are often *in flow*, and they have a special way of talking about what they do. When Rodin made his incredible sculptures, he said that he took a piece of marble and chipped away until enough was gone.
4. Joyful physical feedback	It is especially pleasurable when you are doing a task and there is immediate sensory information. For example, when you're knitting, you can feel the wool or cotton yarn running over your hand.
5. Being in comfortable command	Bliss will be blocked if there is a feeling of being out of control. When we are at our personal best, we feel in control, but not controlling.
6. Recreational work	Personal best activities don't seem like work at all. This happens when you lose yourself in the task and become one with it. It's a matter of *being* the work, not *doing* the work.
7. Timeless pleasure	You lose all sense of time. No drinks of water, no trips to the kitchen for food, no phone calls. You sit down to work and look up and it's five hours later!
8. We get the most out of it when we are least aware of trying to get the most out of it	If we concentrate on reaching our Personal Best Zone, or intentionally try to attain it, we ruin it because we've let our will and Self intrude between the action and ourselves.
9. We get the most for ourselves by giving of ourselves	When you give yourself over to the task and become lost in it, that is the point at which you are *in flow* and receive all the benefits that come from it.
10. We can let it happen	If you are open and allow it to take place, without trying to make it happen, it will happen on its own.

Adapted from CoachVille Top Ten at www.coachville.com

SMARTER PERSONAL BEST

Activity   Being, Doing and Having

One of my favorite phrases is: "You have to be before you can do, and do before you can have." In short, you have to be a person of character and do the right things, and then you can have a life that you really want. First, look at what you have to DO in order to accomplish your career and life goals, and then examine yourself and determine what kind of person you have to BE so that you can HAVE. To make the "Be-Do-Have" theory valid, believable, and usable on your part, look at your own life now.

Directions

- In the **HAVE** column, list all of the things that you really want in life, whether it is an education, good family relationships, a beautiful new home, more money, better health—you name it.

- In the center column of the page, identify what you have to **DO** to acquire the things in the *Have* column. Let's say you want a successful marriage. You must be willing to share your innermost thoughts and concerns with your mate. You must carry more than your share of the workload and encourage your mate when he or she is down. You need to remember special occasions. And the list goes on. Consider each thing you listed in the *Have* column and what you must *Do* to acquire them.

- Now, go to the **BE** column and identify what you need to *Be* in order to *Do* so that you can *Have*. For example, to *Have* a successful marriage, you must *Be* faithful, attentive, loving, caring, helpful, empathetic, encouraging, persistent, committed, kind, thoughtful, considerate and responsible. Not having all of these qualities is okay because they are skills, and skills can be developed.

BE	DO	HAVE

Adapted from *Success For Dummies* by Zig Ziglar

Strengths

Chapter 4

My BestFit Life

As discussed in the previous chapters, your strengths—whether they are problem solving, intuition, inspiring action, relationship building, empathy or initiative—are fueled by your passion. We also discussed what needs to be present in your environment to allow you to effortlessly express these strengths.

> Career success and significance is more like sculpting and editing, rather than accumulating or building.
> —*Cynthia Kivland*

Since your strengths and natural talents are reinforced positively whenever you use them, this will lead to a more confident and competent self (there will be more about *self-efficacy* in the next chapter).

Most people are attracted to jobs, assignments or projects where they can use their strengths. Why? Because everyone wants to shine! But what happens when you are selected for a *new* assignment, project or position because of your strengths? These same strengths may not be optimized under new conditions, or in different situations. Why not? Because something about the new environment, the people, the performance tasks or the profession just doesn't fit with your core passion and purpose.

The key to sustaining career significance and success is to know and understand the BestFit factors that allow you to utilize your assets. You have to say *no* to opportunities if you won't be able to use your natural talents, even when a new position appears to be challenging and offers possibilities for growth, prestige and development.

This requires identifying strengths and seeking BestFit opportunities that allow you to express them. It also requires you to understand your weaknesses and avoid being involved in roles that are not your forte. This can be difficult. Nobody likes to turn down a promotion or a challenge. To accept such challenges will only leave you emotionally drained and unfulfilled. It is SMARTER to focus and develop your strengths, rather than stretch yourself to overcome a weakness.

According to research from the Gallup Organization, and authors Marcus Buckingham and Donald Clifton (*Now, Discover Your Strengths*), it does not make sense to stretch yourself with new and challenging assignments if it involves doing things for which you are not passionate and lack natural talent. Buckingham contends you will not feel energized (personal best) when you focus on your flaws. People who feel successful and significant have the SMARTER mindset to choose their work wisely. They are unwilling to tolerate aspects of a job that do not allow them to shine, and they also seek ways to delegate or avoid certain tasks that drain positive energy.

The longer you put up with aspects of your life that don't play to your strengths, and that

> Discover what you don't like doing and stop doing it!
> –Marcus Buckingham

are not aligned with your core values and purpose, the less successful and significant you will feel. It is just that simple. When you focus on your best talents, you'll find that your career path is exactly where it should be, on purpose, and aligned with who you are.

BestFit Career Star

No one manages your career life but you, even if you are fortunate enough to have a trusted mentor, parent, manager or coach. Most individuals will move between organizations, college majors or careers throughout their life. This may be due to company upheavals, family relocation or a personal significant event. With each change comes a moment for personal reflection, and is a good time to ask yourself, *Where can I find a career life that fits?*

> You cannot know where you are going before you know who you are!
> –David Campbell

This is a question asked by most clients who seek career counseling or coaching. I created the *BestFit Career Star* to guide individuals through an annual assessment of their BestFit factors in relation to five key components.

At times, your *BestFit Career Star* will be just right and shine bright for you. However, at other times, one area may need development or adaptation as you encounter life or work changes. When your BestFit components align with your career passion and performance results, you are being your personal best! The first step to career satisfaction and performance success is self-awareness. The *BestFit Career Star* is a self-awareness tool to assess your BestFit factors.

The BestFit Career Star
PassionFit

PurposeFit   PerformanceFit

ProfessionFit   PeopleFit

PassionFit	PerformanceFit
How well do your natural interests and motivators fit with performance tasks? Does your work or home environment encourage development and alignment of your career passion with current and emerging goals?	How well do your current skills and knowledge align with business, personal, team and career goals? How well do your stakeholders (your school, teachers, family or organization) support skill development that aligns with your career passion and enhances your global employability, inside or outside of the organization?

PurposeFit	ProfessionFit	PeopleFit
How well do your core values and life's purpose fit with your passion, performance, people and professional fit? What core values, lifestyle needs, family/friends, finances and spiritual components impact your life's purpose at this time? How do these components compliment and enhance your career satisfaction and performance results?	How aligned are your natural career passions with your profession's culture? What are the work trends that may affect skill or knowledge development of your profession? How well is your organization providing skill and knowledge development for you to stay ahead of the curve in your profession?	How well do the important people in your life (leaders, family, friends and management) inspire and support your performance results, career satisfaction and future employability? How does the people culture align with your life's purpose and lifestyle needs?

SMARTER STRENGTHS

BestFit Self-Assessment Tools

It takes more than just ambition for you to be your personal best. Reaching sales goals, receiving rewards, and attaining status is usually not enough—and certainly not for long. We must be connected to our core values and intrinsic motivators in order to be truly fulfilled. Determining your BestFit factors is not an easy task. A professional coach, teacher, parent, manager or mentor can assist with this quest.

There are many formal and informal ways in which you can assess your *BestFit Career Star*. Reflections on your past successes are excellent starting points. Make a list of when you are at your best, whether at work or school. What activities do you love doing, and what makes you so engrossed that you lose track of time?

Similarly, you can also identify areas in which you struggle, and therefore discover where your weaknesses lie. Knowing how your skills, accomplishments, knowledge, aspirations and workstyle align with business outcomes and industry trends is just plain SMARTER! For the employer, assessments increase organizational knowledge about employees' accomplishments, aspirations, talents and emerging interests. This knowledge helps to align talent with current and future business or societal needs. It also provides focus for what needs to be developed—and what needs to be leveraged!

BestFit Questions to Ask and Answer

- What drives your career passion?
- What natural talents lead to your performance excellence?
- What competencies are critical to perform job-specific tasks?
- What self-leadership behaviors do you do well, and what behaviors need to be developed?
- What is emotional intelligence, and does your EQ rate?
- How does your workstyle personality impact your BestFit work environment, motivators and career focus?

A few tips about assessment tools

Standardized Assessments require interpretation by licensed counselors, psychologists or qualified coaches/trainers who have completed a specific certification program. These assessments provide in-depth knowledge about your career fit and workstyle needs. Standardized assessment tools have undergone extensive research on both reliability and validity measures.

Self-administered Assessments and activities do not require professional interpretation, but it is highly recommended. Some of these tools are free and others are fee-based. Some can be completed online while others are in paper format.

The Buros Institute has brief and comprehensive reviews of assessment tools at http://www.unl.edu/buros/bimm/index.html.

The following tools are published by CPP, Inc at www.cpp.db.com

Here are my favorite types of tools and activities that you can use to assess your BestFit factors.

Myers-Briggs Type Indicator® is the most widely used personality inventory to assess workplace style to improve leadership, interpersonal and professional effectiveness. Specific career applications include communication, conflict management, team development, change management, problem solving and decision making. *Requires professional interpretation obtained through degree or certification program.*

Strong Interest and Skills Inventory® is based on the most widely used model of career development. It helps individuals at high-school level and older explore the natural passions in their lives (interests), and how these passions align with their self-perceived skills. *Requires professional interpretation obtained through degree or certification program.*

The FIRO-B® provides insight into your interpersonal wants and needs. This assessment provides self-awareness into a key element of emotional intelligence: The ability to read interpersonal situations and interact for mutually rewarding results. This assessment helps you understand how much you want to be included or include others, how you want to express and receive personal feedback and how you want to manage others or be managed. *Requires professional interpretation obtained through degree or certification program.*

Thomas Kilman Conflict Inventory® has been the leader in conflict resolution assessment for the past 25 years. This self-scoring assessment takes about ten minutes to complete online or in printed form. *Professional interpretation is not required, but is recommended.*

SMARTER STRENGTHS

Join the Smart2Smarter Community and learn to CONTRIBUTE SMARTER!

The following BestFit Discovery Tools have been developed by Cynthia Kivland, and are available at http://www.smart2smarter.com

Personal Best Zone Assessment is a dynamic process that requires regular **Discovery** (self-assessment), focused **Commitment** (written and supported development plan) and **Forward Action** (learning and feedback) to align natural passions with performance tasks to achieve career significance and performance mastery. This activity and guide allows you to discover and visualize what needs to be present to achieve your potential, and comes with a coaching guide and development-planning tool. *Professional interpretation is not required, but is recommended.*

Workplace Engagement Values allows clients to discover which values drive their passion. Work engagement—or *flow*—is being energized, focused, positive, blissful and absorbed in the activity in a seemingly effortless and fluid way. *Professional interpretation is not required, but is recommended.*

Career Health Inventory and Development Guide determines how well you are creating a healthy career lifestyle that establishes behavior habits and a mind-set of continuous improvement (growth) and resilience (change management). This tool will provide an annual check-up on your individual career development needs. *Professional interpretation is not required, but is recommended.*

International career, EQ and coaching experts have developed the following tools

The Emotional Quotient Inventory 2.0 (EQ-i 2.0) is an assessment that measures workplace competencies based on human interaction (inspirational leadership, customer service, being a team member or a leading salesperson). Each competency demonstrates humanity and is related to emotional or social intelligence. *The EQ-i 2.0 is based on the Bar-On Model of EQ and consists of 15 EQ Competencies most wanted in workplaces.* —(training) www.smart2smarter.com, or (information) www.mhs.com

Emotional Intelligence 2.0 provides a practical and compelling look at the other side of smart. Each copy includes a FREE code to take the best-selling Emotional Intelligence Appraisal™ test online. *Professional interpretation is not required, but is recommended.* —www.talentsmart.com

Career Anchors: Discovering Your Real Values (Revised edition, by Edgar H. Schein, Jossey-Bass) is an instrument designed to help you identify your anchors and to think about how your values relate to your career choices. *Professional interpretation is not required, but is recommended.* —www.wiley.com

Career Value Card Sort is a tool that allows clients to prioritize 54 variables of work satisfaction, such as time freedom, precision work, power, technical competence and public contact. This is an effective tool for job seekers, those fine-tuning their present jobs and career changers at all ages and stages. *Professional interpretation is not required, but is recommended.* —www.careertrainer.com

Motivated Skills Card Sort is a quick and easy way to prioritize 48 transferable motivated skills that are central to personal and career satisfaction and success. The cards assess your proficiency and motivation in each skill area. *Professional interpretation is not required, but is recommended.* —www.careertrainer.com

SEI™ is focused on self-development. The SEI is the only test based on Six Seconds' EQ-in-action model: Know Yourself, Choose Yourself, Give Yourself. The test measures eight fundamental skills in those three areas, including emotional literacy, navigating emotions, intrinsic motivation and empathy. *Certification required.* —www.6seconds.org

StrengthsFinder is the product of a 25-year research effort by the Gallup Organization to identify the most prevalent human strengths. Gallup introduces 34 dominant themes and reveals how they can be translated into personal and career success. Gallup has conducted psychological profiles with more than two million individuals to help you learn how to focus and perfect these themes. *Professional interpretation is not required, but is recommended.* —www.gallup.com

Creatrix Assessment Creativity, risk taking and innovation are found in the SMARTER skill of Evolving. The assessment measures eight Creatrix® Orientations, their creativity strengths and potential hindrances, and provides insight on how to increase innovation in the workplace by learning the seven drivers of innovation. —www.creatrix.com

Please feel free to recommend other Self-Assessment Tools on the Smart2Smarter *website.*

Work Behavior Inventory (WBI) assessment helps you to better understand your style of work, leadership, influencing or selling, personality characteristics, emotional intelligence, and includes indicators for occupational success. The WBI Career Development Report includes both a profile and narrative report detailing potential assets and cautions to assist people in career assessment and development. It can also be used for employee selection and team building. *Professional interpretation is not*

SMARTER STRENGTHS

required, but is recommended. —www.aai-assessment.com

Well-Being Finder This tool was developed by the Gallup Organization and assesses well-being on five variables: Career, Social, Financial, Community and Physical. *Professional interpretation is not required, but is recommended.* —www.gallup.com

Resilient! 360© is a comprehensive leadership assessment tool that compares and contrasts your self-assessment with the assessment of your managers, peers, direct reports and clients. Feedback is specific on 28 competencies in resilience with detailed behavioral scores and personal comments on your strengths and development needs. *Requires professional interpretation obtained through degree or certification program.* —www.resiliencei.com

Emotional Intelligence Skills Assessment 360 (EISA 360) The EISA instrument quickly and accurately measures emotional intelligence of both individuals and organizations. This 50-item assessment gauges strengths and areas for development, compares the results to normative data, and indicates areas in the workbook for relevant activities. It measures emotional intelligence based on five core factors that can be developed to maximize emotional and social functioning: Perceiving, Managing, Decision making, Achieving and Influencing. This tool was developed by Pfeiffer in cooperation with MHS, author of the EQ-1. *Professional interpretation is not required, but is recommended.* —(training) www.smart2smarter.com, or (information) www.pfeiffer.com

AAI 360 A leadership development tool developed by Ron Page, Assessment Associates International, based on 17 core behavioral competencies in five cluster areas: Interpersonal, Achieving Results, Management, Leadership and Self-Management. *Requires professional interpretation obtained through degree or certification program.* —www.aai-assessment.com

The Conflict Dynamics Profile assesses what triggers conflict behaviors in individuals in the workplace, as well as how they respond to conflict. It also provides practical approaches for improving behaviors that promote more effective workplace conflict resolution. *Requires professional interpretation obtained through degree or certification program.* —www.conflictdynamics.org

Everyone Wants to Leave Footprints

People who experience high levels of success in their careers state that there is an alignment between what they do and who they are. They somehow manage to attain that magic blend of their purpose in life with what they do in their jobs.

The power of self-awareness is heightened by knowing our life purpose. We all seek meaning in life; everyone wants to leave footprints. Yet finding and clearly defining your footprint can be elusive. The key to acting with purpose is to connect the needs of the world to your unique talents in the form of a career—or a calling.

Without purpose in our lives, or without knowing what that is, one's career life will lack direction and joy. Many experts believe that we can identify our purpose by looking within ourselves. Regardless of our spiritual or philosophical beliefs, most people agree that when we act in alignment with our strengths (talents and desires), there is a sense of heightened energy and *flow*, and we become our personal best with the world—and ourselves. Therefore, when our purpose is aligned with our career, we become more driven and motivated in all aspects of our lives.

Assessing BestFit factors does require emotional intelligence and intuition, enough to hear our own signals when it is time for *purposeful pausing*. To put it simply, call a "time out" to listen to your physical, mental, emotional and spiritual cues or signals. Purposeful—not idle—pausing is a necessary SMARTER skill in our fast-paced, ever-changing global society.

In the words of an anonymous Chinese scholar and philosopher, "When there is no time for quiet, there is no time for the soul to grow. The man who walks through the countryside sees much more than the man who runs."

Join the Smart2Smarter Community *to access the following activities and additional* STRENGTHS *resources and assessments online at* www.Smart2Smarter.com

BestFit Career Life Wheel book and website
BestFit Affirmations book
BestFit Year Reflect and Envision book and website
Career Health Inventory and Development Guide website

Activity   BestFit Career Life Wheel

Directions

The eight sections in the *BestFit Career Life Wheel* represent key factors to being your personal best (you can change the section names if you'd like). If the center of the wheel is zero (lowest) and the outer edges are ten (highest), rank your current level of satisfaction with each area by drawing a curved line to create a new outer edge. The new perimeter represents your *BestFit Career Life Wheel*. How balanced are the attributes in your current job? Which attributes are priorities, and which would you most like to change?

PassionFit
The work I do matches my current and emerging career interests and motivators. *Does leadership encourage development and alignment of my career passion with current and emerging business goals?*

PurposeFit
The work tasks, organization's values and corporate policies are aligned with my core life and work values. *What core values, lifestyle needs, family, friends and spiritual components impact my life's purpose at this time? How do these components compliment and enhance my career satisfaction and performance results?*

PerformanceFit
The work I do requires my best talent, skills, knowledge and abilities. *How well do my current skills and knowledge align with business, team and career goals? How well does my manager and organization support skill development that enhances my employability inside or outside the organization?*

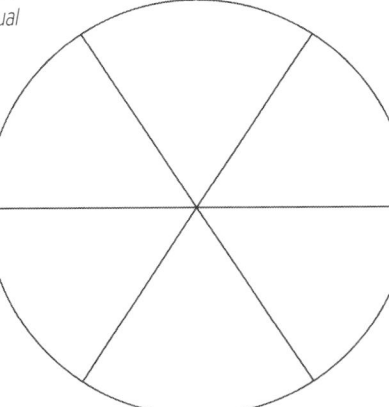

LifestyleFit
The compensation package is competitive, meets my lifestyle needs and provides non-monetary and monetary rewards for contributions. *Do the working conditions (e.g., hours, benefits, life/work balance) and physical environment align with my lifestyle, physical and emotional needs?*

ProfessionFit
Opportunities exist to develop professionally and advance my career. *How aligned are my career passions with my profession's culture? How and what trends are impacting job security, such as outsourcing skill and knowledge development within the profession? How well is my organization providing skill and knowledge development to stay employable?*

PeopleFit
The people, culture, leadership, management and associates enhance my performance results, career satisfaction and future employability. *Does my manager encourage my development through coaching, training and special assignments?*

Activity   BestFit Affirmations

1. **Do what you love for a living!** If you don't love what you do, you won't perform at the top of your game.

2. **Think of yourself as self-employed**—even if you work for someone else. You can no longer count on your employer to manage your career for you. What is your marketing plan? What is your R&D strategy for future skills development?

3. **If you are seeking a new job now**, develop a network that goes outside of your existing industry or profession, and don't be afraid to ask people for help. A great approach is to state, *This is my goal...* Then ask, *Who do you know that I should be talking to?*

4. **Learn a new skill** We live in an era of lifelong learning, and if you don't hone or learn skills, the challenge and fun of your job evaporates into the staleness of daily routine.

5. **Find ways to be more valuable** Take on a new project, head a committee or set up meetings with people to learn more about what they do.

6. **Demonstrate your value proactively when annual review time comes** Rather than relying on vague statements that state you have improved over the past 12 months, keep a record (file, folder or computer document) of your accomplishments during the year.

7. **Nurture your network** Have lunch with someone you know professionally at least once a month. Keep your name on their "radar screen."

8. **Keep yourself current on trends in your academic interests, profession and organization** Do you know the top 10 companies in your field? Or where the new products or services are headed? This knowledge will make you more valuable, enable you to challenge yourself with new assignments, and facilitate a transition when you need to make one.

9. **Keep your resume up-to-date** See affirmation #6 for tips on this.

10. **Reflect and envision** "If you don't know where you're going, you'll probably not get there," says Dr. David Campbell, H. Smith Richardson Senior Fellow, Center for Creative Leadership (CCL). If you could create your ideal life, begin living it right now and be where you would love to be in five years, what would it look like? (See the next activity.)

Activity   BestFit Year Reflect and Envision

Closure, first. Envision, second. The best way to close out a year is to acknowledge your accomplishments, be grateful for new and old relationships and release any regrets about what might have been. Ideally, schedule time to sit quietly and write these down.

Get into a meditative or quiet frame of mind, breathe deeply and allow yourself to experience the year you want to have. Move month by month through the year ahead, imagining the activities of each month, including vacations and family/friend time. At some point, start writing it all down!

By envisioning the experience you want to have, a life theme will emerge. Themes such as "expanding" or "easy and effortless" may become your life themes or this year's purpose. By envisioning your *best year*, you can then write down your BestFit life and work goals—and commit to them.

Consider these reflective questions as you envision your BestFit Year

- What kind of people do I want to have as part of my journey?
- What kinds of projects, events and activities am I working on?
- How does it feel when I am involved, whether at work, home or in my community?
- What am I doing or learning that ignites my passion?
- Where is the fun and play happening in my life and work?
- What kinds of accomplishments am I striving for to give me a sense of purpose and significance?

Whatever your gifts and talents, you hold an important place in the orchestra of work, family and community. *Play the music that lives inside of you.* Play it to the best of your ability. Resolve to give your all this year.

Join the Smart 2 Smarter Community
and learn to *BE* SMARTER!

Mastery

Chapter 5
Thrive or Survive

Choose Hope Over Fear

According to Joshua Freedman, Director of Programs for Six Seconds EQ Network, fear and faith both have something in common: A future that has not happened. Fear believes in a negative future. Faith believes in a positive one.

This chapter will pose the question: *If neither the positive or negative future has happened, then why not choose to believe in the positive future?* The key word here is *choose*! You have to make a choice, and your choice determines whether you *Thrive* or *Survive*. The key is *how you choose to manage* your emotional brain.

When an event takes place that appears to threaten or intrude upon our normal state of being (*flow*), a reaction kicks in to defend against it. Primal instincts are our natural defense mechanism against threats to our lives or well-being. This primal instinct can also refer to disruptive reactions that occur in response to non-life-threatening events. These responses are not only emotional, but result in behaviors ignited through emotions, such as slamming the phone, withdrawing or yelling. To choose the path to thrive means being aware of real or perceived threats, and mastering the skills to not become distracted, diverted, frustrated or, at worst, emotionally crippled.

80/20 Survival Rule

Joshua Freedman admits that we all have some fear. A healthy dose of fear causes you to examine your situation and plan for the future. When used wisely, it

SMARTER MASTERY

allows you to manage risk and make better decisions. However, many people spend as much as *80% of their day in a fear or survival mode.* I'm sure there are better things you can do with your energy.

Imagine that you hear a loud bang as you read this sentence. You probably would cover your head and crouch instantly, and only then would you look up to see where the sound came from. You would have taken those actions without your conscious mind considering what to do. This rapid instinctive reaction could have saved your life.

Most of us have learned to fear things in our lives. It is all about what is under our iceberg. People, events, experiences or even the media may have taught you to be fearful of certain things. Fear generates anger, which is a learned feeling. Therefore, your anger is *yours.* Why is it that what makes you angry may just annoy me? Because our sense of fear or hope comes from our learned response to external events.

Let's look at how we process information

External Event Someone cuts you off while driving to work
Interpretation or Beliefs That person is a jerk and needs to be taught a lesson
Feelings These thoughts and beliefs are making me angry
Behavior So I yell at the other person
Next External Event And the cycle continues!

External events only provide raw information. It is our interpretation of these events through our stories, scripts and learned fear/anger that impacts our emotional response and behavior. Your thrive or survive response is thus influenced by learned responses, your personal history (iceberg), and programmed messages about how the world is and your ability to influence it.

Anger is an energy that gets stirred up within and causes one to fight or flee from the fear. To explore what your anger is about, find the fear(s) associated with it. Ask yourself what that angry energy is about, and what might be underneath the anger (often, it's some kind of hurt). Then ask what you need to say or do in order to release that anger.

Dr. Albert Ellis' premise from his research in 1955 on Rational Emotive Therapy is that we all have stories about fear and power and what we will do if we think we'll lose personal power, safety or security. The fear of losing any of these causes individuals to act instinctually. The body prepares itself for danger—real or imagined. The emotional brain shuts down.

John Gottman's research on couples headed toward divorce states that as the stress of divorce (or any major change) increased, the body and mind adapted. He found that when a couple's pulse increased, his or her ability to listen diminished. Even a 10 percent increase inhibits our ability to hear what others are saying. When a person's pulse reaches 100 beats a minute (below aerobic level for most people), conversations become terribly strained. Have you ever said, *I am so mad I can't think straight*?

Living in constant fear keeps you operating (and living) in the survival path. All of your emotional energy is focused on *protecting yourself* as opposed to *expanding yourself.*

To move from Fear (Survive) to Hope (Thrive), try these actions

- Learn about the origin of your fear/anger trigger points, then consider how they are serving you today.
- Notice when you are too tired, lonely, hot or hungry—all of which increases a fear and survive response from yourself and others.
- Inquire: *Who or what drains positive energy from my life, and how do I let it happen?*
- Remove yourself from the fear trigger situation if and when possible.
- Restrain and challenge your iceberg stories.
- Own your anger and fear. Say, *I am getting angry because...* rather than, *He's making me furious!* No one can make you angry unless you agree to it.
- Learn words. Frustrated people cannot put their feelings (of fear/anger) into words. It becomes a feeling without a name, but still holds power. Name it, and it is yours to manage.
- Be relentless and adamant about forgiving yourself and others— for your benefit, not theirs.
- Watch for catastrophizing. Ask: *Is _____ really the end of the world or the worst disaster? Could it be a difference of opinion, a miscommunication, an unintentional slight or a bad day?*
- Try saying to someone in an argument, *You are absolutely right,* and see what happens.
- Be *curious.* When someone's ranting, instead of joining in, get curious. Say, *So it's your impression that I missed that deadline because I wanted to cause trouble for you? Tell me about that.*

Road to Thriving

But what if you choose the road to thriving? With this belief, you make SMARTER choices and actions that create your positive future. You invest in yourself, in your environment, and you build your reserves. You are focused and committed to your vision and purpose. You identify opportunities in the midst of the challenges, and you focus on solutions instead of fixing problems. Most importantly, this energy spreads to others through your emotions; thus, everyone around you is inspired to travel down the road to thriving.

We all have emotional intelligence, but that does not mean that all of our emotions are intelligent.

According to Freedman, the first step is to recognize this: "If I don't deal with feelings, they will cause me problems." The second step is to learn that "feelings are valuable in and of themselves." Dr. Antonio Damasio, author of *The Feeling of What Happens: Body and Emotion in the Making of Consciousness*, states that our awareness of our own thoughts is created by emotion. "It's your feelings that create the awareness of your life." Damasio says that, "without emotion, we would actually lose all perspective of what's important, and of our role in the continuity of our lives."

Think about what is challenging for you. It usually boils down to some belief about what you are *supposed to do or be*. From an EQ perspective, this interaction between thoughts, feelings and actions is the *key to thriving*.

Furthermore, because the brain actively looks for input from outside of ourselves, we are also influenced by the thoughts, feelings and actions of others. This means we are all interconnected, and we constantly influence one another. Finally, most of us grew up learning that feelings get in the way of clear thinking, so we learned to put them aside. Therefore, it makes the work of really listening to our emotions more challenging. Tuning in to the way you experience and use emotion is a first step. The next step is to make a commitment to focus on and observe how emotions impact your own life and the lives of those around you. The good news is that you do not have to wait for some "big moment" to look at how you experience emotions.

Take the opportunity right now to review where you are on the *Emotional Spectrum of Thrive or Survive*. On the next page, place a (**C**) to indicate your **Current** Survive or Thrive choice, and an (**I**) on your **Ideal** Survive or Thrive choice (where you want to be three months from now).

Emotional Spectrum of Thrive or Survive

Stuck vs. Flow

I am stuck in one emotion, constantly   ...I let emotions flow and
recreating the same feelings, or...   change with the situation

1	5	10

Suppress vs. Feel

I put my emotions aside, or bury   ...I experience emotions daily
them until they are hijacked, or...   as a source of intelligence

1	5	10

Forceful vs. Gentle

I use emotions as a force to control,   ...I let emotions flow gently, looking for
avoid or dismiss other people, or...   congruence, connection and reciprocity

1	5	10

The Thrive or Survive Emotional Framework

As you begin to explore how you experience and use emotions, you may begin to resist actually feeling some feelings. You are simply relying on past stories that say to feel something is wrong or bad—or dangerous. The intelligence of emotions comes from our feelings that provide information and "weight" to influence decision making. You can block that information by resisting or suppressing these feelings. If you've decided that sorrow is dangerous, you may find yourself doing almost anything to avoid feeling sad. We resist by undermining, side-tracking, attacking or retreating. It's hard to experience feelings that we perceive to be unsafe.

The *survive response* is what Dr. Daniel Goleman called "hijacking the amygdala." The amgydala is the primary emotional center in the brain, and one core function of it is reacting to perceived danger. As Dr. Peter Salovey says, this reaction is actually an example of the intelligence of our emotions—a kind of "emotional logic" is followed and decisions are made with little or no cognitive thought. When our brains perceive a threat, they react to protect us; it is a survival response built into the limbic brain (or *emotional brain*). Depending on biology and experience, when threatened, you may choose to survive by fighting, fleeing, freezing or flocking. Remember, your emotions are seeking safety. When you have a strong reaction, know that it's a message that some part of you feels unsafe. When someone else has a strong reaction, know that she or he feels unsafe. You may become defensive by attacking back, retreating, evading or ganging with others. Depending on your reaction, others may respond defensively as well.

What constitutes a threat from the amygdala's point of view? Almost any external or internal event where you perceive harm (real or imagined) will trigger the survival response. This harm takes the form of shaming, blaming, embarrassing, judging, discrediting, dismissing and dividing. This interaction occurs whether at home, at work or at play. You want to be right, or the best, or the smartest, so you blame, judge, put down or, at worst, fight with others. The other person reacts in survival mode, and the situation escalates.

In research at UCLA, Professor Emeriti Dr. Albert Mehrabian found that only 7% of communication comes in our words—the rest is tone, body language and expression. Dr. Paul Ekman's work on facial expression reinforces this conclusion. Ekman has found that people display a massive amount of emotional information through "micro expression." While most people notice general patterns of these micro expressions, Ekman says very few can accurately "read" a stream of micro expressions. We may be able to notice that someone is upset and trying to hide it. The nonverbal cues never lie; the body always tells the truth. We may then imagine their displeasure is directed at us, without proof or evidence.

Why then, when you do put aside your feelings and act calmly, do people still respond as if you've attacked them? According to Freedman, this comes from another survival mechanism in our limbic brains, which he calls "Danger Radar." The limbic brain constantly seeks out emotional radar that indicates danger such as anger, frustration, fear and anxiety. (*Note:* Anxiety is a major issue in today's stressful environment, and it will be discussed later in this chapter.) To summarize:

The Survive Path
- You defend yourself to retain safety, security or personal power
- Your amygdala is on the lookout for emotional cues that signal danger, such as anger, fear or a mismatch between words and nonverbal expression
- Prolonged anxiety or stress increases the "danger alert level," and you live in a reactive and defensive mode to survive

The Thrive Path

- Let go of the belief that *to flow* is weak
- Let go of the fear that emotions will overwhelm you
- Let go of the terror of choosing a different route
- Let go of your hurry to know it all now
- Let go of the embarrassment of being wrong

You have had a lifetime to learn to protect yourself by using emotions in a certain way. You may have learned to manipulate or mask feelings rather than really listen to the intelligence of those feelings. The SMARTER choice is to listen, and to learn.

Building SMARTER skills is about using the intelligence of your emotions to build and experience success and significance in your life and work. Everyone has his or her own definition of success and significance; in general terms, success is more easily defined by tangible measures, while significance is more easily defined by intangibles (how we feel about what we've done and the greater impact to the world). Your framework for success and failure has an impact on the actions you take—and don't take.

> Thriving is a lifelong process of letting go of primal fears.

Join the Smart2Smarter Community
and learn to *THRIVE* SMARTER!

The interplay of our feelings, thoughts and actions is illustrated in the following Thrive or Survive Frameworks. The intelligent use of emotions is to move from *Is there something wrong with me?* or *Is everyone out to harm me?* to *What are my emotions really telling me—and what is really behind the fear?* Consider that you might be choosing the road to surviving because you have learned that it's easier to turn off those emotional signals than to listen to them. The diagrams on the next page illustrate the Surviving and Thriving Frameworks.

Diagram: Fear and Survive Framework

	Internal or External Event Derail Your Destiny	Fight • Shout, Explode, Tension, Bully, Demand, Push, Power-Plays, Threaten, Dismiss or Intimidate, Protect Turf
Emotions • Fear • Negative Energy • Hijacked • Anxiety, Anger and Angst • Silence or Violence	• Low Trust and Closed to Learning • Resist, Protect and Defend • Excuse, Attack, Blame, Shame, Withdraw, Project, Rationalize, Stay Silent • Isolates • Win-Lose Mindset • Enhances Others' Power	**Fear Behavior** • Fight, Flight, Freeze or Flock • Protect and Reject • Resist • Blame and Games • Problems
		Flight • Withdraw, Sarcastic Humor, Silent, Passive-Aggressive, Shame, Guilt, Deflect, Incriminate Others

Diagram: Hope and Thrive Framework

	Internal or External Event Master Your Destiny	Hope Behavior
Emotions • Hope • Positive Energy • Flow • Optimism, Inspiration and Faith • Happiness	• High Trust and Open to Learning • Shift Expectations, Eliminate Tolerations, Check Reality of Perceptions • Collaborates • Win-Win Mindset • Enhances Own and Others' Destiny	• Experiment and Evolve • Accept and Connect • Persist • Possibilities or Solutions • Forgive • Resilience

Blind Spots and Drama Roles That Keep You Stuck

One thing that stops people from making SMARTER choices is *emotional blind spots*. In this section, we will explore how blind spots and life roles may have you traveling the path of surviving, instead of thriving.

Consider the blind spots that occur as you drive your car. Do most people look to the blind spot before changing lanes in a car? Of course not. We can change lanes without incident by carefully checking our rearview mirrors perhaps 90% of the time. The problem is that the other 10% of the time can result in an accident when we don't see what's in the blind spots.

In his book, *Discover Your Blind Spots: How To Stop Repeating Everyday Business Mistakes*, Dr. Bob Smith presents a model with specific tools to discover and eliminate our blind spots. Dr. Smith describes six different areas of our brain that process information. Three areas determine how we see the world, and the other three specify how we see ourselves. In addition, he explains the following *four methods we use to process information:*

1. **Reacting** Use of one dominant area of thought that is driven by impulse and designed to protect us from danger

2. **Responding** Use of two or three areas of thought that are triggered after we have had a moment to process different elements of a situation

3. **Reflecting** Ability to use four or five areas of thought, which we achieve when we are focused on solving problems

4. **Relating** Capacity to use all six areas of thought, which we attain when we relate with other individuals while in deep thought, searching for alternatives and solutions—*the SMARTER way!*

Eighty to ninety percent of our time is spent in *Reaction* and *Response* mode, where we utilize a small portion of our brain. The intelligent use of emotions is to take time to *Reflect* deeply and *Relate* with others in search of solutions. This helps to discover our blind spots (past stories, habits or thoughts that hijack our personal best).

Another obstacle in making SMARTER choices is role playing. *Role playing is hard to avoid.* You may have been practicing certain roles since childhood (consciously or unconsciously), and they have become automatic responses to events. These roles have short-term payoff, even though in the long term none of them will help you thrive.

The Karpman Drama Triangle states there are *three roles people play:* Victim, Persecutor or Rescuer. Most people have a default role, the one they are most comfortable playing (for me, it's the *rescuer*), and a second role they will commonly switch to (for me, it's the *victim*). The leftover role is the one in which people are most afraid, and the one they get manipulated by most easily. When you are in a role, you feel yourself behaving in a manner that you don't really like, but somehow you do it anyway. This is because when you're playing one role, you're in a drama with someone who is playing one of the other roles.

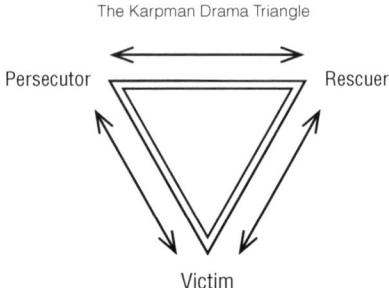

The Karpman Drama Triangle

Persecutor — Rescuer — Victim

Learning about role playing is a first step in breaking out of the Drama Triangle. Look at the three roles. Which one(s) do you play? With whom? What is the win to move out of the role? To stay in it?

Playing the VICTIM

Victims live in the "poor me" and "I cannot do anything about it" space. They feel powerless and weak—and part of them loves that because it removes responsibility. They feel persecuted and picked on, which means they can feel like martyrs and wallow in their suffering. Victims attract rescuers and persecutors.

Step out of Role Remove yourself from the situation. Problem solve. Repeat to yourself that there are options to choose from that give you hope (power) over fear (victim).

Playing the RESCUER

Rescuers jump into "let me help you" and "I will make it okay." They try to smooth everything over and keep things calm. For the rescuer, there are no uncomfortable conflicts. Doing all that rescuing makes them feel good—all those people really need them. They are often meddlers, but justify it with what they claim as good intentions. Rescuers love to save victims.

Step out of Role Take no action until requested. Resist the short-term win to feel good, to jump in and fix it or to "just help out."

Playing the PERSECUTOR

Persecutors love to waggle the finger—"it's all your fault" and "you're no good/ you're stupid." They use orders and threats and often vent their anger. They have to do everything because no one is good enough to get it done. They use anger and shame-and-blame as tactics to stay in control. Persecutors love picking on victims.

Step out of Role Disengage! Step away from the situation and let others sort it out, even if at first they stumble. Watch for shaming or blaming language!

A Few Thoughts About Anxiety

Where fear is a psychological and physiological response to a real threat, *anxiety is a psychological and physiological response to a perceived or anticipated threat.* Almost everybody has some anxiety—it's just part of life. The physical elements include things such as sweaty palms, accelerated heartbeat and a queasy stomach. The mental elements include self-doubts and excessive worry. According to Barbra Sundquist, a certified international Mentor Coach, there's no solution that will satisfy a highly anxious person in the moment. Their arousal level has to subside before they can consider options. Also, be aware of the *reciprocal anxiety spiral,* when someone behaves in an anxious way toward you that may trigger your own anxiety. Barbra discusses the *seven faces of anxiety* that can keep you stuck on the road to surviving or, at worst, in stagnation alley.

Seven Faces of Anxiety

1. **Angry Outbursts** Angry outbursts are a manifestation of that *fighting back* response.

2. **Constant Worry** A classic anxiety symptom is feeling threatened or anxious because something might go wrong (such as showing up late for an interview). Often the threats that we worry about are things we can only control in the present. Visualize yourself showing up on time and stay positive.

3. **Controlling and Uptight** Controlling people may look as though they are in control, but they are actually feeling very anxious and unsure of themselves.

4. **Irritability** This is often a result of overstimulation. When people are anxious, they are hypersensitive to sensory input. Noise, temperature, visual stimuli and touch are all exaggerated. This overstimulation leads to irritability. Of course, in addition to physical overstimulation, there's psychological overstimulation, which can also result in irritability. So a person who is experiencing a lot of demands on them may feel overwhelmed and react with irritation.

5. **Nervous Talking** Some people talk and talk because they are feeling anxious and ungrounded. You may imagine that they don't care about you, or they think they know it all, but they may be feeling insecure.

6. **Ultra-Cautious** People who are hypervigilant may be afraid to take action unless they are absolutely sure that nothing bad will

happen. This avoidance behavior is mostly seen in the *flight* or *flock* response.

7. **Reassurance-Seeking** High anxiety often leads to a decrease in self-esteem and lack of confidence (efficacy in one's talents), which leads to an increased need of reassurance.

Strategies to master anxiety are to relax your mind and take a "time out," relax your body through yoga or breathing, or simply slow down whatever you're doing by relaxing with self-care such as music. When dealing with other people's anxiety, recognize what's going on, detach or unhook with compassion (leave and let them know when you'll be back), and don't reinforce their behavior (decide where you draw the line between support and reinforcement).

Anxiety can also show up in different types of fearful thinking, such as catastrophizing (imagining the worst), polarized thinking (no middle ground) and overgeneralization (assuming that just because something bad happened once, it will happen again). Listen to your *what if* statements *(What if I forget my speech? What if I don't win?)*. Remember, *what if* thinking is both a cause and a symptom of anxiety. Be aware of how anxiety shows up in other people. Stop and reflect: *What am I noticing about the other person's behavior, and what am I imagining?* Consider other explanations for their behavior: They may be reacting that way because they feel anxious.

A Final Thought *Do What You Fear*

Dr. Susan Jeffers discusses five truths about fear in her book, *Feel the Fear... and Do It Anyway: Dynamic Techniques for Turning Fear, Indecision, and Anger Into Power, Action, and Love.*

- **Truth 1** The fear will never go away as long as I continue to grow
- **Truth 2** The only way to get rid of the fear of doing something is to go out...and do it
- **Truth 3** The only way to feel better about myself is to go out...and do it
- **Truth 4** Not only am I going to experience fear whenever I'm in unfamiliar territory, but so is everyone else
- **Truth 5** Pushing through fear is less frightening than living with the underlying fear that comes from a feeling of helplessness

Dr. Jeffers further recommends that you change your relationship with fear.

How? Copy these *five truths*, post them, and read them once a day for the next month. Begin to see those situations that you fear as they really are, and think of them as opportunities to stretch and grow stronger.

I agree with Dr. Jeffers' premise that *to move from pain (fear) to power (thriving) is to take action.* Take a baby step outside of your comfort zone, set yourself up for a small success and build on that. Then repeat the process, step by step, again and again.

Author Bill Treasurer, *Courage Goes to Work: How to Build Backbones, Boost Performance, and Get Results*, also discusses how to replace fear with courage. He states that, by using courage, we can push our comfort zone and expand it over time. Some key take-aways from his book to move from fear to courage are:

> Do one thing every day that scares you.
> *–Eleanor Roosevelt*

- Stretch your comfort zone, then push more (modulation)
- Reward courageous behavior for yourself or others, even if it falls short of the desired outcome (reward *falling forward* mistakes)
- Develop an area of courage that is new (discernment of needs)
- Create positive energy by interchanging the words "courage" and "fear"
- Ask yourself why you get up, rather than what keeps you awake at night
- Master the survive default style of being "com*fear*table"

Join the Smart2Smarter Community *to access the following activities and additional* **MASTERY: THRIVE OR SURVIVE** *resources and assessments online at* www.Smart2Smarter.com

Imagine Your Fears book and website
Choose Thrive Over Survive book and website
Re-Route That Thought! book and website
Stop the Fear Noise book and website
Emotional Spectrum of Thrive or Survive book
What Drama Game Are You Playing? website
Six Steps to Mastery website
Self-Defeating Behaviors website

Amygdala Hijacking website
Thrive and Survive Incident Form website
The Hope and Thrive Mastery Framework website
High and Low Emotional and Social Intelligence website
18 Minutes Back to Flow website

Activity   Imagine Your Fears

Exhibiting frequent and repetitive fear behavior may indicate a response pattern based on the survive path. SMARTER people may exhibit the survive response pattern some of the time, but not most of the time. SMARTER people face their fears by choosing a new route, and moving step-by-step to evolve into their personal best.

Imagine a major accomplishment in your life, something of which you are *really* proud. Recall an image of what was present before you achieved this accomplishment and answer the questions below:

- What challenges did you face?
- What did this fear look like while working toward this achievement?
- How did you overcome this fear?
- What did it feel like to conquer this fear and complete the achievement?
- How are you stronger because of having overcome this fear?

The following chart shows common areas where fear shows up. Use the list of *Common Fears* on the following pages to name your fear(s) and to consider new actions to challenge it.

Fear of Being	What My Reaction May Look Like to Others	SMARTER Reflect and Act	Other Behaviors
Controlled	Control freak, over-organizer, compulsive, mistrusts authority, closes off data.	To be SMARTER is the ability to lead and be led.	
Insignificant and Intimate	Gossip, center of attention, condescending, talks about self, hordes information, conditional relationships.	Intimacy is non-conditional. Intimacy is the ability to be a tolerant, nonjudgmental person who respects the needs and wants of others.	
Disrespected	Demanding, arrogant, seeks status.	How am I showing respect in my day-to-day interactions?	

Fear of Being	What My Reaction May Look Like to Others	SMARTER Reflect and Act	Other Behaviors
Criticized and Judged	Hypercritical of others, blame game, victim role, averse to risk, short impulse, projection.	Does the fear that others are constantly judging you keep you from doing what you want and need, or from going after your dreams and goals?	
Rejected	Guarded self, small comfort zone, superficial relationships, picks fights, quiet, victim, personal attacks.	Rejection does not mean you are not worthy, talented and significant. View rejection as a single event where what you had to offer was not a good fit. Keep creating positive work and social contributions.	
A Failure	Perfectionism, averse to risk, workaholic, overcompensates, indecisive.	Does everything you do have to be entirely successful?	
A Success	Hides wins, exaggerates mistakes, understates and underrates, passive-aggressive, self-sabotages, unpredictable appearance.	Does success mean more responsibility, more attention, more liability and pressure to perform at a high level?	
In Conflict	Over-accommodating, them first-me second, overly confrontable or agreeable.	What is another way to look at this situation or person?	
Alone and Abandoned	Over-scheduled, workaholic, impulsive, needy, passive, codependent, does not speak true feelings.	What are you doing to build a strong self-concept and efficacy? Offer your best self to the world and the fear of being alone will fade.	

sMARTER MASTERY

Fear of Being	What My Reaction May Look Like to Others	SMARTER Reflect and Act	Other Behaviors
Embarrassed	Shame, exclusion, withdrawal, sarcastic humor.	You have the choice to allow yourself to live and to not be concerned with the judgments or opinions of others.	
Expressive of Feelings	Passive or aggressive communication, codependent, low EQ in self-awareness.	Honest, open communication delivered in a respectful and empathetic manner is a learned habit.	
In the Unknown	Small comfort zone, limited relationships, low intimacy, anxiety, overcompensates, avoids the present, focuses on past or future, many *what if's*.	Use your values, passions and talents to guide you in the present, challenge your stories and build EQ reserves.	

Activity   Choose Thrive Over Survive

Review the following list of activities provided by Joshua Freedman (www.6seconds.org) to move away from the road of surviving and create new pathways on the *road to thriving*.

- **Tune into your own "Danger Radar"** feelings to learn what triggers your *fight, flight, freeze* or *flock* response. For the next day or two, notice yourself as you either get angry, frustrated, afraid or defensive. What other feelings do you have at the same time? When do you find yourself wanting to fight? To flee? To freeze (shut down)? To flock or herd? What physical sensations do you have—in your palms, your gut, your neck, back or shoulders?

- **Play the "silent movie game"** at lunch, on the bus or in an airport. Watch people and see if you can guess what's going on inside of them. The game is more fun when you have someone playing along—each of you observe the same scene, then compare notes on what you think each person was feeling.

- **Look at your own micro expressions.** Get someone to videotape you doing an activity that causes a variety of feelings (such as talking to your boss). Then watch the tape, pausing every few seconds. If you are feeling bold, invite your "silent movie game" partner to watch with you; you are likely to be amazed at how much she or he is able to see.

- **Create a "stress-o-meter."** It can be as simple as an index card with a scale from 1-10, and a paperclip you slide up and down. When you are really fatigued, stretched, at the "end of your rope" or anxious, put the clip near number 10. When you are cool and collected, put it near number one. A few times each day, check in with yourself, notice your stress level, and mark it on the stress-o-meter. Do not do anything to manage the stress right now—just notice it.

- At the same time, **notice how your own level of reactivity changes** along with the stress-o-meter. Again, do not judge it or change it, just notice how your stress-o-meter level affects your Danger Radar. You can make this more fun by putting a bunch of pennies in one pocket, or on the corner of your desk. Every time you feel reactive, put one penny in a jar.

- **Check your own congruence or authenticity.** When you are saying something you do not truly mean, what are you feeling emotionally and physically? When you are not completely congruent, how does that affect your voice, posture, energy level, neck pain, ability to sit still and clenching of muscles (such as your toes)? Once again, the exercise is not about being more congruent, it is about noticing the subtle signals that go along with hiding (or trying to hide) some parts of your feelings.

Activity   Re-Route That Thought!

The Work of Byron Katie® is a great way to *work with issues before they become issues.* This process can be done with events that have already happened, but it can also be used around events for which we are afraid, worried about, or doubting our capabilities (things in the future).

- Write down the worst-case scenarios for a current or future job, career or life situation

- Next, write down what you are thinking (those iceberg stories)

- Next, write down what you are feeling when you think about the possibility of each worst-case scenario happening, and then...

- *Stop the thought* using the four questions below
- Then turn it around to a potential thought (look for opposites that might be as true as, or truer than, the original statement)

    1. Is it really true?
    2. Can you absolutely know that it is true?
    3. How do you feel when you think that thought?
    4. Who would you be without that thought?

This process works directly with your thoughts that impact your emotions and guide your behavior. Remember, it is not the perceived, possible and actual events that are stressful, but the *thoughts about those events* that cause emotional stress and hijacked behavior.

Activity   Stop the Fear Noise

Fear can paralyze us. It can prevent us from making decisions, from taking any action, from asking for what we want, and from realizing what it is that we truly value, need and want in our life. The following list describes common areas where fear shows up. A famous quote that is very helpful to remember when facing fears is: "Fear knocked at the door and faith answered, and no one was there."

1. **Fear of Failing** This has traditionally been one of the things people say they are most afraid of when asked why they did not do or try something. It is *based on old ideas* that everything we do has to be entirely successful (or even mildly successful), and that there *exists* such a thing as a real failure!

2. **Fear of Success** As with fearing failure, many people are just as afraid of succeeding. To them, success could mean more responsibility, more attention, perhaps more liability and a *continued pressure to perform* at a high level. Many of us were taught to be prepared for failure; therefore, we are more afraid of success.

3. **Fear of Being Judged** We grow up wanting the approval of our parents and peers. This can carry through to adulthood, and can hijack our best if the fear of judgment *keeps us from doing what we want or need to do*, and from going after our dreams and our goals. Judging others or ourselves is a waste of time and serves no positive purpose.

4. **Fear of Emotional Pain** This, like all fears, is one where we can only suffer or allow ourselves to *feel pain if we give permission for it*. Life

is full of lessons, and within those lessons people make mistakes and errors and experience some kind of letdown. The letdown does not have to turn into emotional pain or suffering unless we give it the green light to do so.

5. **Fear of Embarrassment** Most people do not like the feelings associated with making mistakes publicly, usually because they allow themselves to feel ashamed, or they assume people view them as foolish. *This again is a place where we have the choice* to allow ourselves to live, and to not be concerned with the judgments or opinions of others.

6. **Fear of Being Alone/Abandoned** For many, the fear of being alone keeps them in relationships (personal and business) even though they are abused or miserable. Others fear speaking their true feelings for fear their friends, colleagues or loved ones will turn away from or abandon them. Realize that we are never really alone, and that *if people reject us or leave us because we are honest about our feelings, we are better off without those people in our lives.* There will always be new friends, new colleagues and new projects we can become involved with which will keep us connected to others—we need not ever feel alone. As one builds a strong sense of their self-worth and what they have to offer the world, the fear of being alone fades.

7. **Fear of Rejection** When we take a social or professional risk, there is the potential that what we say, or the ideas we present, might be rejected or not accepted as we had hoped. The rejection of an idea, or even the rejection of us personally, does not mean we are not worthy, talented in our work or otherwise desirable. It means that a person or group of people view(s) something differently than we do. So rather than take it to the heart and feel like a leper who has been shunned, or an idiot whose ideas are all bad, it is productive to *view it as a single incident where what we had to offer was not compatible with what others were wanting—and move on.* We have many other people to meet who will accept us freely, and we also have many others who might like our idea that someone else rejected. We need to move on, not take it as a personal attack, keep being ourselves and create what we know to be positive work and social contributions.

8. **Fear of Expressing Our True Feelings** Lack of good, clear, honest communication has ruined more than one relationship, business or business transaction. It is vital, if we are to be successful in our life, to be able and willing to express our true and honest feelings to our loved ones, our colleagues, our adversaries and even to ourselves. If

we do not know how we feel, we need to take time to discover that. If we need help, we need to ask for help. *Honest, open communication delivered in a non-abusive and non-violent manner is a learned habit.* Once learned, it is much easier to do. Practiced regularly, it does more to enrich and keep our lives in balance than almost any other thing we can do.

9. **Fear of Intimacy** While many think of intimacy as strictly having sexual connotations, it encompasses much more. *It is actually the highest and best form of being and communicating with other people (or another person).* Most importantly, true intimacy is unconditional love for the people with whom we share it. Unconditional love is not easy for many to learn and master, but it is essential if one wants to learn to be a tolerant, nonjudgmental person who respects both the needs and the wants of the people in their life.

10. **Fear of the Unknown** Life is full of unknowns. The best any of us can do is to know what our values, needs and standards are and use that to determine what we are willing to spend our time and money on throughout our life. This includes some risks, but so does driving a car, crossing the street or playing a sport. If we stay in the present moment timeframe, we will not allow the fears of anything that happened or that we heard in the past to influence us. If we do not allow ourselves to think into the future and worry *(what if)*, we will not allow ourselves to incorporate any needless anticipatory and totally speculative anxieties into our mind. The unknown can be exciting and vast in a very positive way, especially if we use our common sense, our intuition and heartfelt feelings, and our values and standards barometer to guide us from moment to moment, day to day and project to project. *More often than not, that which we fear might happen never does, and if it does, we are much more prepared for it than we imagined we would be when we were worrying.*

Original submission: Dennis R. Tesdell, author of *Self-Care Weekly,* a weekly email newsletter, plus numerous other articles on personal growth, self-care and life balance.

Join the Smart 2 Smarter Community
and learn to *LIVE* SMARTER!

Attraction

Chapter 6

Attract Your Personal Best

According to Peter Salovey and John Mayer, researchers of EQ, there is evidence that emotions are a motor activity. *Emotions bridge thought, feeling and action*—they operate in every part of a person, they affect many aspects of a person, and a person affects many aspects of them.

In general, researchers agree that there are different kinds of emotions and feelings. Mayer's research shows that some emotions are more biologically oriented, and then there are complex emotions that are saturated with thoughts and cognition. From an educator's viewpoint, this interaction between cognition and emotion opens a portal to endless learning and potential.

In this chapter, we will explore the power of *attraction* in relation to self-efficacy, expectations, optimism, stored memories and greatness.

> You cannot consistently perform in a manner that is inconsistent with the way you see yourself. *–Zig Ziglar*

Signals and Expectation

Most people perceive smart people as having high self-confidence and self-efficacy. Furthermore, Dr. Nathaniel Branden, father of self-efficacy, inquires: "How can one be a good leader if s/he distrusts his/her own capabilities, and how can one bring out the best in others when s/he feels insecure in interpersonal exchanges?" In other words, "A mind that does not trust itself cannot inspire greatness in the minds of colleagues and subordinates."

In 1911, two researchers named Stumpt and Pfungst had a horse named

Clever Hans that could add, subtract, multiply, divide and solve problems involving musical harmony. To perform, the horse needed to be cued by his owners. However, Clever Hans would also answer questions when the trainer was not present. But if the horse could not see the questioner, Clever Hans was, well, not so clever. When the person asking the question did not know the answer, the horse would not either. Why? A wrinkled forehead signaled doubt, and the horse would keep tapping in uncertainty.

So what does a horse have to do with becoming SMARTER and mastering your career success and significance? As humans we are always giving out signals that let the other person know what we "expect" of them. When the trainer signaled via verbal tone or facial expression that he knew the answer, the horse answered correctly!

Esteem is defined as appreciation, worth, and a self-estimate of one's value. Self-esteem is the package of beliefs that you carry around in your head that you have accepted to be the truth about yourself (these are your iceberg stories).

According to Dr. Branden, "Self-esteem is the disposition to experience oneself as being competent to cope with the basic challenges of life and of being worthy of happiness." The head and heart agree, *I am worthy of being valued and accepted*, and this is demonstrated through behaviors that say, *I respect and accept myself.* You expect life to present disappointments, successes, setbacks and obstacles. However, you continue to try new things even when mistakes are made or when events expected to occur don't happen. You feel worthy of career significance and success. You know that an exaggerated or wounded self will impact your ability to become SMARTER.

However, in my coaching practice, I often hear smart people state they wish to feel as confident and worthy as everyone's perception of them. Conversely, some smart people only define their self-worth through accomplishments or setbacks. They hold either negative or exaggerated assumptions about themselves, and they are often overly self-critical or overly arrogant. Finally, some smart people were shielded from childhood disappointments, or they were coached by parents (often called *helicopter parents* for hovering over their children's success) from early childhood, and learned that success is defined by the best schools, highest grades, or the bumper sticker displayed on the car that reads: "My child is an honor student!" These smart people worry about what other people think of them, agonize over not "making the grade" or the sport team list so visibly displayed in the hall, and often worry about what's going to happen if they do not finish first. Individuals with low self-efficacy stay stuck in the past or are paralyzed with anxiety about moving toward the future.

Robert Merton from Columbia University studied social theory and social structures. He found that expectations of self and others are "hardwired" in our mind. Even if the expectation is false, we tend to believe and act consistent with it. Thus was born the self-fulfilling "get what you expect" prophecy. According to Greek mythology, Pygmalion was a statue created by an artist who wanted to create the perfect woman. The artist fell in love with the statue and prayed for it to come alive—and it did! The statue became Venus and they married. The movie "My Fair Lady" plays off of this fable when Dr. Dolittle turns a flower girl into a cultured lady in everyone's eyes. The difference was not the new dress or manners, but that others now treated her as a lady; thus, she became a lady!

The bottom line is that we are constantly forming expectations of people, events and ourselves through the lens of past expectations of people and events. We communicate and receive messages about expectations through emotions that impact our behavior. We then react or adapt our behavior according to the emotional response of these expectations. If not challenged, these expectations can become our *truth*. And we continue to attract people or experiences that align with this truth.

In 1971, Dr. Rosenthal of Harvard University told students that he had developed a strain of super intelligent rats that ran mazes effortlessly. He distributed the rats randomly, telling half of the students that they had the super bright rats and the rest of the students had normal rats. The rats that were thought to be brighter ran faster and more accurately, while the other rats did not leave the starting point. The rats were the same. The only difference was what the students were told about the rats, and how they communicated through their emotions and behavior their confidence of *expecting them to succeed.*

Positive and hopeful emotional energy is created when we communicate with words or behavior a message of high, attainable expectations. Dr. Rosenthal repeated his experiment with elementary school students. Teachers were told randomly that certain students were the brightest. These students had gains of two to seven points on their IQ scores. There was no difference in the time spent between the teachers and the students whom they thought were the brightest, and the teachers and the other students. The only difference was in *how* the teacher interacted with the students they expected to be bright. The teachers called on the students more frequently, looked at them more positively and communicated more positive remarks.

We tend to be most comfortable with people who meet our expectations. It makes us feel good. We tend to avoid people who do not meet our expectations; they make us feel not as good. The reality is that we all pre-judge based on our iceberg stories of past experiences, beliefs and others' expectations of us. Forming expectations is unavoidable and natural. Once expectations are formed, they will become a self-fulfilling prophecy unless challenged ("chip away" at your iceberg stories).

You can control your emotional response to these pre-judgments. Start to record what you pay attention to and what you do not pay attention to. Ask, *Am I listening because I expect this person to be interesting? Am I attracting interesting people or distracting interesting people because of my expectations? How can I create a climate of positive expectations through my emotions?*

What the Experts Say

Warren Bennis, author of numerous books on leadership, states that "knowledge workers, in particular, can be creative and productive and happy only in an environment that nurtures and attracts self-efficacy." Research studies validate that self-efficacy (the belief that one has the skills to succeed) is a key factor to enhance performance success and career significance.

Employees with high self-efficacy are

- More intrinsically motivated and optimistic (Bandura & Cervone, 1983; Deci & Ryan, 1995; Harackiewicz & Larson, 1986; Harter & Jackson, 1992)
- More creative (Domino, 1970; Mackinnon, 1965)
- More apt to work harder in response to significant negative feedback (Brockner & Elkind, 1985)
- Less negatively affected by chronic stressors such as role ambiguity and conflict (Mossholder, Bedeian & Armenakis, 1981)

Employees with low self-efficacy

- Set lower expectations for their performance that lead to reduced effort (Coopersmith, 1967)
- Underestimate their capabilities and subsequently establish less challenging or mediocre goals for themselves (Heatherton & Ambady, 1993)
- Tend to blame either the situation or another person when things go wrong (Bandura, 1997)
- May discover a capability to learn or cope more effectively with the challenges and demands of one's work (Bandura, 1997)

Leadership and self-efficacy

- Leaders typically have higher levels of self-efficacy than non-leaders
- Self-efficacy plays a critical role in decision making by inspiring people and garnering trust
- Leaders with high self-efficacy are generally decisive, assertive, willing to make tough decisions and exhibit high but realistic expectations of their followers, which becomes self-fulfilling

---

Your diamond mine is between your ears.
By taking charge of your mind, you can achieve your greatest dreams.

Did you know?

- Self-efficacy is not dependent on the approval of others
- You are not born with healthy self-efficacy; it is a set of skills that is learned over time
- When self-efficacy is wounded, it is not gone for good; most times it becomes hardier
- Self-efficacy is about tolerating uncertainty
- No one can give you self-efficacy except yourself
- Self-efficacy does not disregard or disrespect others
- Self-efficacy is not egotism, arrogance, narcissism or feeling superior to others
- Self-efficacy is not tied to external events such as a job promotion, other's opinions, making the team or setbacks (although it may be temporarily wounded or elevated by these events)

Join the Smart 2 Smarter Community
and learn to BE YOUR GREATEST SELF!

The Positive and Negative Attraction Loop

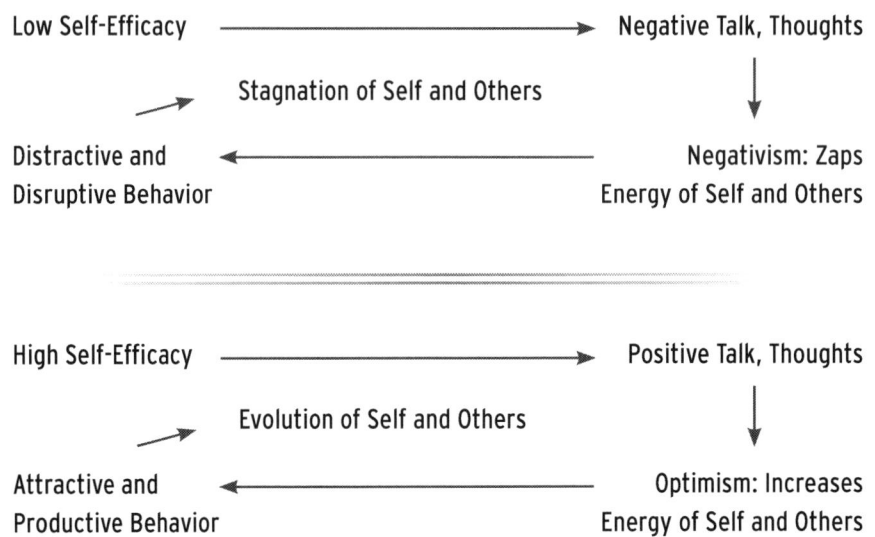

Negative Attraction Loop	Positive Attraction Loop
Past-oriented	Future- and present-oriented
Failure, or gloom-and-doom syndrome	Optimism and possibility mindset
Perfectionism is the only choice	Ability to move on and learn from mistakes or failures
Critical tapes and messages	Creates new tapes, messages and stories
Chronic comparison to others	Able to help others and accept help
External locus of control	Internal locus of control
Unable or unwilling to move on from setback or disappointments	Exhibits self-confident optimistic behaviors
Uncomfortable asking for or giving guidance	Gives and asks for forgiveness and guidance
Exhibits distracting emotional and social intelligence skills	Exhibits SMARTER emotional and social intelligence skills
Exhibits self-destructive or other behaviors	Exhibits positive energy and constructive behavior

Attraction and Career Success and Significance

On average, four out of ten individuals have a career issue they wish to discuss with their manager, and *don't*. Furthermore, most business owners and managers think people stay in their job based on their compensation (wage, salary levels or other incentives). But the real "attraction factors" are how much a manager's actions make the employee feel successful, secure and appreciated. According to Leigh Branham, author of *The Seven Hidden Reasons Employees Leave*, to inspire people to stay and contribute their personal best, leaders need to attract employees to "believe in the leader's vision, to share a workable plan and demonstrate the competence to achieve it."

Workers with low self-efficacy demonstrate behaviors that range from marginally productive to fully distracted, often distracting—and *not attracting*—positive and productive work from others. They let themselves and the business chug along. They do not provide positive emotions to propel themselves or others forward. To attract the best in self and others, design an environment that allows everyone to:

1. Feel valued
2. Feel competent
3. Feel safe and secure
4. Feel empowered

Branham offers several techniques to attract the personal best from employees in the workplace:

Provide Coaching and Feedback

- Hold managers accountable for onboarding coaching and feedback

Provide Career Advancement and Growth Opportunities

- Keep employees informed about the company's strategy, direction and talent forecasts

Make Employees Feel Valued and Recognized

- Ask new employees for input, then listen and respond; keep employees in the loop
- Design the physical environment to provide the right tools, climate and resources

Reduce Negative Energy from Life/Work Imbalance and Overwork

- Initiate a culture of "giving before getting"
- Design a culture that values spontaneous acts of caring
- Build social connectedness and cohesion among employees

Inspire Trust and Confidence in Senior Leaders

- Inspire confidence through a clear vision, a workable plan and the competence to win
- Demonstrate trust and confidence through words and actions

SOURCE: Excerpted from *The Seven Hidden Reasons Employees Leave* by Leigh Branham, ©2005. Published by AMACOM Books, a division of American Management Association, New York. Used with permission. All rights reserved, http://www.amacombooks.org

Attraction and Greatness

Greatness is a state of being that is experienced when you attract the people, experiences and outcomes that bring out your personal best and the personal best of others. The universal *Law of Attraction* states that you attract or distract everything that happens in your life—and you can deliberately attract more of what you really want. It is *not a condition of achievement.*

Attraction is a skill that allows you to attract the best people, ideas and opportunities. According to Thomas Leonard, author of *The Portable Coach: 28 Surefire Strategies for Business and Personal Success*, attraction is success without striving. Attraction is an intentional choice of managing your emotions to attract a social climate to *be* your greatness. You do this by attracting:

1. Behaviors that, when present, push you forward

2. Energy that motivates and inspires you and others

3. People who energize and support you to move toward goals despite setbacks, speed bumps and change

4. Optimistic environments within which you feel valued and accepted

---

A feeling is the response, or *attraction*, part of the emotion. Emotion is an umbrella term which includes the situation, your interpretation of the situation, and the response or feeling related to your interpretation of the situation.

When attracting a state of greatness you

- Trust and act on your intuition
- Have freedom from the past and the future
- Are totally present living in the moment
- Are free of judgments
- Are free from the grip of an emotional hijacking
- Have the willingness and capacity to feel anything and everything
- Attract by intentional choice
- Create and enjoy more free time (space)
- Create and experience less stress (flow)
- Create and have more energy (synergy)
- Want to take better care of your body (choice)
- Nourish your own and others' spirit (better connected)

Attraction works similarly to how a chiropractor reduces blockages, or how an airplane flies in the less-resistant atmosphere, or how a flower always points to the sun, or a magnet attracts iron.

Attraction and Optimism

According to EQ research, people who attract success and significance in life measure high on assessments of optimistic attitudes. It would be easy to presume they are optimistic because they are successful, but research shows that *optimism precedes success.* Traditional wisdom puts forth the idea that to be successful you must have two things:

> Success is measured by your ability to maintain enthusiasm between failures. A pessimist sees the difficulty in every opportunity; an optimist sees the opportunity in every difficulty.
> *—Sir Winston Churchill*

    1. Talent or aptitude

    2. Motivation

More recent research shows that a third element contributes strongly to people's success:

    3. An optimistic attitude, particularly in the face of adversity

High scores for optimism are predictive of excellence in everything from sports to health, elections, and sales. When Metropolitan Life used an assessment of optimistic attitude to select and hire salespeople, they saved themselves millions of dollars in personnel selection. Those highest on the optimism scale outsold others in their first year by 27 percent. At American Express Financial Advisors, a pilot test of optimism training increased sales enough after only three months to make it a standard part of training.

Optimists are more resistant to infectious illness, and are better at fending off chronic diseases of middle age. In one study of 96 men who had their first heart attack in 1980, 15 of the 16 most pessimistic men died of a second heart attack within eight years, but only five of the 16 most optimistic men died.

Dr. Martin Seligman, researcher, author, psychologist at the University of Pennsylvania, and founder of Authentic Happiness, has shown that optimists not only do better educationally and in their careers, they also enjoy superior health and longevity. Data from cancer patients show a definite association between pessimism and mortality for those under 60.

Dr. Seligman has spent a lifetime studying why some people are more resilient than others. He has developed several assessments that measure overall happiness and optimism. In one study of school children over several years, those scoring highest for pessimism were most likely later to suffer depression. To assess your level of optimism, visit Dr. Seligman's website at www.authentichappiness.com.

A Few More Words About Optimism

Are you a dynamic or passive optimist?

Most people say they are optimists, and many will say they are optimistic, but with a dose of reality. Max More, Ph.D., has proposed an interesting concept about two distinct kinds of optimists: Those who are *dynamic* and those who are *passive*. Dynamic optimists have an active, empowering attitude, which creates conditions for success by focusing and acting on possibilities and opportunities. Passive optimists simply tell themselves that all will work out just fine.

A passive optimist, while more effective than a pessimist, sees no need to take action. While the pessimist focuses on problems, pains and pitfalls, the passive optimist sees only what is encouraging and enjoyable. They expect that other people and organizations will solve the problems. They think positively but don't know how to turn thoughts into actions. They are blinded to potential obstacles which lead to missed opportunities or limited success. At its worst, passive optimism leads to unhealthy emotional and social connections.

Those who are really dynamic in their optimism turn their thoughts into proactive behaviors. Dynamic optimists notice different things, experience different motivations and emotions, and take different actions.

They dwell on the constructive and enjoyable while de-emphasizing pain, difficulty and frustration. Such a person can look at a frustrating event, fully accept its reality, and then choose to interpret the event in a way that leads to action, growth and mastery. They recognize dangers, but have a wider vision open to solutions, possibilities and assisting forces.

What Happens When an Optimist Hits the Wall?

Think about the times during the day that you are distracted, blocked and feel discouraged, as if you've run up against a brick wall. What do you do when you hit that wall?

Optimistic individuals persevere and persist. They view procrastinating as a lack of optimistic emotional energy to start and finish a task. They do not see procrastination as laziness. Optimists know the root of the problem is to stop the *negative attraction loop* (refer to page 76) of a person facing an unpleasant, routine or challenging task. A pessimist first thinks negative thoughts when facing such tasks. The optimist thinks positive thoughts that actually encourage and energize.

Everyone has their own wall (point of discouragement). What you do when you hit this wall can mean the difference between attracting helplessness, guilt and a sense of failure, or attracting success and feelings of accomplishment.

Here are *three important tools* for learning to cultivate and attract an optimistic attitude:

1. **Notice what you focus on when a bad event happens to you—are you seeing only one side of the situation?** Are there opportunities that you can focus on, rather than mistakes? Would a dynamic optimist look at this situation and see different things? How else could you view this? Are you looking at this as permanent or temporary? Are you looking at this as global, or specific to this one event only? Do you assign blame personally, or to some external person or thing? *Action* Review your *Positive and Negative Attraction Loop* (page 76)

2. **Talk to yourself with kindness** If something goes wrong, pessimists tend to have hopeless thoughts. They tell themselves, *I'll never get it right*, or *There I go again, I always screw up.* Even worse, they label

themselves with a global declaration of negativity: *I'm a stupid fool.* The goal here is for the person to speak to themselves with kindness and compassion as they would a friend. The optimist might say something like: *Ouch! That didn't go very well today, but I can learn from this. Some of what I did can be corrected. I can do better tomorrow.* To counteract the negative labeling, the person can reframe his or her self-talk by saying, *I know I feel like a stupid fool, but I'm not. I'm a lot better than I was when I first started this job. I'm learning quite quickly and I'm not going to get everything perfect all of the time.* **Action** Examine your internal dialogue, then change what and how you speak to yourself

3. **Distract yourself with pleasurable activities** The other technique for overcoming pessimism is distraction from negative thinking. It's important to not ruminate about bad events that happen to you, at least not immediately. Studies show that if you think about problems in a negative frame of mind, you actually come up with fewer solutions. By boosting mood and self-esteem, and by participating in activities that are pleasurable, you can break the pessimistic cycle and free yourself to think more creatively. Distraction with pleasant activities will free your mind to think more optimistically as you move forward. **Action** Practice *18 Minutes Back to Flow* (www.smart2smarter.com)

Positive Attraction and the Bottom Line

Studies have actually produced data to prove how important a positive climate is in creating good business results. At one insurance company, a researcher found that positive attraction influenced service climate among agents, accounting for a three to four percent difference in insurance renewals—a seemingly small margin, but one that made a huge difference to the business. In a study of nineteen insurance companies, the climate created by the CEOs among their direct reports predicted the business performance of the entire organization, in that, in 75 percent of the cases, climate alone accurately sorted companies into high versus low profits and growth categories.

One study of 62 CEOs and their top management teams assessed how upbeat they were (through their enthusiasm, energy and determination). They were also asked how much conflict the top team experienced in the form of personality clashes, friction in meetings and emotional conflicts (in contrast to disagreements about ideas). The study found that the more positive the overall moods of people in the top management team, the more cooperatively they worked together—and the better the company's business results. The company's market returns declined for the management team that did not get along. This is a clear example of the power of attraction.

Common sense would predict that employees who feel good will make more efforts to please customers, and in return produce increased revenues. Since emotions are contagious, all employees, whether the CEO, manager or head of a team, have a responsibility for attracting positive emotions.

Attraction and Emotional Images

In his book, *Transforming YourSelf: Becoming Who You Want to Be*, Steve Andreas explored how one develops an attractive self-image. He states that our inner self has a structure of images, emotions, and memories of attractiveness. How strongly you feel about a particular attractive quality (such as empathy) is directly related to how vivid your memory is about that quality.

Andreas learned that the strengths of our images and memories are related to how strongly we believe in the capability and value of a particular personal quality. For example, if you believe and value the personal quality of empathy, your images and attractiveness will be that much stronger.

He suggests using kindness as an example of a personal quality. Then, answer this question: *Are you kind?* Most people know the answer to the question, and begin to feel or see a sound or image that symbolizes kindness. Now answer this question: *How do you know you are kind?* If you attract kindness, then a series of memories and stories will emerge of recorded scenes of your kindness. Therefore, if you want to be seen as kind, create more memories and stories of kindness.

What often occurs is the minimizing and downplaying of a personal quality that you once valued and at which you are quite good. Andreas purports that if our reference experiences are not vivid and in bold colors, like a motion picture, then our emotions will not record the full attractiveness of the quality. And if you do not receive reinforcement of the attractiveness of the quality, the memory will not get stored as significant and valued. For example, if you have displayed the quality of assertiveness, but your Gremlin is saying that you are being selfish, the attractive quality of assertiveness will not have as many vivid stored positive memories.

When researching the concept of self, Andreas discovered that a robust self-image that is open to feedback, reflects a person's competence, and will not collapse when challenged, is most conducive to attracting the best in self and others. Stored memories also have counter-examples of when a quality was not used, with vivid images and emotions that remind you of consequences, what not to do, and how to go back to the desired attractive quality. To increase memories of attractive qualities, Andreas suggests these exercises:

1. To develop an attractive quality, go back through your life and find examples, stories, images and pictures of when you showed this quality.

2. Write a paragraph about this image. What was important? Who are the players? What did you learn? Make your story a 3-D memory with emotions, people and actions!

3. If you are unable to remember your own stories, ask others what stories they have witnessed of you displaying this quality.

4. Another tip is to write a scene about when you witnessed this quality in others.

5. After you have some positive stories, recall counter-examples of when the quality was not displayed.

6. To increase confidence in the quality, and attractiveness to it, ask yourself and others what you can do to stretch this quality a bit further—create more scenes!

Conclusion

The ability to attract positive feelings in others is just SMARTER. When people feel good, they work better, are more creative and more productive. Good feelings are like lubrication to the brain: Mental efficiency goes up, memory is sharpened, and people understand directions and make better decisions.

One way to attract greatness is to understand what you are doing—or not doing—to create a climate of positive energy. It can be as simple as being more empathetic and less judgmental (understand what another person may be dealing with, and how that can affect their behavior). Another way is to be crystal clear about your values (things that guide your *significance* compass).

Do you feel fully or somewhat engaged in your current job, college major or career path? Do you feel you are contributing your personal best, or do you feel you would be better off somewhere else? If you answered yes to the latter part of the question, can you define what "better off" means for you?

Work Engagement Values are what drive the passion a person brings to his or her work. Passion is the natural energy, motivation and enthusiasm about how you contribute in the world of work. Work engagement—*flow*—is when you feel energized, focused, positive, blissful and absorbed in an activity in a seemingly effortless and fluid way. When a Work Engagement Value is satisfied, an individual is fully engaged to attract their personal best. When absent or neglected, the engagement spark is missing. For example, when teachers believe in the value of the subject, it often sparks the commitment and energy they bring to their work.

> Surround yourself with the kind of people you want to be like, and you will become that kind of person.

To sum up, a great way to clarify what attracts and engages your *work flow* is to understand what you value. Your values are the foundation of any SMARTER development plan. Values inspire you to attract the life/work satisfiers you want, and often need, to contribute your personal best.

Join the Smart2Smarter Community *to access the following activities and additional* **ATTRACTION** *resources and assessments online at* www.Smart2Smarter.com

Attract Optimism book and website
My Personal Attraction Statement (PAS) book and website
Attraction and Behavior book
Five Steps to Attract Greatness book and website
Managing My Gremlin book and website
The Positive and Negative Attraction Loop book and website
Gremlin Speaks website
Intentional Optimism website
Design Action to Attract Your Greatness website
28 Principles of Attraction (learn to apply principles to attract your greatness) website
Workplace Engagement Values Assessment and Guide (learn what values
    attract your personal best) website

Activity Attract Optimism

This is a self-measure of your optimistic or pessimistic attitude. **For each section below, circle 1, 2 or 3, and add up your score.**

When something *good* happens to me, I tell myself that:

A. 1. This kind of thing always happens

2. These things happen sometimes

3. This never happens

B. 1. This event happened because of something I've done

2. This happened because of me, but I was lucky (in the right place at the right time)

3. What happened is really due to someone or something else

C. 1. This is a great example of the way things always go for me

2. This event is great, but it is limited to this one specific situation

3. This event is a quirk; it will never happen again

When something *bad* happens to me, I tell myself that:

A. 1. Wow, how unusual! This never happens!

2. This may be just a quirk; it normally doesn't happen

3. Here we go again...this is typical of what always happens

B. 1. It's not me—it's them

2. Maybe I could have done better, but so should they

3. I should have done better—it's my fault

C. 1. Well, this is only limited to this one situation

2. This is too bad, and it could easily happen again

3. This is awful; it will ruin everything

The lower your score (close to 6), the more optimistic you are. The higher your score (close to 18), the more pessimistic you are. If you scored in the mid-range, you may be optimistic, but passively so. In order to achieve more, be more successful, maintain good health and possible longevity, you may want to work on how you can raise your score and develop a more dynamic optimistic attitude.

Activity   My Personal Attraction Statement (PAS)

Your Personal Attraction Statement (PAS) states how you attract others to live your greatness. Your PAS communicates what is your greatness, how this greatness looks and how your greatness serves others. This is important because it focuses your intentions, actions and results. When you use the energy of attraction, you are paying attention to what is going on inside of you, yet it shows up outside of you.

The way you respond is a reflection of your belief about your work and your life. If your answer is vague, then others will not be attracted to your energy. However, when you respond in a passionate manner with a clear benefit for your work, the message becomes a powerful magnet that draws others to you. You can express yourself or depress yourself. You can be interesting or boring. You can attract or distract.

How to communicate your Personal Attraction Statement (PAS)

- **People are attracted to me** because…
- **What this looks like** to those I attract is…
- **The benefit** to me, and the benefit to others, is…

Cynthia Kivland's Personal Attraction Statement

Clients are attracted to work with me as a coach because I create a climate where they can connect to their greatness through the energy of my skills, passion, knowledge and experience. *What this looks like* is an invitation to my clients to discover their greatness, commit to a plan and begin to practice forward actions that encourage them to be their personal best. *The benefit to me* is being a successful and significant coach, and *the benefit to clients* is gaining the SMARTER tools, behaviors and knowledge to be their personal best.

On the next page, write your Personal Attraction Statement…

Write your Personal Attraction Statement (PAS)

Activity   Attraction and Behavior

Choose a Response

Consider these situations and reflect: *Who would bring out your personal best?* (Remember, we are all leaders of our careers)

Someone who...

A. has all the answers

B. asks the right questions

Views asking for help...

A. as a sign of weakness

B. as a sign of strength

Views self-knowledge activities...

A. as a waste of time

B. as the foundation for self-efficacy

(Answering "B" to all of the above is the SMARTER career choice.)

Activity   Five Steps to Attract Greatness

The first step to greatness is to intentionally increase positive attraction moments. Therefore, greatness is a SMARTER habit. It starts with knowledge of what positively *(flow)* or negatively *(hijack)* influences self-acceptance and respect. Next, listen to your body, emotions and thoughts. All provide cues about your self-efficacy. Listen, and then inquire: *What do these cues say about my competence and confidence to cope with life's challenges?* Trust your gut about what these cues are telling you. Then ask, *What strengths, abilities or SMARTER skills can help me manage this challenge or story differently?*

> You are educated when you have the ability to listen to almost anything without losing your temper or self-confidence. *—Robert Frost*

1. **Body Awareness**
   Self-efficacy is signaled through your body—you just need to listen. Notice physical cues, such as shortness of breath, neck, shoulder, or back pain, a queasy stomach or a recurring headache. What are these cues saying about your confidence and capability to manage the situation now?

2. **Emotions: Who is Your Gremlin?**
   As mentioned in Chapter 2, your emotional brain directly impacts how you think and act. Signals from your emotional brain may include anxiety, fear, sadness, panic, anger and happiness. Your brain is wired to *react* when you feel threatened—whether that threat is real or imagined. The SMARTER behavior is to short-circuit the emotional hijacking. Remember the phrase: *I am so mad/scared/anxious that I cannot think straight!* Then tap into your rational mind and inquire: *Is there something about this situation that is similar to a previous anxiety-provoking situation? Is this emotional reaction telling me something about the people in this room, or about a story I need to give up?* Step back, or literally step out—it is hard to make good decisions when you are emotionally hijacked (see *Managing My Gremlin*, page 91).

3. **Thoughts: Challenge Your Stories**
   Your personal story impacts what you think about and how often those thoughts attract or distract your greatness. According to Brian G. Jett, you can determine how confident people are by listening

to what they *do not say* about themselves. Your story has evolved from real and perceived events that have molded your self-efficacy in good, and not so good, ways. Self-efficacy develops over a long period of time—just like an iceberg. Your parents, environment, ethnicity, economic status, education level, significant life events, mentors or lack of mentors influence your inner images. These factors impact your self-efficacy, creating a "thought" filter. The background noise impacts how you feel about yourself, what you pay attention to and how often. It also impacts how you talk about yourself and how you behave around certain people or events. For example, do you say: *I am such an idiot, I should be..., I never..., What is wrong with me? I should not be feeling..., It must be my fault...* or *Why am I not able to get over this?* What personal story is it time to give up? What tapes need to be erased? What words need to be zapped from your vocabulary? What new chapter in your "book of life" needs to be closed, and what chapter needs to be written? Ask yourself, *Does what I'm currently thinking make me feel better or worse about myself?* Then say out loud, or write down: *How long am I going to allow this thought to impact my greatness?*

4. **Play Bigger**
   Often my clients replay the same tape about some person or event that wounded their *possibilities*. If your world is small, it may be time to invite new characters, expand your environment and create a new script. "Playing bigger" requires expanding your social and emotional experiences. What are you doing with others that build you up? Are there people in your life that "tell it like it is" and still support you? Are there people in your life that you support? Self-reflection or coaching can help you to understand your purpose, get a sense of the big picture of your life, and keep your other problems contained in a "smaller" perspective.

5. **Keep Life Real**
   Attract the life you deserve by answering a series of "get real" questions before or after a significant event (see next page).

Join the Smart 2 Smarter Community
and learn to *ATTRACT* SMARTER!

Self-Inquiry

- What did I do right? How do I define right?
- What could I have done SMARTER?
- What lesson did I learn?
- Write the SMARTER ending
- Share your story with others
- What do I really want to attract from this experience or event? Best possible outcome? Potential costs?
- Where does this experience or event fit into attracting my personal best *now*?
- What value was expressed? What inner representation or movie will be stored?

Activity   Managing My Gremlin

Our Gremlin is a creature developed by beliefs and feelings to maintain our status quo. It often operates as if to protect us, when in fact it keeps us from moving forward and blocks us from getting what we truly want. The Gremlin is neither good nor bad; it just *is*. The Gremlin loses its power when we identify it for what it is.

The Gremlin often precipitates an emotional hijacking. It can be that inner voice of beliefs that hijacks our confidence and capabilities to manage life's challenges or initiate opportunities. It will have a favorite language: *I should..., They will not respect or like..., I cannot...* Our Gremlin is creative and persistent; therefore, it is important to identify self-sabotaging behavior (via the Gremlin) that may impede your progress and stall attracting your greatness.

Date _____   Gremlin's Name _____

When does your Gremlin show up most? (A Gremlin is whatever may be hijacking your own or others' personal best efforts to protect the status quo.)

_____

_____

From what is your Gremlin protecting you (usually a fear)?

_____

_____

What do you want to have? What is your Gremlin preventing you from achieving?

_____

_____

What type of person elicits your Gremlin to appear?

_____

_____

What are you most likely doing when your Gremlin appears?

_____

_____

What do you gain/lose from *self-managing* your Gremlin?

Gain _____

Lose _____

What do you gain/lose from *not self-managing* your Gremlin?

Gain _____

Lose _____

What do you need to learn or do better to manage your Gremlin? What can you do to interfere with an emotional hijacking prompted by your Gremlin?

_____

_____

Resilience

Chapter 7

What is resilience? Resilience is a belief and a skill. It is to first see and feel the hope and possibilities rather than the obstacles and doom. It is to live from a place of significance, and not from a place of meaninglessness. EQ research finds resilience to be a top predictor for career success and significance.

Resilience is under your control. It is a skill upon which you can learn and improve. As you learn to become more resilient, you will profoundly change how well you handle setbacks. You will embrace challenges and have confidence to step outside of your comfort zone. Some of us are born into circumstances that forge resilience early. However, most of us can learn how to build more or better emotional reserves to be resilient.

> Resilience is the ability to persevere and adapt when things aren't going the way we'd like. It is mentally, and often physically, stepping back to examine and reflect on a situation and to determine the best action. When we act resiliently, we act from a proactive place of hope instead of a reactive place of fear.

This chapter will explore resilience as a proactive—not reactive—mindset and behavior. At the core of resilience is the ability to *persist* even when things are happening just like you expected them to, to *navigate* through uncertain and unpredictable times, to *transcend* common problems and barriers, and to build *reserves* to thrive in the future. Resilience is how you choose to respond to an expected or unexpected event. It is what you do when you feel stuck. Let's explore how healthy and diverse your resilience reserves are, and how to apply the intelligence of emotions through the seasons of your life.

Resilience and the Two Wolves Fight

An old Cherokee is teaching his grandson about life.

"A fight is going on inside me," he said to the boy. "It is a terrible fight between two wolves."

"One is evil—he is anger, envy, sorrow, greed, regret, lies, self-pity, arrogance, guilt, resentment, inferiority, false pride, superiority and ego."

"The other is good—he is joy, peace, love, hope, serenity, humility, kindness, benevolence, empathy, generosity, truth, compassion and faith."

"This same fight is going on inside you—and inside every other person, too."

The grandson thought for a minute, and then asked his grandfather, "Which wolf will win?"

The old Cherokee replied, "The one you feed."

Author Unknown

Resilience is using the intelligence of your emotions to adapt, reinvent and renew—to feed the SMARTER wolf. Resilience is not how you initially choose to respond to a change event, but how you manage the intelligence of your emotions to navigate the transition. William Bridges, author of the bestselling book, *Transitions: Making Sense of Life's Changes*, explains the two parts of any change event.

First is the change itself, which happens at a certain point in time. The change can be planned or unplanned, happy or sad. Changes are a fact of life. Second is the transition. The transition usually starts well before the change and continues long after. The *change is largely factual*. The *transition is largely emotional*. It is also internal. We can understand the change with IQ, but understanding the transition takes social and emotional intelligence.

A transition is an event or non-event that impacts your emotions, thinking and behavior. Most transitions are associated with significant life events—changes to the individual's role or environment that challenge the individual's comfort zone. This includes positive life events (e.g., college graduation, marriage, birth of a child or a new job) along with real or perceived negative events.

According to Nancy Schlossberg, psychologist and expert on the social and emotional impact of transitions, a resilient response is more viable when an individual has acquired knowledge, experience and behaviors to manage the following parts of a transition: Context, Scope and Type.

1. **What is the *Context* of the transition?**
   - How does the transition impact self (*Intra*personal) and relationships (*Inter*personal)?

2. **What is the *Scope* of the impact?**
   - What are the pre- and post-events? How much of your life will be impacted?

3. **What is the *Type* of transition?**
   - Was the transition anticipated (new baby) or unanticipated (loss of a job)?
   - Is it a chronic hassle (traffic jam or annoying co-worker)?
   - Is it a non-event (something you thought would happen, but didn't)?

Navigate Resiliently Through a Transition

According to Bridges, there are common phases of any transition process:

The Ending

It is important to understand that mourning is a natural reaction to loss, and part of the healing process. During endings, people crave information, but may not assimilate it very well. They want to know what will happen, when it will happen and who will be affected. The information may need to be repeated often, and through different mediums.

An activity that goes on inside of people during an ending is a *sorting* process that involves what is actually over (that which they can let go) and what still exists. Often a timely and symbolic action, such as a ceremony, can dramatize the ending, communicating the message that it is time to let go of some of the old ways of being and doing.

In the Neutral Zone

In the neutral zone, people feel *emotionally naked* and confused. This is a time when people are tempted to move to the survive path, and protect "number one."

They are missing the comfortable ways of doing, knowing and being. They do not have a clear vision or direction of what will carry them into the future. The neutral zone is a natural time to experiment. It is a time to reflect on an area in which you can be comfortable experimenting. Coaches, counselors, teachers, leaders, family and colleagues can help you during your time in the neutral zone. Use the acronym of **CUSP** to stay focused on what you and others need when in the neutral zone.

Control over the future; provide people with the explanations that will enable them to feel a sense of control and to **U**nderstand why they are feeling what they are feeling; do what you can to provide them with some **S**upport at this vulnerable time; and give them a new sense of **P**urpose when the old purposes are being called into question.

During the Beginning

This is a place where people begin to feel they have input into, and control over, what happens next. They feel someone is listening to them. When people are trying out new behaviors that do not yet feel normal and natural, recognition and reward can have a calming and positive effect. Some people need a general description of what has changed. Others need a concrete and realistic picture and need to see things in terms of specific behaviors and examples. Also, some individuals (often leaders) are likely to let go before others are even aware of the transition. They are out of the neutral zone and ready for the new beginning just when others wake up to the reality that they have to let go of the status quo.

After the Transition Has Ended

Throughout life, we often move from one change to another, and in different areas of our lives. It is important to learn what worked, what didn't, and remember what life lesson was gained from the transition process. Completing a timeline of the change event is important. Use a timeline to reflect and record what behaviors, actions or people served you best. What do you wish you did? What are you glad you did? And what were you hijacked (or not) into doing? Also, take time to assess how your reserves (social, community, career, physical, spiritual and technical resources) were a support or hindrance.

> Begin with the possible; begin with one step. There is always a limit, you cannot do more than you can. If you try to do too much, you will do nothing.   —P.D. Ouspensky & G.I. Gurdjieff

Hardiness and Social and Emotional Resilience

When coaching clients around the subject of resilience, I often ask them to recall and reflect on a challenge or adversity in their life. Then I ask them to jot down the essence of the situation and recall the social connections and emotions surrounding the challenge. Recalling emotional signals and social connections surrounding a current or past change creates awareness about the people or habits that hold you back or push you forward.

In the chapter on Mastery, you learned that when a change event takes place, a primal reaction kicks in to defend against it. Primal instincts are our natural defense mechanism against a threat or change to our lives or well-being. Some primal reactions at the beginning of a change event are slamming the phone, withdrawing or yelling. Primal instincts keep you in the *Fear Path*. Staying in the Fear Path keeps you stuck—unable to bounce back or move forward.

Shifting from the Fear Path into the *Hope Path* requires what researchers Salvatore Maddi and Deborah Khoshaba (2005) describe as "emotional and social hardiness." Their studies indicate that emotional and social hardiness contributes to resilience. They identified *three emotional and social hardiness choices* that accelerate the transition process. I added two more that are aligned with the SMARTER skills of *reciprocity* and *tolerance*.

1. **Challenge vs. Threat** Emotionally hardy people view stress as a challenge, which motivates them to address changes in positive ways. This proactive and hopeful approach is contrasted with the *fear approach* where change is viewed as a threat (an unfortunate, overwhelming and often paralyzing force that keeps one stuck).

2. **Personal Control vs. Powerlessness** Emotionally and socially hardy people accept challenges and believe that they have the personal power to overcome and master them (the key word here is *believe*). Their beliefs fuel positive energy and thoughts such as, *Even when a situation is not possible to control (the loss of a job, for instance), I can attract people and possibilities to move me forward.* The opposite of

this is a feeling of powerlessness. This is when the individual believes that they have no power to change what has happened. Powerlessness keeps one in the Fear Path. People who feel powerless look for others to "fix" problems and tend to play the role of *victim* (see the *Karpman Drama Triangle*, page 60).

3. **Commitment vs. Alienation** Often a change event causes an individual to ask: *What is my purpose?* Emotionally and socially hardy people persist longer than others because they have a clear definition of their career or life significance—they feel that their life is significant, and they find purpose in their life in spite of adversity. This commitment to their purpose motivates them to seek support and persevere even when their first attempts don't work. Individuals who alienate themselves from others, or have a vague purpose in life, tend to stay in the Fear Path longer. They lack the desire and motivation to be involved with the people or events that can move them forward.

4. **Community vs. Isolation** Hardy people who bounce back quicker tend to have a community that supports, consoles and inspires them to "reach higher." Their community accepts their humanness, and is a source of strength during times of adversity. Conversely, individuals who isolate themselves from social connections when faced with adversity lack the SMARTER skill called *reciprocity* (see Chapter 10). Reciprocity is the ability to give and receive, teach and be taught, and lead and be led.

5. **In Context vs. Endless** Tolerance is the ability to see change events within the context of a bigger Self and universe. *Context is a key trait of resilience and hardiness.* It is the ability to step back and look at the change from a different angle within the context of the particular situation. It is also the ability to see the change as an event that may impact some parts of their lives, but does not have to take over every part of their life. Conversely, those who choose only to see the change as endless, without any particular context, tend to think that a change in one area of their lives will impact *all* areas of their life. This *thinking style* becomes overwhelming and hijacks the person into a "why bother" or the "world is against me" mindset.

A tool I find useful to help assess hardiness characteristics is the *Emotional and Social Hardiness Spectrum* on the next page. I provide brief definitions, then ask the client to reflect on their change and where they are on the spectrum. The reflection and dialogue helps the client to identify what is needed to move forward and to begin challenging the beliefs that may be holding them back.

Emotional and Social Hardiness Spectrum

1) **Challenge**   **Threat**

     View change as instrumental in opening up new pathways for living a fulfilling life

2) **Personal Control**   **Powerlessness**

     Choosing to influence the outcomes of events and changes in your life from a position of hope, not fear

3) **Commitment**   **Alienation**

     The desire and motivation to be involved with the people and events in your life

4) **Community**   **Isolation**

     Asking for help and engaging others to overcome adversity rather than alienating themselves

5) **In Context**   **Endless**

     Place changes into a broader context and explore how one's *thinking style* impacts moving forward

What Are You Thinking...Gloom, Doom or Bloom?

Resilience asks the mind to reconstruct and adapt to a new reality. During change, the mind goes through a rewiring, which is often short-circuited by the emotional survival response. This survival response has you holding onto beliefs, expectations and behaviors that support the past. The resilient mind rewires new pathways. The resilient mind integrates the cognitive, emotional and behavioral self to be creative, confident, optimistic and energized.

Shakespeare wrote, "There is nothing either good or bad, but thinking makes it so." The key speed bump in resiliency is how we think about a situation and what we tell ourselves about it. It is not an event or person that causes problems in our life—it is *what we tell ourselves about the event* that determines our feelings and beliefs about it, both positive and negative. How we choose to interpret the event triggers our action or reaction.

Dr. Seligman researched the direct connection between a person's thinking style and how one explains negative events. He describes this research in his book, *Learned Optimism: How to Change Your Mind and Your Life.*

Self-talk is the internal monologue we have inside of our

When adversity happens, do you tend to blame yourself, or do you tend to blame others? Do you tell yourself this always happens to me or things will never change?

head (the thought bubbles that you see in cartoons). Self-talk triggers emotional responses to an event that lead to reactions (what we say and do). Self-talk is a powerful component of resilience. *Our self-talk is largely determined by our thinking style.* When adversity happens, what do you tell yourself? Do you give yourself a pep talk or tear yourself down? People who are low in resilience explain negative events as:

- *It's my fault* (Personalization)
- *This is going to ruin my life* (Pervasiveness)
- *It will always be this way* (Permanence)

Dr. Seligman further describes these *three thinking styles* that people use to explain adversity:

Style #1

Personalization Internal vs. External (Me/Not me)

Internalizing (seeing adversity as a result of me and my actions)
vs.

Externalizing (seeing the cause of the event as external to me)

When adversity strikes, do I blame myself, or do I blame other people or circumstances?

Style #2

Pervasiveness Universal vs. Specific (Everything/Not everything)

Seeing the impact as universal (affecting all areas of my life)

vs.

Seeing the impact as specific (affecting a specific part of my life)

Do I see the negative event impacting all of my life, or is the impact isolated to a specific event or person?

Style #3

Permanence Ongoing vs. Temporary (Always/Not always)

Seeing the dilemma that I face as ongoing (continuing forever to impact my life)

vs.

Seeing the dilemma that I face as temporary (having an impact for a very short duration)

Do I see the event as persisting in my life, or do I see it as short-lived?

People who are high in resilience

- Accurately assess their contribution and the contributions of others to the adversity or change; they also recognize when an event is beyond their control **(Personalization)**
- Specifically identify the extent of the impact that the adversity or change will have in their life; they do not catastrophize or minimize **(Pervasiveness)**
- Can tell when the adversity or change is temporary, and when they have to cope with something long-term **(Permanence)**

To assess your thinking style, take the **What Are You Thinking Assessment** *(p. 115)*

Thinking Style and the ABCD's of Resilience

Imagine this scenario

Michael and Jane have been co-workers for about three years. They get along, but with a recent downsizing, the uncertainty about job security, and little explanation from senior management, tension has begun to build, straining their relationship and trust. Recently, Jane questioned the numbers that Michael had given her for a report. Michael became angry and stormed off. He was certain Jane doubted his professionalism, and that she was trying to get him fired.

What triggered this reaction in Michael? It wasn't what Jane said. Michael's reaction was triggered by his assumptions about Jane's intentions.

The question to ask when facing an adversity is, *Am I seeing the real picture here?* How accurate is your self-talk when facing adversity? Are there common behavior, thinking or emotional traps or habits that you fall into?

Andrew Shatté and Karen Reivich have identified eight common traps in their book, *The Resilience Factor: 7 Keys to Finding Your Inner Strength and Overcoming Life's Hurdles.* The most common trap in our thinking is jumping to conclusions. We do this when we make assumptions without the relevant data. It's the umbrella-thinking trap, since all of the traps involve making an assumption. Other traps include magnifying the consequences, personalizing the causes, and mind reading by assuming that you know what the other person is thinking or intending by their actions.

Disputing Our Traps

A key to resiliency and interpersonal effectiveness is to improve the accuracy of our thinking by minimizing these traps. We can be more accurate by questioning the assumptions (or self-talk) we make as we engage another person. To improve the accuracy of your thinking, you must avoid mind traps by disputing self-talk and beliefs.

Disputation involves actively questioning the conclusions that we have drawn. There are *four important ways* to make your disputations credible:

The first two ways apply to our beliefs about the causes of the adversity.

Evaluating the evidence Disputation by showing that the belief is incorrect (not accurate). The most convincing way of disputing negative traps is to show that it is factually incorrect. Play the role of a detective and ask, *What is the evidence for this belief?*

Generating alternatives Scan for all of the possible contributing causes for the adversity. Focus on alternative explanations that are non-personal, changeable and specific. Ask yourself if there are any less destructive ways to look at this situation.

The final two ways work with our beliefs (often based on our iceberg story) about the implications of the adversity.

Review the implications (decatastrophize) Put the situation in perspective. Maybe the self-talk is correct in this situation. So what does that imply about your ability and you? And how likely is the worst-case scenario?

Determine the usefulness of the trap Even if the belief is true, is the situation changeable? What can you do to deal with this and get around it? Identify behavior changes or actions to change the situation.

The ABCD Model

Albert Ellis is often considered the father of research on how emotions interact with rational thought. He developed a model on how to use the intelligence of your emotions to dispute adversity, anger or worry. He called his model the *ABCD Model* (or *Rational-Emotive Model*).

The *ABCD Model* will help you to intentionally choose how to respond at a problem-solving level rather than at a blaming, shaming or complaining level. Using the *ABCD Model* helps you to be aware of the *thinking style* you use to explain events. Research has shown that using a more optimistic way of explaining events increases our ability to bounce back—this is the hallmark of being resilient. A SMARTER thinking style is within your control.

A Describe the *Activating* situation or trigger event. Objectively describe the who, what, where and when of the situation. Avoid emotionally-laden terms or language designed to justify your reaction to it.

B Identify the assumptions and *Beliefs* you had about that situation. What were the iceberg stories and images that went through your mind during and after the event? What do you tell yourself about the event (your self-talk)? What are your beliefs and expectations of others on how they should act or not act?

C Identify the *Consequences* and emotions tied to the event. What are you saying and doing as a consequence of the triggering event? What emotions were evoked as you explored the consequence of your decision?

D *Dispute* self-talk and beliefs. Disputation involves questioning conclusions, alternatives, implications and usefulness. Examine your beliefs and expectations. Are they unrealistic or irrational?

If you want to stay focused on what really matters, practice your ABCD's for the next month by identifying one thinking trap per day. Write four columns on a sheet of paper, labeling the first *A*, then *B*, then *C*, and then *D*. Use it as a worksheet to improve your awareness of good and bad resilient habits.

Reserves and Resiliency

Imagine a sponge or a coil and how they can get bent out of shape but are able to spring back. Being resilient means having reserves that help you bounce back. Just like putting money aside for a rainy day, financial reserves help you navigate any seen or unforeseen "financial storms." Reserves free up space mentally, physically and spiritually, and allow you to focus on what really matters. Building reserves is the act of saving for a rainy day in multiple aspects of your life.

The following reserves are important *to build resilience*. When reviewing the list, consider which factors are present in your life and which are absent.

- **Economic security** Surplus resources, no debt, stable income, own home or employment contract
- **Emotional security** Supportive partner, emotional well-being and mental health, and resolved regrets, guilt or shame
- **Self-Care** Physical and mental fitness, balance, quality time for leisure, engaged passions
- **Resilient skills** Experiences that increase skill development
- **Supportive work environment** Clear role and contract terms, adequate resources, time demands, manageable and clear life/work boundaries, and good relations with boss and team
- **Significant relationships** Personal relationships and social support networks
- **Participation** Confidence and active participation in the change event with an opportunity to huddle/plan
- **Priority and time management** Staying ahead of deadlines, removing clutter, keeping aligned with values
- **Spirituality** Space and time for spirituality, meditation and reflection
- **Evolving** Regularly puts oneself in a position to initiate, innovate or improve (e.g., starting a new hobby or project, or taking a course)

Linda Nash, author of *The Bounce Back Quotient: 52 Action Oriented Ideas for Bouncing Back From Any Change or Setback in Life,* has developed a personal assessment tool that measures your ability to bounce back from changes and set-backs. Another tool you can use to build resilience is the *Reserves and Resilience Action Plan* (pages 109-110).

Finally, practice the art of *pruning*. When pruning my garden, I get rid of the old and damaged pieces to allow more room for growth, to shape the plant in a certain way, and to keep it compact and exposed to the sun. In coaching, we call this *getting rid of tolerations*, which we will talk about in the next chapter.

Resilience and Career Success

If you want to be your potential, and have the career success and significance you deserve, then career resilience is required. Resilience specific to your career has the following benefits:

1. Helps you in a current career crisis to identify underlying issues, discuss coping strategies and develop a commitment plan to adapt, reinvent and renew

2. Provides an opportunity to review and challenge your iceberg story (education, life and career crises that undermine your self-confidence and efficacy)

Do you know what career resilience competencies are necessary to obtain employability for new graduates, to make a career shift or to secure a promotion? Do you know which skills you need to develop to ensure your employability? Career resilience competencies are skill sets that are in compliance with the standards set by the National Career Development Association (NCDA), an international professional association that benchmarks competencies specific to career development.

> When we don't prune in the garden, nature does it for us through wind, ice, hail, fire and flood. One way or another, the boughs will be shaped or strengthened. If we don't prune away the stress and plow under the useless in our lives, pain will do it for us. Make no mistake, I think pain is a wretched gardener. Her cuts stun and sting. But after pruning, and preferably voluntary, we're able to discern what's real, what's important, and what's essential for our happiness. *−Sarah Ban Breathnach*

Five Career Resilience Competencies

1. Know Your Strengths
2. Manage Your Transition
3. Seek Information
4. Embrace Exploration
5. Promote Self and Accomplishments

Assess Your Career Resilience

Start to develop an action plan by taking the *Career Resilience Assessment.* The purpose of this assessment is to increase individual awareness for skill improvement. The outcome is the basis for a career development plan and a commitment to *forward action.*

Visit www.Smart2Smarter.com **and click on**
RESILIENCE to take the *Career Resilience Assessment*

Resistance and Resilience

Resistance is any force that slows or stops forward movement. Resistance is the opposite of resilience. It is a natural part of change and can occur during any stage of the transition process. Rick Maurer, a world-renowned resistance expert (www.beyondresistance.com), and author of *Change without Migraines,* has identified three levels of resistance.

Level 1 *Based on information*

Resistance at this level is a disagreement or mistrust based on information such as facts, figures and ideas. It is based on rational analysis or action. *Level 1 emotional resistance may stem from:*

- Lack of information
- Disagreement with the idea itself
- Lack of exposure
- Confusion

Level 2 *Physiological and emotional reaction to this change*

Level 2 is an emotional and physiological reaction to change. Blood pressure rises, adrenaline flows and the pulse increases. It is based on the fear or survival response. Level 2 can be triggered without conscious awareness.

Maurer suggests, "Imagine a client talking to her staff about a proposed re-structuring." Her staff respond with Level 1 questions: *How much will it cost? When will it begin? What's the timeline?* She then tells her staff about the possibility that this could result in downsizing. Suddenly, two-thirds of the room drops to Level 2 resistance. She may as well quit speaking to the rational mind, since people are now responding from a different part of the brain—the amygdala. *Level 2 emotional resistance may stem from:*

- Loss of power or control
- Loss of status
- Loss of "face" or respect
- Feeling of incompetence
- Feeling of isolation or abandonment
- Sense that nothing else can be taken on (too much change)

Level 3 *Bigger than the current change*

People are not resisting the change, they are resisting you—or rather, who or what you represent. They may resist because of their relationship with you or with people like you. Level 3 resistance can occur due to cultural, religious or political differences. When operating in Level 3, we minimize or dismiss others' ideas and opinions. *Level 3 emotional resistance may stem from:*

- Personal history of mistrust
- Cultural, ethnic, racial or gender differences
- Significant disagreement over values
- Transference (the person being resisted represents someone else, e.g., mother or father).

In another of Maurer's books, *Beyond the Wall of Resistance: Unconventional Strategies That Build Support for Change*, techniques are offered to manage your own and others' resistance to change. Consider those who have been, or will be, impacted by a change event.

1. Imagine the world from their point of view and ask yourself, *Why might they resist my ideas or me in particular?* As you brainstorm and write down some responses, think about the following questions:

    - If I were in their shoes, what might I experience as threatening by this change?

- What would cause me to resist this person who is initiating this change?

2. Once your lists are completed, underline all the responses that are Level 1. Using a dotted line, underline all those that are Level 2. With a wavy line, underline all the Level 3 responses.

3. Review your lists and consider resilient strategies to manage the level of resistance identified.

> Faced with the choice between changing one's mind and proving that there is no need to do so, almost everybody gets busy on the proof.   –John Kenneth Galbraith

Listen and Learn

Are you or others agreeing to a change, but your emotions, or theirs, are saying something else? Listen from the heart as well as the mind. Since most resistance stems from your fear or survival response, you must be willing to listen to the *whole self*. When interacting with others, *listen beyond the words* to see if you can pick up information from their tone of voice, eye contact, choice of words, how they hold their bodies or where they choose to sit.

What you are not saying may be more important than the words you speak.

Join the Smart 2 Smarter Community *to access the following activities and additional* RESILIENCE *resources and assessments online at* www.Smart2Smarter.com

Reserves and Resilience Action Plan book and website
Get Unstuck Now book and website
Ten Questions to Get Unstuck book and website
Stress Warning Signs book and website
What Are You Thinking...Gloom, Doom or Bloom? book and website
Hardiness Resilience Factors book and website
Career Resilience Inventory website
Ten Stages of a Career Transition website
Key Questions to Lead Change website

Activity   Reserves and Resilience Action Plan

Review the following list of life reserves

1) Put a (+) by the top five reserves of which you have plenty and know how to get more. 2) Put a (-) by reserves of which you have very little. 3) Put a (?) by reserves that you need to collect, create or store more of in your life. 4) Complete the *Reflect and Develop Questions* at the end of the checklist. 5) Print this out, tack it up, carry it with you, invite a friend or colleague to review it, and build your reserves!

Life Expectations for Success and Significance

___ I have the skills and support to persevere despite challenges or setbacks

___ I get the message *you can succeed* at work, home or school

___ I know what I am good and competent at doing

___ I take initiative and know how to tap the "fire in my belly" to motivate myself

___ I am perceptive, and exhibit insightful understanding of people and situations

___ I believe in my talents, and give myself positive messages to accomplish goals

Opportunities for Meaningful Participation

___ My voice (opinion) and choice (what I want) is heard and valued

___ My opinions and ideas are listened to and respected at work or school

___ I provide service in my community, faith organization or school

___ I feel connected to a shared purpose with people at work or school

___ I have a community that gives unconditional love and is there for me

___ I believe and have faith in something greater than myself

Clear and Consistent Boundaries

___ My relationships have clear, healthy boundaries (mutual respect, personal autonomy, giving and receiving)

___ I experience clear, consistent expectations at work or in school

___ I stand up for myself, don't let others take advantage of me, and say *no* when I need to

___ I adapt and, as needed, distance myself from unhealthy people or situations

___ I stretch my comfort zone to positively cope with situations

___ I do not tolerate distractions that pull me off course—I adjust, bend and continue to climb

Life Skills

___ I have (and use) good listening, honest communication, and healthy conflict skills

___ I have the education, training and skills to perform at work or school

___ I know how to set a goal and take steps to achieve it; I expect a positive future

___ I have a love of learning (capacity for and connection to learning)

___ I know how to express myself through artistic and creative methods

___ I have a sense of humor, and am able to laugh with others and at myself

Self-Care

___ I participate in daily exercise to get blood pumping and endorphins flowing

___ I limit caffeine, alcohol and sugar intake during times of stress or uncertainty

___ I fall asleep easily, sleep soundly, and average six to eight hours of sleep

___ I schedule time and space for fun and leisure activities where I can laugh or simply "chill out"

___ My work or school environment is healthy to my psychological well-being, and I know how to manage toxic people or bullies

___ I eat three to five small meals a day with a balance of fruits, vegetables, grains, fish, meat and water

Reflect and Develop

Plenty in the Reserve Bank
List the five statements where you have plenty of reserves (+) in your life

- In which category are most of these reserves located?
- How have you made this a priority?
- How can you use these resiliency builders to manage current problems or stressors?

Start to Gather and Save
List two or more areas where you need to build or store more reserves (-) and two or more areas where you have few reserves (?) in your life

- In which category are most of these reserves located?
- How can you make replenishing or gathering these reserves a priority?
- How will acquiring these resiliency builders help you to manage current problems or stressors?

Activity Get Unstuck Now

In their book, *The 12 Bad Habits That Hold Good People Back* (formerly published as *Maximum Success*), authors James Waldroop and Timothy Butler, Directors of MBA Career Development at The Harvard Business School, identify the 12 habits, or Achilles' heels, that can keep you from getting ahead in your career. Which pattern best reflects aspects of you? Your co-workers? Your friends? Review the actions on the next pages to *get unstuck now*.

1. **Never Feeling Good Enough**
   Symptom Feeling not good enough to deserve a promotion; unconsciously self-sabotaging it once it's received

2. **Seeing the World in Black and White**
   Symptom Resents that the world demands negotiation and the selling of ideas, believing that if something is *right*, that should be enough

3. **Doing Too Much, Pushing Too Hard**
   Symptom Pushes hard and does too much; causes others to burn out and is destructive within an organization; leaves behind a trail of "dead bodies" of co-workers who couldn't keep up with the pace

4. **Avoiding Conflict at Any Cost**
   Symptom Always avoids conflict, but not a peacemaker; fears change and prevents innovation

5. **Running Roughshod Over the Opposition**
   Symptom Runs roughshod over colleagues and clients, or willfully defies authority to get attention

6. **Rebel Looking for a Cause**
   Symptom Always looking for a cause that doesn't exist

7. **Always Swinging for the Fence**
   Symptom Swings for the fence, and has unrealistic ambitions; always disappointed at failures, but would have more successes if they could settle for hitting a few singles

8. **When Fear Is in the Driver's Seat**
   Symptom Focuses on the downside, is defensive or risk-averse, and obsesses over what can go wrong

9. **Emotionally Tone Deaf**

   Symptom Sometimes clueless when it comes to thinking about how others feel and knowing how their behavior impacts others

10. **When No Job Is Good Enough**

    Symptom Thinks that no job is ever good enough, and life is full of near misses

11. **Lacking a Sense of Boundaries**

    Symptom Always talking out of turn, and lets things slip

12. **Losing the Path**

    Symptom Work is without meaning; lost passion about a job, but stays on without energy

---

Whether you're a college student, recent graduate, or *generation whatever*, it is important to create new pathways to be resilient and get unstuck.

- Pay attention and observe your own actions, thoughts and feelings; reflect on the causes and impact of your reaction to the change

- Set up a buddy system to help you monitor your behavior at work and outside of work to give you brutally honest feedback about what you might not see

- Deliberately create new ways to apply your personal power and strengths

- Decide which behaviors you want to change to *be your potential*—and start today

- Engage an objective outsider to help you identify your strengths, blind spots and an action plan to take your personal potential to the next level

- Notice how you respond emotionally to everyday situations, especially the habitual ones

- Take mini-breaks to focus on things that you appreciate or care about

- Ask yourself if the energy you're expending while reacting negatively to a situation is really worth the emotional and physical price

Activity   Ten Questions to Get Unstuck

1. **What am I resisting?** What we resist most are the things that force us to grow the most

2. **What is the lesson here?** To evolve, we have to seek out the lesson to be learned

3. **Have I been here before?** Is it just a different name and face, but the same situation?

4. **Am I losing energy to this?** Every negative thought is measured in decreased energy, reduced immune function and sometimes heightened depression or illness

5. **Am I holding on to something of which I need to let go?** Resilience is bouncing back and letting go of certain outcomes and our need to be right or in control

6. **Am I in the present?** Regretting the past or worrying about the future is losing the potential of the present; staying in the present is a full-time job

7. **What do I need to do now?** The truth is that deliberate inaction is action, and it's often a way to allow a cloudy situation to become clear

8. **Who is in control here?** There are times to recognize that you are not always in control; paradoxically, this recognition and your acknowledgement of it can free you from the need to always be in control

9. **What is my responsibility here?** Your responsibility is a level of detachment that will allow you to see the situation and how—or if—to be involved in the problem

10. **Am I at peace with this?** Being at peace is when you can look at an issue, person or problem and feel no charge, no subtle or sudden surge of emotion; the peace-check is a key element in gaining closure when the transition is complete and no longer holding you back

Join the Smart 2 Smarter Community and learn to BOUNCE BACK SMARTER!

Adapted from writing by Paul Shale, a contributing author of www.selfgrowth.com

Activity   Stress Warning Signs

The first step to reduce a negative stress reaction in your life is to be able to recognize the signs of emerging stress. The following are warning signs that stress is present in your life, and most likely others are also feeling your stress.

1. **Thoughts racing out of control** If you notice that you cannot seem to stop your mind from racing from one thing to another like crazy, and/or you find that you cannot seem to focus on any one thing, you may be on the cusp of being stressed to the max.

2. **Muscle tightness, tension or twitching** Are your shoulders rising up to your ears? Or is your back or stomach tightening up into a knot? Or is your eye muscle twitching like crazy? These are all possible signs that you are internalizing stress.

3. **Shallow breathing** How is your breathing? Is it quick, little breaths? People tend to hold their breath and breathe shallowly when they are getting stressed.

4. **Low-grade or sudden nervousness, anger, sadness or guilt** Do not ignore these obvious signs of stress in the making.

5. **Chewing nervously on lips, fingernails, pencils, toothpicks or food** Are you trying to chew your stress away on whatever you can get in your mouth?

6. **Negative or fearful thinking** You become what you think. Thinking negatively and fearing possible future outcomes is a sign of stress!

7. **Increased heart rate and/or blood pressure** Your heart rate and blood pressure may be signs of stress. Notice your breathing.

8. **Change in appetite** Your appetite is a great indicator of your level of stress. If your appetite suddenly increases or disappears, perceived or real stress may be present.

9. **Clutching things in your hands with a tense grip** Squeezing the daylights out of whatever is in your hands may be an indicator of ignoring something stressful.

10. **Spacing out** A lot of people have adopted the survival mechanism of spacing out when they feel stressed. If this sounds like you, check in on whether you have checked out.

Originally submitted by Ronya Banks, Mind Power Leadership coach and popular author of Mind Power articles, rbanks@ronyabanks.com.
©2000-2004 CoachVille, LLC. May be distributed if full attribution is given and copyright is acknowledged.

Activity   What Are You Thinking...Gloom, Doom or Bloom?

Please note: This tool uses an informal approach to assessing positive and negative thinking, and is designed to help you focus on SMARTER approaches to attracting the life that is your potential. It has not been validated through controlled scientific tests; therefore, treat results as indicative and interpret with common sense.

The tool is based on Dr. Seligman's theory that individuals have a default style of explaining events. Seligman says we explain events using three basic dimensions of *Permanence*, *Pervasiveness* and *Personalization*.

For each statement below, circle the numerical value that most speaks to you. Notice that the numerical values are in different order for some questions (12345 or 54321).

I tend to think like this question...					
Not at All	Rarely	Sometimes	Often	Very Often	
1. When my boss asks to speak with me, I instinctively assume he or she wants to discuss a problem or give me negative feedback.					5 4 3 2 1
2. When I experience a real difficulty at work or home, other aspects of my life tend to be painted with the same negative brush.					5 4 3 2 1
3. When I experience a setback, I tend to believe that the obstacle will endure for the long-term (e.g., *The funding did not come through, so I guess that means they hate the project. All that work for nothing...*).					5 4 3 2 1
4. When a team I am on is functioning poorly, I believe the cause is short-term and has a straightforward solution (e.g., *We are not working well. If we can fix _____, we will do better!*).					1 2 3 4 5
5. When I am not chosen for an assignment I really want, I believe that I just don't have the skills they are looking for right now, as opposed to thinking that I am generally unskilled.					1 2 3 4 5
6. When something happens that I do not like or appreciate, I tend to conclude that the cause is widespread in nature and will continue to plague me (e.g., *My assistant did not 'cc' me on that email she sent to my boss. Administrative assistants are all out to prove how much smarter they are than their supervisors.*).					5 4 3 2 1
7. When I perform very well on an assignment, I believe that it's because I am generally talented and smart, as opposed to thinking I'm good in that one specific area.					1 2 3 4 5

I tend to think like this question...					
Not at All	Rarely	Sometimes	Often	Very Often	
8. When I receive a reward or recognition, I tend to figure that luck or fate played more of a role than my actual work or skill (e.g., *They asked me to be the keynote speaker at the conference next year. I guess the other guys were all busy.*).					5 4 3 2 1
9. When I come up with a really good idea, I'm surprised by my creativity. I figure it's my lucky day and caution myself not to get used to the feeling.					5 4 3 2 1
10. When something bad happens, I see the contributions that everyone made to the mistake, as opposed to thinking that I am incompetent and to blame.					1 2 3 4 5
11. After winning an award/recognition/contract, I believe it's because the competition is not as good as I am (e.g., *We won that large contract against two strong competitors. We are simply better than they are.*).					1 2 3 4 5
12. As the leader, when my team completes a project, I tend to attribute the success to the hard work and dedication of the team members, as opposed to my skilled leadership.					5 4 3 2 1
13. When I make a decision that proves to be successful, it's because I have expertise on that particular subject and have analyzed the problem well, as opposed to being a generally strong decision maker.					5 4 3 2 1
14. When I achieve a long-term and personally challenging goal, I congratulate myself and think about all the skills I used to be successful.					1 2 3 4 5
15. When I don't get a second interview, I believe I am just too young or old. I might as well give up.					5 4 3 2 1
Total					

Score Interpretation

My overall score is: _____ out of 75

Score Comment

15-30

Yikes! It must feel as if there is a rain cloud that hangs overhead all day. You have gotten into the habit of seeing things as your fault, and you have learned to give up your control in many situations. Taking this quiz is the first step toward turning your pessimism around.

31-50

You try to be optimistic and positive; however, some situations get the better of you.

51-75

Great job! You have a generally positive and optimistic outlook on life. You do not take things personally and you are able to see that setbacks will not ruin the rest of your life.

How to Turn Negatives Into Positives

The first step in changing negative thinking is to be aware of it. For many of us, negative thinking is a bad habit—and we may not even know we are doing it! Consider this example: You think that the guy on the subway who just made a face is surely directing his behavior at you. When the receptionist does not greet you in the morning, you must have done something to anger her…again! You head straight to the coffee machine because it's Monday morning and you just know you will be solving problems until lunchtime. When you finally get to your desk, your assistant is waiting for you. *Oh no*, you think. *What has he done now?*

If you are feeling bad after reading this, imagine how it would feel to surround yourself with that much negative energy. Then ask yourself if this is the way you tend to think in your own life.

As mentioned earlier, Dr. Seligman has done extensive research on thought patterns. In particular, he looks at the impact of an optimistic versus pessimistic outlook on life and success. He says we explain events using three basic dimensions of *permanence*, *pervasiveness* and *personalization*, with optimistic people on one end of the scale and pessimistic people on the other. Let's look at how you rated yourself on these three dimensions.

Re-Shape Your Thinking

Mastery is the art and science of optimizing your emotional brain to impact rational thought. It is breaking down your iceberg, directing a new story and intentionally *stopping* the thinking habits that derail your personal best. Your total scores on *Permanence*, *Pervasiveness* and *Personalization* can show whether you have a positive or negative pattern of thinking. They are also great starting points to become more aware of your thoughts—and the effect they have on your life.

Fill in your scored answers in the tables in the next pages and calculate your total.

Permanence, Pervasiveness and Personalization Scores

Permanence (Questions 3, 4, 9, 11, 15)

Question	Score
Question 3	
Question 4	
Question 9	
Question 11	
Question 15	
Total	

Total out of 25

19-25: High optimism Doesn't think that the event will last forever or is ongoing

15-19: Situational optimism Sometimes thinks that the event may be permanent

14 or less: Low optimism Thinks that the event will never end

Your score shows how much you believe that something you are experiencing is either permanent or temporary. A low score implies that you think bad times will carry on forever. A high score shows confidence that you will be able to get things back on course quickly.

Pessimist I lost my job and I'll never find one as good again. No point in even looking!

Optimist I lost my job. Thank goodness there are other opportunities I can explore!

Pervasiveness (Questions 2, 5, 6, 7, 13)

Question	Score
Question 2	
Question 5	
Question 6	
Question 7	
Question 13	
Total	

Total out of 25

19-25: High optimism Doesn't think that the event will impact all areas of one's life

15-19: Situational optimism Sometimes thinks the event will impact all areas of one's life

14 or less: Low optimism Often thinks the event will impact all areas of one's life

Your score shows how far you believe that situational factors cause an effect, as opposed to the view that the effect is evidence of more universal factors at work. A low score shows that you tend to think that if you have experienced a problem in one place, you will experience that problem wherever you go.

Pessimist I lost my job. Companies are all the same...all they care about is money. I don't know why I bother putting in any effort at all.

Optimist I lost my job. The company has to reinvent itself to stay competitive. Thankfully, I learned some great transferable skills.

Personalization (Questions 1, 8, 10, 12, 14)

Question	Score
Question 1	
Question 8	
Question 10	
Question 12	
Question 14	
Total	

Total out of 25
19-25: High optimism Doesn't blame oneself entirely for the outcome of an event
15-19: Situational optimism Sometimes blames oneself for the outcome of an event
14 or less: Low optimism Often blames oneself for the outcome of an event

Your score shows how far you believe that *something about you* influenced the outcome, as opposed to *something external to you* causing it. A low score indicates that you tend to blame yourself for bad things, rather than attributing the cause to more general factors.

Pessimist I lost my job. If I had been a decent employee, they would have found a new job for me.

Optimist I lost my job. I gave it my all, but they just can't use my skill set right now.

Remember, career resilience requires creating lifelong behavior habits to consistently and regularly sharpen and strengthen your career competency skills. Congratulations for focusing on your skill development and taking the first step to becoming a competent and resilient career manager!

Tolerance

Chapter 8

This chapter will explore how to develop tolerance. Tolerance is the ability to *accept, acknowledge* and *appreciate* different cultures, people, ideas, perspectives and beliefs. Put simply, it is the ability to cultivate opportunities through diverse people, events and experiences. Tolerance is also the ability to recognize and eliminate behaviors, thoughts and habits that hold you back from being your personal best.

Acceptance *Tolerance and Comfort Zones*

A comfort zone is an emotional magnetic field that provides limitations on how you act or react to events, people, challenges and setbacks. It acts as a magnet that either pulls you forward to perceived safety, or one that pulls you back. *Tolerance is an emotional state of being comfortable with being uncomfortable.* For example, a client makes a positive first impression at a job interview. Near the end of the interview, the interviewer asks the question: *Where do you see yourself in five years?* This question reminds the client of being asked by a teacher what they will be when they grow up. The client shrinks back into a familiar comfort zone of surviving, drifting back to a "smaller" self, and is unable to answer the question.

Whenever you start something new, such as work, college, a relationship or a project, your emotional comfort zone is activated. When you tolerate events, people, habits or behaviors that hold you back, you are retreating to the safety of your current comfort zone. Everyone has a comfort zone. Everyone also expands his or her comfort zones through tolerance. Conversely, the presence of unhealthy tolerations, such as unhealthy physical habits, can hold you back.

Your comfort zone is crafted from your iceberg story. This story allows your comfort zone to expand or contract, and thus will directly impact your emotions, reasoning and behaviors. A restrictive comfort zone prevents you from taking the required action to achieve career significance or success. When you are honest about your comfort zones, you will begin to accept your tolerations that are holding you back, and learn what you need to tolerate to move forward. When you start to uncover your tolerations (your hidden beliefs, stories, fears and lost hopes), you can begin to be SMART-ER in both your life and your career.

> Talent, skills or personality do not explain why some of us continue to thrive and evolve. When you reach for your goals or dreams and comfort zones expand, amazingly you will find ways to breathe.

Comfort zones also impact your business roles, whether as a leader, individual or team. A leader that does not allow input creates a comfort zone of risk-adverse behavior and silence. An individual who only hears negative feedback has a comfort zone that sabotages their personal best by creating obstacles to success. Individuals who consistently stretch their comfort zones continue to excel. They also expect to perform well, while those with restricted comfort zones tend to have lower expectations.

How Comfort Zones Are Formed

A restricted comfort zone is formed through experience and repetition, and it turns into a negative emotion and belief—or Gremlin (see Attraction chapter). We keep our comfort zones stable by recreating these limiting experiences. We reinforce and give power to our Gremlin by saying, *I knew this would happen,* or *I knew I'd only get this far.* Our comfort zones become our unspoken self-fulfilling expectation. Remember, expectations of ourselves and others impact self-efficacy.

A comfort zone is composed of emotional pathways with direct connections to our thoughts and behaviors. Let's look at the layers of an emotional *Comfort Zone.* I will use the example of a twenty-something career professional who is considering changing jobs. The first, or inner, layer is where you are now (what is comfortable, safe and predictable). Bob is comfortable working at a consulting firm performing financial audits; however, he lacks passion for his work and does not feel significant or successful. Bob wants to expand his career choices, and chooses to consult my services as a career counselor. He has now entered the *Possibility Zone.* As Bob explores his passions and talents, he discovers he wants to use his accounting skills in a smaller consulting firm working with small businesses. Bob begins to explore possible companies and firms. He is offered a job in another state, far from family and friends. His emotional pathways are pulling in two directions. The *Fear* path feeds his head with messages about being lonely, leaving his mom and not having friends around. The *Hope* path feeds his head with energy and optimism of meeting new people and gaining new skills and experiences to further develop his greatness.

Which path does Bob choose? Does he continue to tolerate the old messages and scripts and choose to stay comfortable? Or does Bob choose to stop tolerating traveling down the same path and explore a new direction? Bob did choose the *Hope* path, and expanded into the *Potential Zone*. Was this expansion easy? Of course not. However, by eliminating tolerations that held him back, he was able to evolve into his greatness. He learned to be comfortable with being uncomfortable.

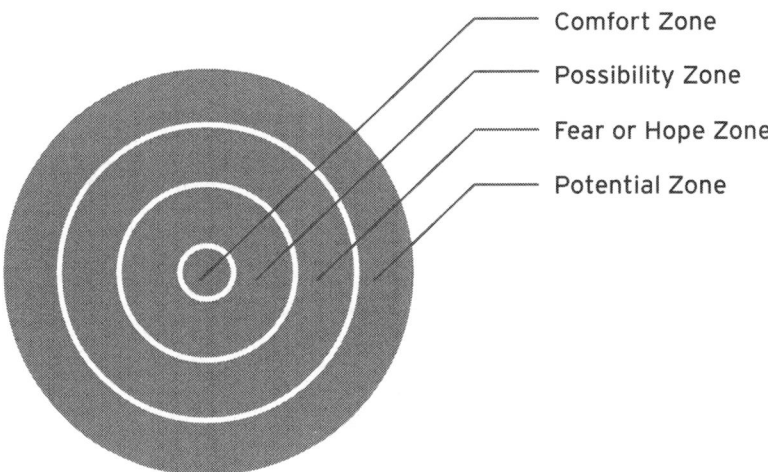

Comfort Zone

Possibility Zone

Fear or Hope Zone

Potential Zone

Expand Your Comfort Zones

1. **Accept and challenge yourself** If you have a fear or limiting belief about yourself, a task or situation, accept it—then challenge it. *Is this belief really a true reflection of my talents or skills, or just a Gremlin that is limiting my potential?*

2. **The past is not today** Your comfort zone has nothing to do with today. It's only a learned habit based on past experience, and it is not a reflection of your potential today.

3. **Take a step** All comfort zones can be broken and expanded. Take a

first step. Just like when a baby learns to walk and leaves the comfort of their mother's arms, that first step turns into another step, and another, and so on.

4. **Ask for support** Eliminating tolerations takes sustained emotional energy. Ask for support from family, friends, peers, a coach or significant other.

5. **Expect setbacks** Eliminating tolerations is not easy. It may feel easier to travel the same route, even if you get bumped and bruised along the way. Reframe setbacks and second attempts as opportunities for self-discovery and growth.

6. **Prune monthly** As mentioned in the previous chapter, a garden needs its weeds to be pruned to flourish, as do your life and dreams. Set aside time each month, or week, to prune away those habits you are tolerating that clutter your "mind garden." It is hard to expand your comfort zones with too many weeds in the way. Pruning can be as simple as cleaning out your closet, updating your resume, having lunch with a friend or answering the mail.

Acknowledge *What Are You Tolerating and What Are Others Tolerating About You?*

When I ask clients to acknowledge what they're tolerating that interferes with their personal best, I hear a variety of answers—or excuses. Some say that they tolerate people who are late, pretentious, judgmental, indecisive, rude, needy or arrogant. Others say they tolerate a bad habit, relationship or an unfulfilling job. Next, I ask them to acknowledge what others are tolerating about them that may hold them back. Most tolerations involve a *should* message or belief: *I should be on time*, or *I should tolerate someone being late*, *I should be nice*, or *I should always get what I want*.

> Our emotions and behaviors are tolerated not by the events, but by how we interpret those events.

What you tolerate will persist. Behavior that is tolerated will repeat itself. If you tolerate someone being late, they will learn that being late is acceptable. If others tolerate you being rude, you learn that being rude has no consequences and your rudeness continues.

Acknowledge *Should I Stay or Should I Go?*

You are faced with a difficult choice. Should you pursue a new position or career, or tolerate where you are now? How do you decide which is the better offer? How can you know you will be happier, more successful and fulfilled in your existing or new position? What does happy, successful or fulfilled mean to you, really?

As discussed, *passion* is the natural energy, motivation and enthusiasm you demonstrate when contributing significance to the world. Passion is present when your talents, skills, interests, values and capabilities are fulfilled—and often stretched. It is easy to do and learn whatever is important and necessary to contribute your personal best. It is an attitude of *I love to do this* and is something from much deeper inside of us—a "fire in the belly," if you would.

Performance is converting career passion into performance success that meets or exceeds agreed-upon individual, team or organizational goals. A performance success reminds us that it is not enough to have the passion for our work, but also to have the skills, knowledge, resources, support and rewards to sustain high performance outcomes.

When passion and performance motivators are fulfilled, you not only are contributing your personal best, but also are aware of what to tolerate and what not to tolerate to sustain the *hope* momentum.

> We became uncompetitive by tolerating mistakes. The moment you let avoiding failure become your motivator, you're down the path of inactivity. You can stumble only if you're moving.
> —*Roberto Goizueta, former Coca-Cola CEO*

The *Career Tolerations Assessment* will help you evaluate between two career options based on the *BestFit Career Model*. The *BestFit Career Model* states that to actualize one's *career potential*, two equally important motivators need to be satisfied: *Passion Significance* (intrinsic motivators) and *Performance Success* (external motivators).

Career Tolerations Assessment: Should I Stay or Should I Go?

This assessment and guide will provide insight and actions to increase awareness of your career tolerations, and will help you design an environment that fuels your personal best.

Visit www.Smart2Smarter.com and click on TOLERANCE to access this appraisal

Acknowledge *Overloaded Circuits*

Frantic, forgetful, fragmented and frazzled. Does this describe you or someone with whom you work? If so, you're not alone. This section will explore the consequences of tolerating overloaded mental circuits.

Technology has given us and others 24/7 access to information—we are bombarded with it via smart phones, texting, twitter and other social media. However, digital communication is not a substitute for authentic human interaction. In addition, positive human-to-human contact reduces blood levels of the stress hormones epinephrine, norepinephrine and cortisol. That is a good thing!

Does your body and mind feel like it's always on standby? You are not alone. Since the mid-1990s, people have increasingly complained of being chronically inattentive, disorganized and overbooked. Most complaints originate from individuals who do not have clinical diagnoses of Attention Deficit Disorder (ADD). Instead, they suffer from what ADD expert Dr. Edward M. Hallowell calls "severe cases of modern life"—a condition he dubs Attention Deficit Traits (ADT) that promotes a fast multitasking environment.

He asserts that ADT sufferers have an environmentally induced attention deficit—a phenomenon he describes as the *F-state*: Frantic, frenzied, forgetful, flummoxed, frustrated and fragmented. The faster we go, the more we take on. The more we take on, the more there is to do. Labor-saving devices create more labor; by shortening the time and energy required to complete any one task, these devices free us to tolerate doing more.

The consequence is that our brain becomes overloaded with data. When a computer becomes overloaded with too much data, it will shut down, often losing some of its data along the way. When emotional circuits in our brain become overloaded, any incoming or outgoing messages are blurry or full of static. Our brain, like the computer, shuts down—whether you know it or not. The SMARTER person intentionally shuts downs, untangles the overloaded circuits, and reboots.

For many people, working in the *F-state* is fun. Some people enjoy the adrenaline surge. Tolerating a faster, frenetic life along with hoarding more data and devices creates an adrenaline high, but does not increase your sense of fulfillment. While tolerating these behaviors may temporarily charge your emotional battery, they eventually hijack your personal best. Symptoms include: loss of personal vitality, an inability to converse, a craving for a computer screen when separated from one, and low-grade depression.

Two important prerequisites to stop tolerating overloaded circuits are a positive emotional environment, and finding the right rhythm. Dr. Hallowell includes a list of suggestions to control Attention Deficit Traits in his article, "Overloaded Circuits: Why Smart People Underperform."

Control ADT at Work

- Have a friendly, face-to-face talk with a person you like every four to six hours
- Break large tasks into smaller, manageable steps
- Keep a section of your workspace clear at all times
- Each day, reserve some "think time" free from appointments, email and phone calls
- Set aside email until you've completed at least one or two more important tasks
- Before you leave work each day, create a list of three to five items you will do the next day
- Pay attention to the times of day when you're at your best—do your most important work then, and save the rote work for when you're less focused or energized
- Do whatever it takes to work in a more focused way: Add background music, take short breaks or a walk—whatever works best for you
- Ask a colleague or assistant to help you stop talking on the telephone, emailing or working too late; recognize and correct your nonproductive habits
- Move around: Go up and down a flight of stairs or walk briskly
- Ask for help, delegate a task or brainstorm with a colleague; in short, do not worry alone

Acknowledge *Stress and Tolerations*

Stress is the body's response to any physical or emotional changes in life. This response includes the release of the hormone adrenaline. Adrenaline causes an increase in heart rate, breathing and blood sugar levels. It also diverts the blood flow from your digestive system to your muscles (brain, legs, arms, etc.). This response prepares you for the *fight or flight* response (the fear response). Stress also sparks optimism, hope and excitement (the hope response). We all experience stress as we cope with everyday events. Daily demands such as rules, responsibilities, decisions, changes, relationships, illness and money can all cause stress.

Everyone tolerates situations differently and experiences stress at different levels of intensity. Your body sends out physical, mental, behavioral and emotional signs of tolerations. Emotional signals of toleration are anxiety, excessive worrying, moodiness, fear, or feeling inadequate. Mental signals of an unhealthy toleration are poor concentration, forgetfulness, low self-confidence and self-efficacy. Behavioral signals of toleration are acting in a defensive, aggressive, passive or impulsive manner, nervous habits (biting nails), loss of interest in activities, avoidance of tasks or people, being easily distracted, withdrawing from social activities or substance abuse. Furthermore, prolonged toleration exposes our bodies to the negative effects of adrenaline that lead to many problems such as decreased immunity, increased blood pressure, digestive problems or depression.

Acknowledge *Tolerations and Life/Work Balance*

A Question of Balance

Some people don't know what a balanced life looks like, or how having one will improve their career fulfillment. They believe they are stuck within their imbalanced lifestyle. Often, they are not aware of how unhealthy and toxic their situation is to themselves, their work, their peers and their families. When a major crisis occurs, they are forced to take a good look at the choices they have been making.

When working with clients around the SMARTER skill of *tolerance*, I often start by asking my clients to finish several incomplete sentences. How the individual replies, or if the individual has difficulty providing a response, gives a starting point to discuss life/work balance.

- I know I'm out of balance when...

- I feel guilty when...

- I expect of myself to be...

- I expect of others to be...

Another balance technique is one provided by Lisa Martin, author of *Briefcase Moms: 10 Proven Practices to Balance Working Mothers' Lives*. She presents the concept of the *Four P's* when coaching clients around life/work balance.

The Four P's

1. **Personal** What is your definition of balance *now*?
2. **Practice** What practices or habits can you do to increase balance in your life?

3. **Pause** Are you investing time to be reflective, present or simply to pause?

4. **Permission** How do you allow yourself permission to invest in your well-being?

Lisa also introduces ten proven practices to achieve a more balanced work life. I have found these ten practices useful for both women and men, young or old (consult her book for additional techniques and resources).

Ten Practices to Balance Life/Work

Simplification How much time do you focus on showing respect versus resentment? What do you really enjoy doing, and what can you outsource?

Lightness Pay attention to the amount of *shoulds* in your life. How much time do you tolerate feeling guilty? How can you move from a *should* state to a *want* state? What do you need to stop tolerating about your definition of "perfection" in all of your life roles?

Well-Being How much time do you invest in enjoying the small stuff (a rainbow, sunny day, movie or family)? How often do you schedule time for self-love or self-pampering? When was the last time you had a health checkup? Do you own a pet?

Self-Discovery Who would you be without your work? How is your work significant? How would others be without your work?

Alignment How do your actions align with what you value? How often do you ask, *Why am I doing this?* Consider your values as billable hours. Are you getting your money's worth? When you are not living a core value, listen to your emotional radar.

Liberation Stop tolerating self-limiting beliefs. Stop tolerating your Gremlin. Liberate yourself!

Protection Do you really believe that you are worthy of taking a vacation or getting a massage? Who do you allow to keep stepping over your boundaries? Consider that when you say *yes* to something, you are also saying *no* to something else. What can you say *no* to and stop tolerating? What is on your *yes* list (your non–negotiables)?

Connection Who is in your system of support? How does your support system protect you? How does it liberate you? How may it fence you in?

Courage What fears do you need to confront to allow you to move forward? What self-talk do you need to challenge and delete? How can you use courage to expand your comfort zones? How can you turn complaints into a request?

Reflection What does *having it all* really mean to you? What does it mean to your significant other? To your children?

Toleration Busters

You may not be able to get rid of all your tolerations, but you can manage them at a level that is SMARTER and healthier. On the next several pages are *toleration busters* that will free up space and time for you to be your personal best.

Plan your time well Give priority to the most important activities and do them first. Break large demands into small, manageable parts. Decide how much time you need for each job. Leave some room for flexibility and spontaneity. Note what you tolerated that took you off-task.

Speak to someone about your tolerations Seeking help is not a sign of weakness. Sharing your tolerations (worries and concerns) with your spouse, family, friend, supervisor, coach or peer helps free up positive emotional energy and provides you with emotional support.

Keep healthy Keep your body healthy and fit by exercising regularly, eating wisely and getting enough sleep. Regular physical activity releases endorphins that give you a natural high. Eating a healthy and balanced diet will provide levels of nutrients needed to boost the immune system.

Be clear about your roles Know your job scope and what is expected of you. Do not tolerate *out-of-scope* tasks just to get things done. Be realistic in what you can do. Consult your supervisor or team to know each other's roles and responsibilities.

Learn to say "no" when necessary Say *no*. Take time for yourself. Take a short break or walk when you feel your toleration level is getting the best of you. Let your emotional brain recharge.

Counter negative thoughts Stop negative thoughts! Stop shaping your future around what you perceive other people will do or think about you. Add helpful reminders to your screen saver, such as *Take a deep breath,* or add an image or picture that makes you smile.

Practice Deep Breathing

Give yourself 5-10 minutes to do this exercise.

1. Find a quiet comfortable place. Switch on some soft and relaxing music. Dim the lights.

2. Sit on a comfortable chair or lie down. Close your eyes. File away worries and concerns.

3. Breathe in slowly, steadily and deeply. Relax all your muscles and let your body go limp.

4. Imagine that you are walking in your favorite place (a park, your yard, or a vacation spot).

5. Feel the cool fresh breeze around you. Take a deep breath in and out.

6. Place one hand on your stomach right above your waist.

7. Take a deep breath in slowly though your nose. Feel your stomach slowly rise.

8. Slowly breathe out gently through your mouth.

9. Focus on your breathing and feel the air moving in and out of your body.

10. Repeat steps 5-9 several times until you feel relaxed. When done, slowly open your eyes.

See a New Path: Visual Imagery

Give yourself 10-15 minutes to do this exercise. For best results, start with the above deep breathing exercise, then continue with this visual imagery exercise.

1. Imagine your special place and, at the end of it, there are white, sandy beaches and pebbles lining the shore. Take a deep breath in and out.

2. Feel the smooth, cool pebbles. Take a deep breath in and out.

3. Breathe in slowly, steadily and deeply.

4. Focus your attention on your hands and fingers. Clench your fists as tightly as you can and count to 10.

5. Notice the pull of your hand muscles. Feel the tension. Then release the tension very slowly by letting your hands unfold as you count to 10.

6. Feel the warm tingling sensation in your hands. Let the tension drain out of your hands.

7. Repeat this exercise with other parts of your body: Face, head and neck, arms and shoulders, abdomen, buttocks, legs, feet and ankles.

8. Continue this visualization until you feel very relaxed.

9. Slowly count to 10 and you will come to a more alert, wakeful and refreshed mind.

Acknowledge *Toleration Signals*

Complete the *toleration checklist* (p. 137). ***Stop tolerating. Start eliminating.***

Acknowledge *Reflect and Redirect*

The following list of questions will increase awareness of your tolerations.

- What are the beliefs that reinforce your tolerations?
- What assumptions are you making about others or the situation that keep your tolerations strong?
- What can you start tolerating without resenting the person or situation?
- What can you accept, acknowledge and appreciate about the situation or person?
- How can you shift the focus to your life instead of theirs?
- Who are you when you're silent and still?
- What is a personal win for you and others when you continue to tolerate the situation?
- Where else does this toleration show up or manifest itself?
- How are you inviting this toleration into your life?
- How are you teaching people to treat you like this?
- Of what do you need to let go to be more tolerant?

Appreciate *Empathy Is Tolerance*

One of the SMARTER employability skills that most employers desire is the skill of empathy. Empathy starts with self-awareness, in that understanding your own emotions is essential to understanding the feelings of others. Lack of empathy is a primary cause of career derailment and interpersonal dysfunction. Our ability to show empathy toward others starts with our ability to have empathy for ourselves.

Empathy is the ability to identify and understand another's situation, feelings and motives. It means *seeing things through someone else's eyes.* It is simply being attuned to how others feel in the moment, recognizing their emotional mood and context, and responding appropriately. Empathy is an emotional and thinking muscle that becomes stronger the more we use it. By expressing empathy, you also create empathy in others.

Empathy is *career currency:* It allows us to create bonds of trust; it gives us insight into what others may be feeling or thinking; it helps us to understand how or why others are reacting to situations; and it sharpens our *people acumen* and informs our decisions.

Empathy can be defined as the ability to see things from the other person's point of view, to be able to "walk in someone else's moccasins." Daniel Goleman, in *Working with Emotional Intelligence*, defines it as the ability to "read" other people. This implies more than a cognitive understanding, more than just remembering a similar situation that you may have gone through yourself. Empathy means that you can recall some of those same feelings based on your own memories—there is a sharing and identifying with emotional states.

In Daniel Pink's book, *A Whole New Mind: Why the Right Brainers will Rule the Future*, he emphasizes that left-brain thinking from "the information age" will no longer serve us in the 21st century, which he calls "the conceptual age." Pink *also* predicts that power will reside with those who have strong right-brain (interpersonal) qualities. He cites three forces that are causing this change: Abundance, Asia and Automation.

> Create loving, accepting space around people and this will put irresistible pressure on them to grow to fill it.
> —Mac Andrews

Abundance refers to our increasing demand for products or services that are aesthetically pleasing; *Asia* refers to the growing trend of outsourcing; *Automation* is self-explanatory. To compete in the new economy, Pink suggests six areas that are vital to our success, one of which is empathy. Empathy is the ability to imagine yourself in someone else's position, to imagine what they are feeling, to understand what makes them tick, to create relationships and to be caring of others. All of this is very difficult to outsource or automate.

Empathy as a competency is poorly understood by those who need it most. Some people believe you either have it or you don't. Some lack empathy because they assume it's too "touchy-feely." Some very smart people walk around blindly using only their powers of intellectual reasoning, wondering why others can't see things their way. Without an adequate understanding of another's point of view, the smart person will lack flexibility, may not work well with team collaboration, and may not relate well with the people who are there to help generate results.

Empathy skills are those that involve paying attention to people—things like listening, attending to needs and wants of others, and building relationships. When empathy skills are high, one is more likely to inspire others. When you truly act to understand others and communicate that to them, you are more liked and respected. Practicing empathy results in better performance: When you are respected, the people you work with will go the extra mile.

Empathy and focus need to be balanced. When they are, career success and significance are optimally effective. According to Goleman, *empathy represents the foundation skill for all the social competencies important for work.*

1. **Understanding others** Ability to sense others' feelings and perspectives

2. **Service orientation** Ability to anticipate, recognize and meet customers' needs

3. **Developing others** Ability to sense others' developmental needs and bolster their abilities

4. **Tolerance** Ability to cultivate opportunities through diverse people

5. **Political attractions** Ability to read political and social currents

Individuals who are high in empathy skills are able to pick up on emotional cues. They can appreciate not only what a person is saying, but also why they are saying it. They understand what might be motivating another person's feelings. Those that do not have empathy have a tendency to misread the other person. They do not ask questions to clarify. They do not pay attention to nonverbal cues. These people listen to the words, facts and figures, and completely miss the underlying meaning of what is being said. Remember, only 7% of the message is carried in the words, and the rest is in the nonverbal cues.

Both managers and employees need empathy in order to interact well with customers, suppliers, the general public and each other. Managers need it even more: When assigning a task to someone who won't like it; offering criticism to someone who may get defensive; having to deal with someone they don't like; dealing with employee disputes; and giving bad news, such as telling someone that they won't be promoted.

Empathy and Tolerant Communication

Tolerant communication is the art and science of empathetic communication. Empathy involves real curiosity and a desire to know or understand people— genuine interest in what the person is saying and feeling is conveyed. You cannot have empathy without asking questions to learn more about someone or something. When you ask questions or seek more information, you are demonstrating empathy through listening. Some typical inquiries are:

1. *Can you say more about that?*

2. *Really? That's interesting. Can you be more specific?*

3. *I wasn't aware of that. Say more.*

4. *I'm curious about that...let's discuss this in more depth.*

5. *Let me see if I understand you correctly. I hear you saying...*

6. *How do you feel about that? What are some of your concerns?*

How do you learn effective empathy if you are one of those smart people who are primarily focused on achievement? The good news is that your achievement orientation and focusing abilities will help you to acquire empathy skills. Empathy skills must be learned experientially, that is, practiced in real-time.

1. **Keep a note of situations** when you felt you were able to demonstrate empathy, and when you were not. Make a note of opportunities to respond with empathy that were missed.

2. **Become aware of incidents** where there may be some underlying concerns that are not explicitly expressed by others. Then inquire to learn about the other person's perspective.

3. **Make a note of possible emotions** or feelings that the other person may be experiencing. Keep an open mind and never assume, merely explore the possibilities.

4. **Develop a list of questions to ask** at your next encounter with that person. Try to make the questions open-ended or provocative (questions that can't be answered with *yes* or *no*).

5. **Practice listening without interrupting** Wait until the other person has shared their point of view before offering yours.

6. **Manage your emotional defenses** such as shutting down, interrupting,

or nonverbal cues like crossing your arms. Create an open dialogue where possibilities can be explored.

7. **Schedule a time and place** for people to express opinions and ideas without judgment.

8. **Practice active listening** Reflect to the person speaking the meaning of what was said. Paraphrasing what was said helps to clear up misconceptions and deepens understanding.

9. **Always bring focus back into the conversation** Optimal effectiveness is achieved by a combination of focus and empathy.

> In contrast to a phone call or talking in person, e-mail can be emotionally impoverished when it comes to nonverbal messages that add nuance and valence to our words. The typed words are denuded of emotional context we convey in person or over the phone.
>
> We tend to misinterpret positive e-mail messages as more neutral, and neutral ones as more negative, than the sender intended. Even jokes are rated as less funny by recipients than by senders.   *–Daniel Goleman*

10. **Work on achieving an effective balance** of focus, goal orientation and empathetic listening.

For more tips and techniques to demonstrate tolerant communication, visit www.Smart2Smarter.com and click on TOLERANCE to download *Tolerant Communication Tips*

A Final Thought *Tolerance and Social Intelligence*

Daniel Goleman says: "New findings [in social neuroscience] have uncovered a design flaw at the interface where the brain encounters a computer screen: There are no online channels for the multiple signals the brain uses to calibrate emotions. Face-to-face interaction, by contrast, is information-rich."

We interpret what people say to us not only from their *tone and facial expressions, but also from body language and pacing*, as well as their synchronization with what we do and say. "Most crucially, the brain's social circuitry mimics in our neurons what's happening in the other person's brain, keeping us on the same wavelength emotionally. This neural dance creates an instant rapport that arises from a number of parallel information processors, all working instantaneously and out of our awareness.

SMARTER TOLERANCE

The skill of empathy is critical to career success and significance in a global and digital economy. Some questions to consider are:

- How do you demonstrate tolerance through digital communications?
- How will social networking build tolerance of self and others?
- How can you increase your face-to-face communications to develop and practice empathy?

Workplace and Leadership Empathy

The focus on empathy in the workplace fits well with the recent emphasis on humanity (Kivland, 2011). Empathy is at the root of humanity. When one displays their humanity, they are interacting with empathy. Empaths (individuals with high empathy) have a natural talent and ability to develop an honest, open and transparent relationship between themselves and others. Ronald Humphrey's research (2004) found that empathy plays a key role in workplace relationships and ethical behavior. He argues that empathic feelings motivate self and others to behave ethically. Further research describes how empathic leaders are more likely to create positive feelings that lead to a compassionate, humane culture (Cameron, Dutton & Quinn, 2003; Luthans & Avolio, 2003). Humphrey looked at interactive empathy and leadership: Interactive empathy was defined as the ability of leaders to communicate their feelings, make others feel understood, and demonstrate their empathy and concern for others. He argues that peer ratings provide a richer perspective on how well leaders display interactive empathy.

Assess how your workplace and leaders measure on empathy with the *Workplace Empathy Questionnaire* (pages 140-141).

Join the Smart 2 Smarter Community *to access the following activities and additional* TOLERANCE *resources and assessments online at* www.Smart2Smarter.com

Signs of Unhealthy Tolerations book and website	What Are You Tolerating? website
Tolerance in Action book	Social Awareness Top Ten website
Development Paths to Empathy book and website	Toleration Busters website
Workplace Empathy Questionnaire book and website	Life Realignment Wheel website
20 Ways to Eliminate Tolerations website	Career Tolerations Assessment:
Stop Tolerating Chaos website	Should I Stay or Should I Go? website

Activity   Signs of Unhealthy Tolerations

The list of questions below will help you realize how your tolerations may affect you. The more you answer *Always* and *Sometimes*, the more likely it is that you have tolerations that are interfering with being your personal best.

	Always	Sometimes	Never
Do you have to live up to others' expectations?			
Do you find that you are not able to concentrate on your tasks?			
Do you suffer from sleepless nights or find it hard to sleep through the night, often waking up feeling tired?			
Do you suffer from shortness of breath?			
Do you suffer from palpitations or tightness in the chest, or stomach cramps?			
Do you suffer from sweaty palms?			
Do you find it hard to say *no* when you are asked to do more?			
Do you feel tired most of the time?			
Do you have less enjoyment about life?			
Do you over- or under-eat?			
Do you find it difficult to pause and enjoy the simplicities of life?			
Do you suffer from digestive problems like constipation or indigestion?			
Do you grind your teeth or clench your fists?			
Do you find it hard to set aside time to have fun and enjoy yourself?			

SMARTER TOLERANCE

Activity   Tolerance in Action

Complete the following questions to expand your *comfort zone* and *tolerations*.

- Who is a friend that has helped you with a difficult project at work?

- Who is someone you can help with a difficult project at work?

- Who has been an influential teacher in your life?

- Who can you start to learn from that you have avoided?

- Who are the people you enjoy spending time with at work?

- Who can you begin to spend more time with to increase your tolerance?

- Who is a mentor who has offered their guidance at work?

- Who can you seek mentorship from that is outside of your comfort zone?

- Who can you mentor that is outside of your comfort zone?

- Who do you pick up the phone for when you see their caller ID?

- Who can you start to pick up the phone for when you see their caller ID?

- Ask your circle of influence what behaviors they may tolerate about you that distracts or hijacks them from being their personal best.

Activity   Development Paths to Empathy

Some people are naturally and consistently empathetic, resulting in positive connections with others. Practice these behaviors to sharpen or further develop your empathy muscle.

1. **Listen**
   Listen with your ears, eyes and heart. Pay attention to body language, tone of voice, hidden emotions and the context (perspective) of what others are, or are not, saying.

2. **Shadow**

   Shadow someone who is known for his or her interpersonal sensitivity.

3. **Invite perspective**

   Intentionally invite others' views and perspectives. Tell others you are developing a higher level of empathy, and ask them for suggestions and feedback.

4. **Default communication style**

   Think back to when your views differed from someone else's. How was your communication received? What is your default communication style when hijacked: Is it critical? Avoiding? Playing the victim or bully? Or do you retreat or stay silent?

5. **Do not interrupt people**

   Do not dismiss others' concerns offhand. Do not rush to give advice. Do not change the subject. Allow people their moment.

6. **Practice the 93% rule**

   Words account for only 7% of the total message that people receive. The other 93% of the message is contained in our tone of voice and body language.

7. **Tune in to nonverbal communication**

   What do actions or silences tell you about how someone really feels, even when verbal communication says something different?

8. **Use people's names**

   Remember the names of significant people in others' lives.

9. **Be fully present when you are with people**

   Avoid your email or phone calls when interacting with others at work. Think about how you would feel if your boss did that to you.

10. **Encourage people, particularly the quiet ones, when they speak up in meetings**

    A simple thing like an attentive nod can boost people's confidence.

11. **Give genuine recognition and praise**

    Pay attention to what people are doing and catch them doing the right things. Say to them, *You are an asset to this team because....*

12. **Show people you care—have monthly lunches with a friend or someone new**

    Remember birthdays and weekly *I care* phone calls.

Activity   Workplace Empathy Questionnaire

In the space provided next to each of the following statements, **circle the number that best describes your agreement with the item,** using the scale below. Then calculate your total and use the scoring descriptions to interpret your results.

5 = Strongly Agree   4 = Somewhat Agree   3 = Neither Agree nor Disagree
2 = Somewhat Disagree   1 = Strongly Disagree

1. My workplace's vision statement emphasizes a culture that attracts and nurtures leaders who are authentic mentors.	5 4 3 2 1
2. Leaders and my peers are passionate about their work and put their *all* into projects.	5 4 3 2 1
3. My workplace embraces leaders and teams who are drawn to making an emotional connection, and are comfortable expressing their emotions.	5 4 3 2 1
4. My workplace rewards the emotionally responsive person who is skilled at active listening.	5 4 3 2 1
5. People at my workplace are encouraged to be in touch with their emotions, which allows them to connect well with customers, peers and leaders.	5 4 3 2 1
6. My workplace teaches and rewards responding in a manner where the customer *feels* that you are working from their agenda.	5 4 3 2 1
7. My workplace encourages others to name their emotions, believing that to be *emotionally aware* helps build social networks, earn interpersonal loyalty, win clients and create alliances.	5 4 3 2 1
8. My workplace encourages the development of skills to "read" others' emotions in order to interpret and build relationships on what is seen and heard.	5 4 3 2 1
9. My workplace has training programs in place to build emotional loyalty.	5 4 3 2 1
10. My work culture encourages the sharing of "people stories" to recognize, reward and reinforce empathy.	5 4 3 2 1
11. When interacting with my leader, I feel she or he values me as an individual.	5 4 3 2 1
12. I get a sense that my leader understands and feels the emotions experienced by others.	5 4 3 2 1
13. My leader makes others feel understood.	5 4 3 2 1

14. My leader is comfortable sharing others' feelings of happiness.	5 4 3 2 1
15. My leader encourages others to talk about how they feel.	5 4 3 2 1
Total	

Score Interpretation **My overall score is: _____ out of 75**

75-60
Your workplace has a clear vision, interactive leaders and performance processes to embrace humanity and the healthy display of interactive empathy.

59-40
Your workplace has some performance processes, some display of interactive leadership, a vague vision to embrace humanity and the healthy display of interactive empathy.

40 or less
Your workplace needs to create and communicate a vision statement, develop leadership programs and design performance processes to communicate, reward and reinforce the healthy display of interactive empathy.

The important lesson one can learn from being an empathetic workplace or leader is the ability to experience the world from another perspective, often the perspective of your customer, peer or employee. Acceptance of others' humanity through interactive empathy needs to be embedded in the workplace culture—from leaders, salesmen, customer service workers to support staff. Remember, empathetic workplaces are more likely to create a psychologically positive workplace, which will lead to increased and passionate performance, higher customer loyalty and predictable bottom line results. As an anonymous English author wrote, *"To empathize is to see with the eyes of another, to hear with the ears of another, and to feel with the heart of another."*

Reflect

- What conversation needs to happen to bring empathy into your workplace?
- What is leadership's role in making this happen?
- What skills need to be developed to have an empathetic workplace?
- What type of work environment will help make the manifestation of the skill development of empathy happen?

Evolve

Chapter 9

The premise of the science of physics is that *everything* is made up of energy. Throughout this book, you have learned that emotions, thoughts, actions or inactions are filled with positive or negative energy. Furthermore, your hopes or fears have energy that either attract or distract people or events. Finally, the process of evolving requires the ability to *not* tolerate any energy that zaps your greatness.

All behavior is driven by emotional energy that moves you toward or away from a desired goal. Emotionally healthy people achieve their goals unless they allow distracting or hijacking energy to sabotage the desired goal. This chapter will explore the process of personal, professional, spiritual and relational evolution by using the intelligence of emotions to thrive—and not just survive. The SMARTER definition of evolution is the ability to continuously *improve, initiate,* and *innovate.* There is no endgame when evolving.

Evolution vs. Conflicting Emotional Energy

A question I often ask when coaching clients is: *What if you are the problem?* Their answer will tell me if there is a *conflicting energy* that is sabotaging their desired results.

Conflicting energy is an unseen or unspoken story or script that has a more negative push *away from evolving* than a positive pull toward it. These energies get into our bodies and minds in many different ways. They result in conflicting beliefs or thought patterns that block the energy to act freely. Often the conflicting energies emerge from our iceberg story. This story (belief) inspires—or stalls—our evolution. *Self-sabotage* is the result of conflicting emotional energies that pull you away from a desired goal—intentionally or not.

Conversely, the energy of evolution intentionally recognizes, redirects or repels any conflicting emotional energies. Why is this important? The benefit of managing conflicting energy (the push-pull, the hope or fear, the *should I?* or *shouldn't I?*) is the following:

- Freedom from being tied to the past and the future
- Free of your own and others' unhealthy judgments
- Free from the grip of emotion that interferes with being your personal best
- Capacity and desire to feel anything and everything
- Skills and energy to evolve
- Skills and energy to help others evolve

Energy of Evolution vs. Energy of Self-Sabotage

Remember, positive energy attracts the environment, people and actions to move you toward your goals, and negative energy hijacks or stalls actions to hold you back or move you away from your goals. When two forces of energy are moving in opposite directions, they:

- Cancel each other
- Expend double the energy
- Create zero net effect

What does this look like in real life?

1. **Positive energy** propels you to take focused action to obtain the desired result
2. **Conflicting energies** stall you, and your actions are slowed down
3. **Hyper-energy** creates *lots* of actions, but not the kind that will lead to the desired result
4. **Negative energy** propels patterns of actions that self-sabotage the desired result!

Conflicting Emotional Energy

"Core Dynamics of Conflicting Energy" was the model that I was trained on through CoachVille (www.coachville.com). I like this model as it provides a tool to identify the hidden energy that is holding you back from achieving your desired goals. The model provides language of positive or negative energy that occurs between your mind (what you think), heart (what you feel) and body (what you know). *Currently this model and training courses are available through* www.innerhumandesign.com.

According to the model, there are *three emotional reactions* that can sabotage our desired outcomes. These self-sabotaging response patterns evolve from limiting beliefs, addictive behaviors, false assumptions, default conditioning, avoidance habits and conflicting intentions.

- The emotional reaction of **Frustration** = Force the outcome
- The emotional reaction of **Overwhelm** = Resist to feel fully
- The emotional reaction of **Isolation** = Looking for yourself where you are not

Each of these emotional responses leads to specific behavioral reactions or non-actions. For example, when you have the emotional reaction of *Frustration*, you may try to have things your way. You will then force the outcome toward what you want. The emotional response of frustration forces an outcome that keeps you safe and secure, and aligns with your past stories (your iceberg). Therefore, you exclude others' perspectives, you manufacture your own interpretation of events or you overreact to events. These are all variations of frustration.

When you have the emotional energy of *Overwhelm*, you protect yourself by resisting to feel anything fully. Therefore, you ignore your intuition (what your gut is telling you), or you become overly judgmental or you simply avoid what is happening in the present. You hold onto the old ways, or you move into the future quickly to avoid the pain of the present. When you are judgmental, you create a world of separateness. If you feel, it means you are connecting, and you don't want to feel connected because it may have an emotional cost.

Another example of the emotional energy of overwhelm is to shut down your emotional radar. It's too uncomfortable, so you pull the *off* switch on your capacity to feel. Avoiding the present is an example of emotional overwhelm. To avoid feeling *now*, you hold onto past scripts, or you get caught up in the grip of emotion and are unable to be present in the moment. Avoiding the present (and your feelings) can result in addictive or repetitive behaviors that numb the feeling in the moment.

Finally, the emotional energy response of *Isolation* results in looking for yourself where you are not. This creates an over-identification with objects, people or events for validation and love. So what do you do? You resist evolving due to a fear of losing an external sense of identity and *love*. You limit your greatness to fit others' perceived expectations of what you should be. You resist accepting that you are okay just the way you are. You archive stuff in your mind to fit a definition of a perfect you.

Each of the emotional energies described above will sabotage your evolution to greatness. The good news is that when you use the intelligence of your emotions, you can evolve into your greatness by making the following shifts from:

- The emotional reaction of **Frustration** *to* the emotional reaction of **Trusting** (clarification of intention)

- The emotional reaction of **Overwhelm** *to* the emotional energy of **Knowing** (feeling things fully)

- The emotional reaction of **Isolation** *to* the emotional energy of **Connecting** (operate from wholeness)

To learn more about conflicting energy, visit www.humandesign.com

Improve

Career evolution includes having the skills and knowledge to manage career satisfaction and performance success, both inside and outside of the organization. Competent career managers know that the business and economic climate will constantly change. This requires annual *career health checkups*.

> What is split off, not felt, remains the same. When it is felt, it changes...If there is in you something bad, sick, or unsound, let it inwardly be and breathe. That's the only way it can evolve and change into the form it needs. —*Eugene Gendlin*

How Is Your Career Health?

What role does *career health* have to do with SMARTER skills in a global economy? Everything! Maintaining your career health is similar to maintaining your physical health. Much like the regular preparation and conditioning athletes use to achieve success in their particular sport, the global worker needs to commit to regular career conditioning (head *and* heart) to thrive in a global economy. From my review of global research on employability factors, and from counseling over 500 global career clients, I have identified six SMARTER *Career Health Habits* (see the chart on the next page).

Awareness	Strengths	Trends
Can you define what career management competencies are needed to sustain your employability?	Can you describe the skills, values, personality style and motivators that bring out your personal best?	Can you describe the industry, economic and market trends that are and will affect your industry and profession?

Practice	Feedback	Culture
Do you have a career practice plan that includes continuous fitness training, learning and skill development?	Do you regularly ask for, receive and give others feedback about work performance and career goals?	Are you in a work environment (this includes your boss) that inspires, promotes and sustains your future employability?

Improve Your Career Health

To evolve, knowledge is required from others or from yourself (through self-reflection or self-assessment). The *Career Health Inventory and Development Guide* is a tool that will provide you with self-knowledge in the six career health competencies, along with development actions to increase your self-knowledge.

Visit www.Smart2Smarter.com and click on EVOLVE to take the
Career Health Inventory and access the Assessment and Development Guide

Initiate

Requests frequently directed at candidates during a job or college interview are: *Tell me about something that you are proud to have initiated* and *Tell me about a situation when you initiated action.* Both requests are seeking examples of how often you stretch out of your comfort zone to solve, prevent or improve a situation. The requests also tap into your ability to work independently (without direct supervision) to achieve results. In our global, virtual and distributed workplace, most employers want employees who will work independently to get the job done, solve problems without prompting and own the results. In other words, they want employees to initiate action without a prompt and without the need for applause.

Initiation is a selfless act. It is other- or outer-directed to make someone's life easier, to keep or retain a customer or to prevent a crisis.

When you initiate, you evolve. When you initiate, you demonstrate

- Confidence in moving forward with uncertain outcomes
- Empathy by putting the other person or situation first—and putting your own ego aside
- Resilience by stepping out of your comfort zone
- Tolerance for others by asking for help or assistance

Can you provide an example of when you initiated an action in the last year?

- Where did this happen?

- What was the circumstance?

- What did you do?

- What was the result?

- Who else benefited?

- How did you benefit?

- Who did you tell?

Innovate

The third path to evolution is the ability to innovate—to go beyond what is, and inquire what could be. Contrary to what you may think, many of our best innovations took flight during challenging times.

> The ability to innovate is only as good as how one can accept changes and take risks.
> *–Franco Paolo Liu Eisma*

The process of innovation is the implementation of new ideas. Innovators go through a series of phases, and each phase requires different strengths and contributions. A resource to better understand your unique approach to innovation is the workbook *Type and Innovation*. Based on type theory, the workbook enables you to identify where and how one can best contribute and have the most positive impact. Visit https://www.cpp.com for more information.

Innovation requires the art and science of questioning. According to Paul

Sloane, global speaker on innovation (www.destination-innovation.com), asking questions is the simplest and most effective way of learning. Children learn by asking questions. Students learn by asking questions. SMARTER people learn by asking questions. Innovators never stop asking questions because they know that this is the best way to gain deeper insights. Eric Schmidt, CEO of Google, said, "We run this company on questions, not answers."

Why don't we stay childlike and continue to ask questions? Some people assume they know what they need to know, and don't want to exert energy to learn more. They cling to their beliefs and remain certain in their assumptions. They stay within their comfort zones.

Some people may think they will look weak, ignorant or unsure. In fact, asking questions is a sign of strength and intelligence, not a sign of weakness or uncertainty. Individuals who enjoy career success and significance constantly ask questions, and are comfortable knowing that they don't have all the answers. Finally, in our "hurry-up to get everything done" mode, we often don't stop to ask questions because it might just slow us down.

Innovators check their iceberg stories, assumptions and unhealthy beliefs at the door. They know that to evolve requires the art of curiosity. Curiosity leads to asking questions that deepen understanding and expand possibilities. Innovators start with broad, open-ended questions, then move to more specific areas to clarify or deepen their learning. As a professional coach, I understand the power of questioning with provocative questions. Provocative questions allow the client to reflect and innovate, leading to a new path of evolving into their personal best.

Examples of provocative questions are

- What is the one thing that you hope I do not ask you?
- What do you want to get out of this assignment?
- What do you want to accomplish?
- How do you get from here to there?
- What was *really* important?
- What are your thoughts on what might have caused this problem?
- What other possibilities could you consider?

Once the provocative questions have been explored, innovators ask questions to get specific information. These are called *reality* or *action* questions because they encourage a "reality check" or a prompt to action.

Examples of reality/action questions are

- When did this happen?
- What did you do first?
- Where is the project right now?
- Did you call the client? What did you say?
- To whom can you send your resume?
- Who needs to play a different role in your supporting cast?

To use provocative and reality/action questions to prompt innovation and create an *Accountability and Evolution Plan*, consult the *Evolving Into Greatness Tool* (pages 158-159).

Why Do People Stop Evolving?

Marshall Goldsmith, coauthor and editor of 19 books (including *The Leader of the Future 2*—a *Business Week* best-seller, *Global Leadership: The Next Generation* and *The Art and Practice of Leadership Coaching*), and Kelly Goldsmith, a Ph.D. at Yale University School of Management, provide insight into the dynamics

Excuses, Excuses.
If you want to do anything, you find a way.
If you don't want to do anything, you find an excuse.

of goal setting and why some clients lose motivation to evolve. Marshall and Kelly discuss *six reasons that people give up on goals* and stop evolving.

1. **Ownership** If you want to really evolve, then you need to understand that ultimately only you can make you better. If you are a coach, manager or counselor, you need to have the courage to test your client's commitment to evolve. The *Accountability and Evolution Plan* must come from within (you) and not be externally imposed by others.

2. **Time** Smart people have a tendency to underestimate the time needed to reach targets. In general, our behavior changes long before the perception of this change is acknowledged by others.

According to Marshall Goldsmith, we hold on to our perceptions of people or events in a manner that is consistent with our previous stereotype, and we look for behavior that proves our stereotype to be correct.

3. **Difficulty** The *optimism bias of smart people applies to difficulty as well as time.* Not only does everything take longer, it requires hard work! Diet books are almost always at the top of the best-seller lists. Why? Smart people underestimate the difficulty in sticking to a diet plan. Long-term change and personal evolution requires sustained effort. Evolving is not easy, and you will face some problems in your journey.

4. **Distractions** Smart people have a tendency to underestimate the distractions and competing goals that will invariably appear through-out the year. One truism to remember is that a distraction most likely will appear. In some cases, the distraction or crisis may result from a problem; in other cases, it may result from an opportunity.

To evolve, one needs to assume that unexpected distractions and competing goals will occur. By planning for distractions in advance, you can set realistic expectations for progress and be less likely to give up when special problems or opportunities emerge.

5. **Rewards** Smart people tend to become disappointed when the achievement of a goal doesn't immediately translate into the achieve-ment of other goals. SMARTER people acknowledge the value of a long-term investment in their own development. SMARTER people see the evolution process as a long-term investment in their career success and significance development.

6. **Maintenance** Smart people often rationalize that, since they put in all of the effort needed to achieve a goal, it can be tough to face the reality of the work required in maintaining a changed behavior. One of the first reactions of many dieters upon reaching their goal weight is to think, *This is great! Now I can start eating again.* SMARTER people understand that evolution is a process—not a state of being. SMARTER people can never "get there," because SMARTER people accept that evolution never stops.

Avoid a "Repairs Only" Mentality

When creating an evolution plan, the first step is to avoid a *repairs only* men-tality in your planning. Good development plans focus first on strengthening your strengths as well as remedying areas of apparent weakness. Also, remember you have limited time and energy, so look for maximum impact when selecting development goals that are personally significant and career-aligned. Ask yourself the question: *Of all the things I could do, what would make the biggest difference right now?* Whenever possible, choose evolution goals that matter to you, that energize you.

Becoming a skilled communicator is an outcome.

> Remember, an evolution goal is an outcome, not an activity. Avoid confusing one with the other.

Attending a communication skills workshop may be an action step, but it is not your evolution goal! Incorporate your preferred learning style as you determine the action steps you will take to achieve your development goal. Are you an experiential, visual, auditory, logical or reflective learner? The action steps also need to include *how* the learning (evolution) will take place. Research shows that 70% of evolutionary learning takes place "in the emotional energy field of life," and 20% through people connections. Only 10% of evolving takes place through lecture-style workshops.

Finally, consider these *three strategies* recommended by the Center for Creative Leadership when creating your *Accountability and Evolution Plan*:

1. **Seek challenging assignments** You need to practice skills and behaviors to help you reach your goal. You will most likely find opportunities to practice new challenges in your current job, home or educational environment.

2. **Seek experiential learning for targeted skills** Seek programs that encourage the application of new skills with immediate personal feedback to accelerate the evolution learning curve.

3. **Seek accountability relationships** Your chances of reaching your goals increase when you invite personal connections into your emotional energy field. You need to identify people who will hold you accountable to your goals, provide a nudge when needed, be a mentor and then a cheerleader to celebrate your success.

Consider these *development paths* as you create your *Accountability and Evolution Plan*:

Observation Schedule time to observe people who have the skills you want to develop.

Networking Schedule time to meet with people from whom you can learn, and who can learn from you. Make use of electronic, project, professional and social networking, along with sports and leisure events to deepen your knowledge and expertise of an area you want to develop.

Practice If you want to get better at performing a task or behavior, you need to ask for projects, activities or "stretch assignments" to practice! Even if you have a natural talent, you need to use it often in order to continue achieving high performance.

Ask for help and feedback Asking for help and feedback is an emotional intelligence competency that bridges personal and social development.

Training Are you the type of person that learns best by taking a class, learning with others in a classroom setting? Find a course that will develop those skills you have targeted, or ask those whom you admire and have the skills you want for recommendations of a course.

Find or be a coach or mentor A coach or mentor can provide advisement, modeling, accountability and encouragement on how to improve your skills.

Keep an emotional awareness journal Each day, take time to record what your emotional brain taught you about the day's events. Look for patterns. Answer: *What was that emotion telling me? What were my senses (smell, sight, sound) telling me? What judgments did I make? Did I jump to conclusions? What action did I take? How did that action work out for me? What do I want now? What can I now choose to do differently?*

A Final Word *Persistence*

In Christopher Peterson's and Dr. Seligman's book, *Character Strengths and Virtues*, they define

> Big shots are only little shots that keep shooting.
> *–Christopher Morley*

persistence as the "voluntary continuation of a goal-directed action in spite of obstacles, difficulties, or discouragement." Just as fear is a prerequisite for courage, challenge is a prerequisite for perseverance. Thomas Edison is purported to have said, "Genius is 99% perspiration and 1% inspiration." SMARTER people know that wisdom (the ability to learn from past efforts), self-esteem and rewards play a critical role in personal evolution. However, Ben Dean, Ph.D., a psychologist, coach, and the founder of MentorCoach (www.mentorcoach.com), purports that the strength of persistence is critical to your evolution. Dr. Dean offers the following advice about persistence and evolution:

- **Impossible goals** Some goals are truly impossible to reach, and some outcomes are simply unavoidable. As Kenny Rogers says, "You got to know when to hold 'em, know when to fold 'em."

- **Self-esteem and task difficulty** As we learned in the chapter on Mastery, people with higher self-esteem are more likely to persist on a difficult task than people with lower self-esteem. If you believe you are a competent person with a good chance of succeeding at most things, you are less likely to quit. However, people also tend to persist longer at solving problems when they are told that what they are doing is easy as opposed to difficult. Why? Because failing at a task that everyone else finds easy can be humiliating and damaging to self-esteem. In contrast, there is minimal shame when one fails a widely acknowledged difficult task (Starnes & Zinser, 1983; Frankel & Snyder, 1978).

- **Rewards** When individuals have been rewarded in the past for sticking with a task, they are more likely to persist on a future task— even if the future task is not directly related to the first (Eisenberger et al., 1992; Eisenberger & Selbst, 1994). However, some rewards undermine persistence. People who perform tasks for money, prizes or awards tend to lose interest in performing a task for its own sake (Deci, 1971; Harackiewicz, 1979). If the reward becomes unavailable, then persistence may drop off sharply. SMARTER people persist to enhance their external and internal self-image of competence, worth and connectivity—all fueled by the emotional brain and positive emotions.

- **Anger and cynicism** According to the book by Williams and Williams, *Anger Kills: Seventeen Strategies for Controlling the Hostility That Can Harm Your Health*, it is important to know when anger or cynicism is interfering with personal evolution. The book provides a roadmap to understand how to stop cynical thoughts that hijack your *emotional brain.*

- **Your environment** Evolution becomes sustainable when we have environments that support our growth. Just like the dinosaurs evolved due to changes in their environment, human beings can choose to evolve or resist as a result of their environments. To persist, and thus evolve, requires environments that work for you. Think of your environments as "evolution partners" that nurture and sustain your growth. Your environments include everything from people, pets, work spaces, rooms, a yard, food and church. When your environment is without distractions or clutter, it is amazing how easy it is to evolve. An ideal environment *feels* safe by increasing predictability, and reducing uncertainty and stress. Design your environment to be self-sustainable and to inspire you. See everything as part of your environment, and stop tolerating parts of your environment that are not sustainable or do not sustain your evolution. Remember, every goal needs an environment to support it.

- **Action blocks** are not about a lack of willpower. Action blocks start with an emotional signal that often triggers a physiological response in your breathing, heart rate, muscles and tendons, or in your sensations like hot or cold, tension, tightness, pain or sweating. Action blocks are similar to a car's warning light that signals you are about to run out of gas. If you don't stop (or pause) and refill, your evolution, like the car, will be stalled. What are the warning signs that tell you it's time to refill? For me, I become hyperkinetic and cannot fall asleep. My body is *on idle*, yet my brain is still running. I know that without sleep, my evolution is stalled. I remind myself to "pull over," look at the emotional or physiological signals, and then take action to remove the block(s).

Some questions to reflect upon when you feel blocked

- Are you currently blocked?
- What are your warning signals?
- How do you normally react to being blocked?
- Is the block *protective, rebelling* or *wanting something else*? How do you know?
- Can you envision a world where you work through your blocks and take action?

Concluding Remarks

Think about your intentional evolution as an investment in your career and quality of life. Where will you get the best return on your development commitment? As you create an *Accountability and Evolution Plan*, first focus on what natural strength or talent you want to amplify that will positively impact career success and significance. Second, choose a behavior that you want to make stronger, minimize or eliminate to increase your career success and significance. Then stop, look and listen for signals that may stall your action. Finally, enlist people who will inspire, nudge and celebrate your evolution!

> *Join the* Smart 2 Smarter Community *to access*
> *the following activities and additional **EVOLVE** resources*
> *and assessments online at* www.Smart2Smarter.com
>
> Evolution and Innovation Habits book and website
> Evolving Into Greatness: Self-Reflection or Coaching Questions book and website
> My SMARTER Evolution Plan book
> Emotional Energy Patterns: Are You Evolving or Sabotaging Your Greatness? website
> Evolutionary Action Planning website
> Evolutionary Distinctions website
> Career Health Inventory and Development Guide website

Activity Evolution and Innovation Habits

Creating new habits requires using the intelligence of your emotions. Before you review the list of habits with yourself or others, first read the five steps below to prepare yourself for accepting, and not rejecting, the feedback.

Prepare Your Physical and Mental State

1. Become physically centered, breathe deeply three times, keep your hands in your lap

2. Ask for and receive perspective, knowledge and suggestions on how you can evolve more into your greatness

3. Silently remind yourself:

    a. This person is sharing their perspective with me; it will add valuable insight for me to evolve or inspire innovation in others

    b. This is their perspective, which may be based on fact or intuition

    c. It's my choice how I choose to emotionally respond to the information

    d. I must remind myself why this relationship and information is important

    e. I must remind myself of what I will gain by listening

4. I will acknowledge and appreciate the information

5. I will communicate on next steps that I'll take to continue to evolve

Habits That Limit Evolution and Innovation	Shift to...	Habits That Attract Evolution and Innovation
Can't or won't say *I don't know*. Until I say *I don't know*, I do not create an opening to receive new information or new ideas.		I'm willing and able to say *I don't know* when I really, or "kind of," don't know.
Forgetting that, like everyone else, I have blind spots. No one person can see all possible consequences or outcomes. When we forget this, we limit our evolution.		I am aware that I have blind spots, and I seek diverse viewpoints of those I respect to fill in the gaps.
Wanting to be clear about everything all of the time. There will be moments of confusion or lack of clarity. Insisting on constant clarity can stall growth and innovation.		I am open to the confusion that exists within environments of change. I choose to accept, and not avoid, environments that are not crystal clear.
Closing off curiosity and questions. Questions about what I don't know can produce more new ideas than statements about what I do know. Stopping others from asking questions will perpetuate more of the same.		I encourage others to ask questions that may challenge the norm. I see questions as progress, not as obstacles to action. I will take action, even if all questions have not been answered.
Being attached to the novelty of new ideas. Never letting a good idea take root by rushing from new idea to new idea without getting the full value of any one idea.		I stick with a new idea long enough to evaluate its value. I recognize that obstacles will appear as the idea is executed.

Habits That Limit Evolution and Innovation	Shift to...	Habits That Attract Evolution and Innovation
Not giving permission to be taught. I create roadblocks or limit authority for others to teach me.		I choose my teachers and I give them the authority to teach me in the domain of their expertise.
Already knowing how and what I need to change. Innovating is rarely a solo act. Insisting that I know what I need will cut me off from the valuable ideas of others.		I grant my teachers permission to help me understand, identify and suggest how to address my development gaps. I acknowledge that what worked in the past may not work today as conditions change.
Believing I can't change, I am not good at change, or I am not creative.		I am capable of evolving, and I am uniquely creative. I share my creative ideas openly.
Confusing having an opinion or an explanation with knowing the answer. If I insist my opinion or explanation is the solution, the incentive to seek or receive new solutions becomes mute.		I recognize that my explanation may be powerful, but it's not the only explanation. I look for the explanation that gives the most leverage to progress.
Not respecting emotions in the innovative process. Change will produce positive and negative emotional reactions in others and in me. Not acknowledging, recognizing or ignoring these emotions will slow or derail the evolution or innovation process.		I acknowledge and respect that emotional reactions that arise during times of change are natural and often spontaneous. I do not ignore them. I seek to understand their source. I am respectful of the humanness of myself and of my colleagues.
Confusing having new information with being able to take new action. Allowing little or no time for reflection. Constant action usually perpetuates the same action. Innovation often requires gaining perspective, which often comes from reflection.		I allow time for reflection to step back from the action, and I encourage others to do the same.

SMARTER EVOLVE

Activity   Evolving Into Greatness: Self-Reflection or Coaching Questions

Self-reflection is a SMARTER evolution strategy that allows one to pause, step back to gather information, visualize a future self, and design an environment and path to move forward. The following questions are presented as being asked by a third party. However, feel free to substitute the pronoun *you* with *I* (e.g., change question #3 to: *Sounds like I want to hold on to the old script. How can I write a new chapter?*).

1. What will happen if you explore other perspectives?

2. How can you anchor another perspective?

3. Sounds like you want to hold on to the old script. How can you write a new chapter?

4. Who continues to enable your current story?

5. Seems like you shifted to a "smaller" self?

6. Would you be open to the possibility that there are other stories?

7. Do you feel that you have the choice of continuing down the same path?

8. Is there anything you are not saying?

9. Why aren't you taking any action on this?

10. Who would you be if this did not happen?

11. Are you sure that you're not getting fixed on an outcome that is blocking all other ideas?

12. Your vision sounds all about you. How does this vision serve mankind?

13. Would you be open to a technique to explore your greatness?

14. What is the win to free yourself from patterns you carry from the past?

15. Sounds like you continue to *play small*. How can you *play bigger* **and** be your greatness?

16. What resources do you need to help you in your development?

17. What projects or teams can provide on-the-job application?

18. Who is an expert in the skill you want to develop?

19. What job assignments will help you acquire skills and experience?

20. What training will provide further knowledge and techniques?

21. What was your biggest triumph this year?

22. What was the SMARTEST decision you made this year?

23. What was the biggest risk you took this year?

24. What was the greatest lesson you learned this year?

25. What was the most challenging thing you did this year?

26. What is your biggest piece of unfinished business for this year?

27. What are you most satisfied about completing this year?

28. Who are the three people who had the greatest impact on your life this year?

29. Where have you held back this year?

30. What do you want to let go of from this past year?

31. What else do you need to say or do to complete this year?

32. For what are you most grateful?

33. Who do you want to become in the next year?

34. What do you want to learn in the next year?

35. What strengths do you wish to use more this year?

36. What will success mean to you this year?

Activity   My SMARTER Evolution Plan

Specific, Measurable, Agreed-upon action, Realistic stretch, Time-bound, Emotional energy and Reward

Be SMARTER

*Use these **SMARTER** questions to review your development commitments*

1. Are your commitments **Specific**?

    a. Goals that relate directly to the advancement of your career success or significance need to be linked to a short-term performance goal or a long-term life/work plan.

2. Are your commitments **Measurable?**

    a. Your commitment goal needs to include metrics for measuring the quality/quantity of progress toward the goal

3. Do you and your support team or coach **Agree** upon how to measure your progress?

    a. Commitment goals need to be developed and agreed upon with your coach/support team

        i. Limit SMARTER goals to one per month

        ii. This will ensure focus on career goals that will enhance your employability, career health and life balance

4. Are your goals a **Realistic** stretch?

    a. Set challenging, but possible, goals to achieve

    b. Discuss what it will really take to complete the *Development Plan* so that your expectations and others' are realistically achievable

5. Is your Commitment Plan **Time-bound?**

    a. Goal milestones should be accomplished within a set amount of time

    b. Milestone indicators are a basis for evaluation when the long-term goal is to be accomplished in a future year

6. Are you using the intelligence of your **Emotions** to fuel your energy?

    a. Assess what you need to stay attracted to the Thrive Path

    b. Build reserves to keep your energy high in order to reach your goal

7. What recognition and **Reward** do you need to sustain positive energy?

    a. What do you need from others to recognize your progress?

    b. What will you do to recognize your own progress?

Reciprocity

Chapter 10

As a mother, I intentionally taught my children the power of reciprocity. Reciprocity is an act of kindness which is best received by returning an act of kindness. Through the power of relationships, this skill helps you and others develop the previous six SMARTER skills discussed in this book.

The cumulative impact of these previous six SMARTER skills is *reciprocity*. Why? Because all relationships are a reflection of the one you have with yourself.

Reciprocity is defined as

- The ability to lead and be led
- The ability to give and receive feedback
- The ability to teach and be taught

> Today we are faced with the pre-eminent fact that if civilization is to survive, we must cultivate the science of human relationships.
> *—Franklin Delano Roosevelt*

The Ability to Lead and Be Led

Your emotions and actions impact those you lead. Research indicates that a ten percent increase in the perception of a leader who creates a positive emotional work climate results in a three-fold increase in performance output and customer satisfaction.

Why should you care about developing the SMARTER skill of reciprocity? When people feel good, they work better and are more creative and productive. Good feelings are like lubrication for the brain: Mental efficiency goes up, memory is sharpened, and people can understand directions and make better decisions. Studies have shown this to be true when it comes to the ability to lead and be led—emotions are contagious.

Individuals form a perception within the first 30 seconds of meeting you about whether or not they will follow you. The next 30 seconds will either confirm or deny their emotional signals to follow, or not follow, your leadership. Their decision has everything to do with the emotional connection between you and them. Clients, partners, employees and friends stay in relationships because they feel appreciated, utilized, enhanced and rewarded.

Think about the relationships you left. You most likely left based on feelings of being limited, exploited, ignored, bored or

> In everyone's life, at some time, our inner fire goes out. It is then burst into flames by an encounter with another human being. We should all be thankful for those people who rekindle the inner spirit.
> –Albert Schweitzer, Alsatian theologian

drained in some way. Reciprocity is not about you or them. It is about a shared emotional connection that elevates performance *flow*. It is about *us*.

Emotions play a key role in attracting or distracting followership. Are you creating positive shared emotional experiences? What images come to mind when others think about you? What images appear when you think about them? Remember, hope and fear are the two primary emotions that attract or distract leading or being led. Utilize the concept of mirrored neurons to understand and activate shared positive emotions. Strive to leave people feeling better than they did before your interaction.

According to Lou Cassara, president and CEO of The Cassara Clinic® (www.cassaraclinic.com), people follow others due to the positive "emotional pull" that increases everyone's confidence to achieve personal wins, significance and success.

Cassara suggests surveying at least five people each year that you value as a client, leader or peer and asking them the following *five questions*:

1. Why did you choose to engage and interact with me?

2. What values or qualities do we share?

3. How have I exemplified these values or qualities?

   It's better to under-promise and over-deliver!

4. In three words, what's the value (personal win) of our relationship to you?

5. Do I deliver what I say I will?

Balancing Feeling Good With Results

Emotional intelligence essentially describes the ability to effectively join emotions and reasoning, using emotions to facilitate reasoning, and reasoning intelligently about emotions (Mayer & Salovey, 1997). The challenge for leaders is obtaining a balance between followers feeling good, having satisfying relationships, and keeping their focus on the goal. The ability of a leader to foster group enthusiasm can determine its success. Conversely, emotional conflicts within a group take attention and energy away from shared tasks, and overall performance suffers.

Since emotions are contagious, then all leaders, whether at school, home, work or in the community, can choose to create and sustain positive shared experiences. Leaders can, by managing their own moods, drive service climate, volunteerism, academic performance and business outcomes.

What the Research States

Research linking positive moods to creativity suggests that positive moods do impact a leader's creativity and the creating of a compelling vision for their group or organization (Isen et al., 1987). Leaders use their positive moods and emotions to envision improvements. They are also likely to be aware that their positive moods may cause them to be overly optimistic (Mayer et al., 1990). Leaders use the intelligence of their emotions to more accurately appraise how their followers currently feel, to understand why they feel this way and influence followers' emotions so that they are receptive to, and supportive of, the leader's goals (Gardner & Avolio, 1998).

Leaders also need to distinguish between the emotions their followers are experiencing and the emotions they express. Leaders with emotional intelligence— *social awareness* and *tolerance*—can decipher when expressed emotions are genuine, understand why they may be faked, and influence followers to experience genuine excitement, enthusiasm, confidence and optimism (Hochschild, 1983; Rafaeli & Sutton, 1989).

Emotional intelligence also contributes to the ability to solve problems with a minimum of stress (Epstein, 1990; Katz & Epstein, 1991). This then leads to creative ideas that settle disagreements, generate *win-win* solutions to problems, and ensure cooperation and trust. Moreover, when a leader realizes that emotions generated by low priority demands are interfering with more pressing demands, the leader's ability to actively manage these distracting emotions facilitates effective decision making (Easterbrook, 1959; Frigda, 1988; Mandler, 1975; Simon, 1982).

Finally, quality interpersonal relationships between leaders and their followers has also been linked to emotional intelligence (Gerstner & Day, 1997; Graen & Uhl-Bien, 1995). Specifically, leaders with high emotional intelligence scores attract higher enthusiasm, excitement and optimism as well as a climate of cooperation and trust.

Transformational Leadership

According to well-documented research from both the Gallup Organization and the Hay Group, roughly 50 to 70 percent of employees perceive the person in charge as responsible for the conditions that directly affect people's moods at work, and ultimately their ability to work well together and create satisfied customers. What separates a good leader from a great leader is the ability to inspire greatness in their followers.

Research conducted by Bernard M. Bass & Ronald E. Riggio, authors of *Transformational Leadership*, found that transformational leaders hold positive expectations for followers. They affect followers' beliefs and values through a sense of commitment, involvement and duty. As a result, they inspire, empower and stimulate followers to exceed their personal best, and tend to focus on and care about followers and their personal needs and development.

Bass and Riggio provide four components to transformational leadership, sometimes referred to as the *Four I's*. Each component includes one or more emotional intelligence competencies.

1. **Idealized Influence (II)** Serves as an ideal role model for followers; the leader "walks the talk," and is admired for this

2. **Inspirational Motivation (IM)** Ability to inspire and motivate followers

The first two *I's* fuel a leader's charisma and positive emotional energy.

3. **Individualized Consideration (IC)** Demonstrates concern and gives personal attention to the needs and feelings of followers

4. **Intellectual Stimulation (IS)** Challenges followers to be innovative and creative

Several tools are available that measure transformational leadership qualities, including the *Multifactor Leadership Questionnaire* (www.mindgarden.com), the *SHL Leadership Report* (www.shl.com) and the *CPI Leadership Report* (www.CPP.com).

What Derails the Capacity to Lead or Be Led?

Several books have identified behaviors that cause smart leaders to fail. The impact is simply that people they once led (their followers) leave. Some derailers are both strengths and weaknesses. The average person has two or three derailers. The stress of being at the top and intense pressures can activate the derailers. In addition, the higher you go in an organization, the less likely other people are to tell you about your derailing (failure-producing) characteristics.

- In their book, *Working for You Isn't Working for Me: The Ultimate Guide to Managing Your Boss,* authors Katherine Crowley, a psychotherapist, and Kathi Elster, a business strategist, identified 20 behaviors that derail one's ability to lead and be led.

- David L. Dotlich and Peter C. Cairo describe eleven derailers that lead to failure in their book, *Why CEOs Fail.* Under stress, these characteristics lead to errors in judgment that can be fatal to a career, and often to an organization.

- Sidney Finkelstein, author of *Why Smart Executives Fail,* researched leadership failures and their causes over a six-year period. The *seven habitual patterns* he found that can steer leaders and followers off the Thrive Path and onto the Survive Path are listed below:

Habit 1 They see themselves and their companies as dominant. On the positive side, this attitude is seen as highly optimistic. Optimism is a primary trait of successful leaders; however, when carried to extremes, it causes one to lose touch with reality.
Warning sign: A lack of respect.

Habit 2 They identify too closely with their place of employment, losing the boundary between personal and work interests. On the positive side, this trait means that a leader works long, hard hours over and above what is expected. But if carried to extremes, a leader may exhibit a sense of entitlement, which can pave the way for unethical or toxic behavior.
Warning sign: A question of character.

Habit 3 They think they have all the answers. High intelligence and an ability to solve problems quickly and decisively are essential for leadership. When a leader does not seek input or adequate information before making and acting on a decision, their decisions may be inappropriate. And just as important, when followers' input

is not sought, followers tend to be less enthusiastic and committed to implementing the decision.
Warning sign: A leader without followers.

Habit 4 They eliminate anyone who isn't completely supportive. When followers are comprised of "yes" people, there isn't enough dissension to evaluate risks appropriately.
Warning sign: The departure of followers.

Habit 5 They are consummate spokespersons. When leaders appear to be promoting themselves more than they promote the group, beware.
Warning sign: Blatant attention-seeking.

Habit 6 They underestimate or dismiss obstacles. Optimism works for motivating and inspiring, but carried to extremes it can hijack adequate risk evaluation and reality checks.
Warning sign: Excessive hype.

Habit 7 They stubbornly rely on what worked for them in the past. The problem is, nothing stays the same. Applying yesterday's solutions to all of tomorrow's problems is just not smart.
Warning sign: Constantly referring to prior successes.

Getting Leaders to Change

Marshall Goldsmith has been called America's foremost executive coach by several leading magazines and newspapers (*Fast Company, Forbes, Wall Street Journal, Harvard Business Review*). His model for behavioral coaching outlines a reliable process to help leaders achieve positive, measurable changes in themselves, their staff and their teams.

According to Goldsmith, it is critical to clarify at the outset *who the client is.* When the coach and the leader understand that the company is the actual client, then ground rules are easier to accept. This is a vital step for gaining and maintaining trust. Once the ground rules have been established, they need to be adhered to by both the client and the coach.

Next, secure an agreement with the client (the organization) and the leader with respect to *two key variables*:

1. What are the key behaviors that will lead to the greatest positive change in leadership effectiveness?

2. Which key stakeholders (accountability partners) should determine (one year later) if this change has occurred?

The coaching agreement needs to clarify *confidentiality, reporting relationships,* and *information gathering.* Goldsmith provides the following guidelines:

1. **Confidentiality, expectations and commitment** Be clear about what will be shared with the leader's boss, and what will be kept confidential.

2. **Reporting relationships** There must be clarity among the three key participants: The organizational sponsor (boss or HR representative), the coach and the leader.

3. **Methods of information gathering** Key stakeholders may be contacted by both the coach and the leader. The coach requests direct help in *three critical arenas*:

    a. Let go of the past. Key stakeholders must agree to focus on a future that can improve, as opposed to a past that cannot.

    b. Be helpful and supportive—not cynical, sarcastic or judgmental. If people don't give the leader a chance, he or she will stop trying.

    c. Tell the truth. Key stakeholders are advised not to gloss over or embellish reports.

4. **Choose an area for self-improvement** The leader will ask for ongoing development suggestions. Stakeholders, too, will be asked to select an area for self-improvement and to solicit suggestions. Stakeholders will serve as "fellow travelers" in the quest for self-improvement.

5. **Making judgments, setting objectives and monitoring progress** The coach helps the leader and key stakeholders maintain objectivity. Coaches must focus on one or two behaviors, without judgment, and facilitate honest sharing about progress.

6. **How, why and when the coaching will end** Success parameters are set at the beginning of the engagement, along with milestones for assessing progress and a completion date (usually 12 to 18 months).

Summary *Leadership Behavioral Coaching Process*

1. **Invite leaders to be involved in determining desired behaviors** Leaders cannot be expected to change their behavior if they lack an understanding of the desired goals.

2. **Leaders identify key stakeholders** When leaders and their managers agree in advance on desired behaviors and key stakeholders, they buy into the coaching process.

3. **Collect feedback** The coach can accomplish this by interviewing key stakeholders and using 360-degree rating systems that collect information from multiple sources.

4. **Determine key behaviors for change** Select only one or two key behaviors that will have the most positive impact on effective leadership.

5. **Have the leader interact with key stakeholders** The leader talks with each key stakeholder to collect additional suggestions on how to improve in the targeted areas. The leader keeps the conversation positive, simple and focused. When mistakes have been made in the past, it is generally a good idea to apologize and ask for help in changing the future. Leaders are advised to listen to stakeholder suggestions without judging them.

6. **Review what has been learned, and help the leader develop a *Commitment Plan*** After listening to suggestions, the leader drafts a plan describing what he or she wants to accomplish. The coach provides guidance to help the leader create a *Commitment Plan.*

7. **Develop an ongoing follow-up process** Follow up should be efficient and focused on the future, incorporating questions like, *Based upon my behavior last month, what ideas do you have for me for next month?* Within six months, conduct a two- to six-item mini-survey with key stakeholders, asking whether the leader has become more or less effective in each targeted area for improvement.

8. **Review results and start again** If the leader has taken the process seriously, stakeholders invariably report improvement. Build on this success by repeating the process for the next 12 to 18 months. This type of follow-up will assure continued progress on initial goals, and uncover additional areas for improvement.

Why Leaders Give Up

When it comes to change, some leaders lose motivation and fail to *stick with the program*. Regardless of a coach's competence, failure to achieve goals may occur for several reasons:

1. **Ownership** The more leaders feel the process is being imposed upon them, or that they are "trying it out," the less likely the coaching process will work.

2. **Time** High achievers have a natural tendency to underestimate the time needed to reach targets. Busy, impatient leaders can be even more time-sensitive and underestimate how long true behavior change will take. Ordinarily, our behavior changes long before our co-workers perceive any change.

3. **Difficulty** High achievers' and leaders' optimism applies to difficulty as well as time. Not only does everything take longer than leaders think, it also requires hard work! Long-term change in leadership effectiveness takes sustained effort.

4. **Distractions** Leaders have a tendency to underestimate the distractions and competing goals that will surface. By planning for distractions in advance, leaders can set realistic expectations for change and will consequently be less likely to renounce the change process.

5. **Rewards** Leaders tend to become disappointed when achievement of one goal doesn't immediately translate into achievement of other goals. If leaders think social or emotional skill improvement will quickly lead to short-term profits, promotions or recognition, they may become hijacked and give up.

6. **Maintenance** Once a leader has put forth the effort required to achieve a goal, it can be tough to maintain behaviors. Leadership involves relationships—and relationships, like people, are subject to change. Maintaining positive relationships requires continuous evolution.

Reciprocity *Ability to Give and Receive*

In the *Harvard Business Review* article, "Social Intelligence and the Biology of Leadership," authors Boyatzis and Goleman introduce the concept of *social intelligence*. They define social intelligence as a set of interpersonal competencies built on specific neural circuits (and related endocrine systems) that inspire others to be effective. To me, this is *the essence of reciprocity*—the ability to give and receive when engaged in interpersonal interactions is as much or even more about emotions as it is about behavior. Key points from the article confirm this premise:

- Your behavior can energize or deflate others through mood contagion. Positive mood contagion unifies a group, and bonded groups perform higher than fragmented groups.
- Mood contagion stems from neurobiology. Positive behavior, such as empathy, creates a chemical connection between you and others.

- Mirrored neurons are dispersed throughout the brain. These neurons mimic or mirror what another person does (a yawn, a smile). When we consciously or unconsciously detect another's emotions through their actions, our mirrored neurons reproduce those emotions. The neurons create an instant sense of shared experience.

- There is a shared group of neurons whose only job is to detect laughter or smiles.

- When we give or receive appreciation, gifts or advice, it is these mirrored neurons that record the positive emotional experience.

- Reciprocity is the ability to intentionally store a positive emotional memory.

The Magic Ratio

As discussed throughout this book, the memories of our lives are recorded in terms of positive and negative visual and emotional experiences. Scientists propose that each day our thoughts and emotions keep track of our positive and negative moments, and the resulting score contributes to our overall mood. Our emotional mood is defined by the number of positive versus negative moments experienced during the course of a day. We rarely record neutral moments.

When you interact with someone, a memory or image of the interaction is filed away in your emotional memory bank. When you interact with this person again, the file is retrieved along with the emotional memory. The emotion then travels to your cognitive brain (thoughts) that accepts or rejects the "reality" of the emotion in the *now*. The logical left-brain is busy searching for words, facts and figures, while the emotional right-brain is "reading between the lines."

According to the Nobel Prize-winning scientist Daniel Kahneman, each day we experience approximately 20,000 "interactional moments" where our brain records an experience. The quality of our days is determined by how our brains recognize and categorize these moments—either as positive, negative or neutral. Over the past decade, scientists have explored the impact of positive-to-negative interaction ratios in our work and personal life. They have found that this ratio can be used to predict everything from performance in the workplace to happiness in a marriage.

Noted psychologist John Gottman researched positive-to-negative "interactional moments" in marriages. It was discovered that five positive interactions are needed to "undo" the effects of one negative interaction. Using a 5:1 ratio, which Gottman dubbed the "Magic Ratio," he and his colleagues predicted whether 700 newlywed couples would stay together or get divorced by scoring their positive and negative interactions in one 15-minute conversation between husband and wife. Ten years later, the follow-up revealed divorce predictions within 94 percent accuracy.

The Bucket and the Dipper

In your personal and professional world, it's not a question of whether you *have* relationships, but rather *what kind* of relationships do you have? In their book, *How Full Is Your Bucket: Positive Strategies for Work and Life*, psychologists Donald Clifton and Tom Rath propose a metaphor of looking at positive and negative interactions during the day.

Imagine we all have a bucket that can be filled with positive or negative experiences throughout the day. Each of us also has an invisible dipper. When we use that dipper to fill other people's buckets—by saying or doing things to increase their positive emotions—we also fill our own bucket. But when we use that dipper to dip from others' buckets—by saying or doing things that decrease their positive emotions—we diminish ourselves. An empty bucket poisons our outlook, saps our energy, and undermines our will. That's why every time someone dips from our bucket, it hurts us. You have a choice every moment of every day: To fill one another's buckets, or dip from them. *How full is your bucket today? How full is the bucket of others you interacted with today?*

Here are five strategies *to increase your Magic Ratio of positive-to-negative moments each day*

1. **Prevent bucket dipping** Increase your own awareness of how often your comments are negative. Work toward a ratio of five positive comments to every negative comment.
2. **Shine a light on what is right** Focus and appreciate first what others do right rather than where they need improvement.
3. **Make and be a best friend** in all areas of your life.
4. **Give unexpectedly** A recent poll shows that most people prefer giving gifts rather than receiving them.
5. **Reverse the golden rule** Instead of "Do unto others as you would have them do unto you," consider "Do unto others as they would have you do unto them." The key is *personalization* when filling others' buckets.

What strategy will you start to use tomorrow?

Reciprocity *Teach and Be Taught*

Finally, reciprocity entails the ability to teach and the willingness to be open to new learning that will expand your greatness. The ability to teach and be taught requires vulnerability and trust. As stated earlier, vulnerability includes the ability to ask for help, say *I don't know*, or simply say *I'll try* without really knowing the outcome. Reciprocity is based on shared vulnerability.

Patrick Lencioni, author of the *Five Temptations of a CEO: A Leadership Fable*, states: "We strive so hard to stay in our 'comfort zone,' but it is outside this zone that we see real growth. It is through the acknowledgement of our weaknesses and finding ways others can compliment you, and you compliment them, that we can find success and growth. Without being willing to step out of that 'comfort zone' of being vulnerable comes 'yes men' and disconnect because of the fear others might have of what they say and do. To be vulnerable requires trust of the process and the people involved." The key word in the above sentence is *trust*.

How do you define trust? When I ask others this question, I hear a variety of answers about trusting based on competence, personality or interests. When I inquire about trust-busters, the responses tend to be more about an emotional wound. This is a negative, shared emotional experience that was recorded, replayed and serves as *trust radar*.

What is clear is that how one trusts and why one trusts is very personal. According to Drs. Michelle and Dennis Reina, authors of *Trust and Betrayal in the Workplace*, "trust affects individual and team engagement and productivity." Based on years of experience and research, they found that the capacity to trust is based on the readiness to trust ourselves and our openness to trust others.

> What and how we trust influences our capacity to trust.

What you focus on first when interacting with others also impacts the capacity to trust and be vulnerable. The Reina's present three *Trust Radars* that impact establishing "mutually beneficial trusting" interactions:

1. **Contractual Trust** (trust of *character*) is when a relationship starts or develops by:

    a. Managing expectations

    b. Establishing boundaries

    c. Delegating appropriately

    d. Encouraging mutually-serving intentions

    e. Keeping agreements

    f. Being consistent

2. **Communications Trust** (trust of *disclosure*) is not hesitating to share information by:

    a. Telling the truth

    b. Admitting mistakes

    c. Giving/receiving feedback

    d. Maintaining confidentiality

    e. Speaking with good purpose

3. **Competence Trust** (trust of *capability*) is acknowledging people's talents by:

    a. Allowing people to make decisions

    b. Involving others and seeking input

    c. Helping people learn new skills

Use the **Teach and Be Taught** *tool (pp. 180-181) to assess your capacity to trust*

Appreciative Reciprocity *Teach and Be Taught*

The Reciprocal Teacher *creates* a climate that promotes emotional *flow*. The Reciprocal Student seeks to *attract* a climate of emotional *flow*. Reciprocity is simply the willingness to teach without expecting anything in return. It is the art and science of appreciation. This is observed by behaviors that focus first on what is positive or good about an individual or situation. The key phrase in the above paragraph is *focus first*.

To better understand the concept of appreciation, reflect on the following

1. Who recently taught you something that expanded your greatness and future possibilities?

2. What did you teach someone in the last week that expanded their greatness and future possibilities?

3. How do others attract you to be a teacher in your life?

4. What is it about you that attracts others to learn from or with you?

5. Who are the people you enjoy spending time with? What do they teach you?

A concept I often introduce to clients is *appreciative inquiry*. Appreciative inquiry was developed at Case Western Reserve University in the early 1990s, primarily as an organizational development methodology. Appreciative inquiry states that *we are more receptive to being taught when we appreciate the positive or the good first, then address what is broken or wrong.* The appreciative learning process has *four stages of inquiry*:

1. **Discover periods of excellence and achievement** Through interviews and storytelling, participants remember significant past achievements and periods of excellence. By telling stories, people recall positive memories that contributed to their peak experiences.

2. **Dream (visualize) an ideal or desired future** In this step, the client taps into past achievements to envisage a desired future. Focus is on the *positive present* to expand one's potential.

3. **Designing new structures and processes** This stage is intended to be provocative—develop SMARTER short- and long-term goals that will achieve the dream.

4. **Deliver the dream** In this stage, the client develops and implements an action plan based on their provocative propositions and mobilized resources to achieve the dream.

> *What can you appreciate about the past to bring into the future?*
> *Who can you demonstrate appreciation to today?*

The Digital Teacher and the Student

People with more than twenty social media connections are thirty-four times more likely to be approached with a job opportunity than people with less than five (http://blog.guykawasaki.com). In addition, all 500 of the Fortune 500 are represented in LinkedIn, a leading professional social networking site. When I work with clients on career issues, I often ask the following *three questions*:

1. What are ways you can research organizations to target during a job search?

2. What types of information would you seek about potential employers?

3. What is the number one way a company gathers information about candidates they are considering hiring?

The answer to the third question tells your *digital story*. Today, most companies use social networking sites to learn about you, whether on Facebook, Twitter or a simple Google search. What is your digital footprint teaching others about *You, Inc.*? What "digital dirt" may be out there that needs to be cleaned up (pruned)?

When all else is equal, like education, work history, and skills, employers often evaluate social media footprints to learn more about the potential hire. Employers rarely hire for skills or experience alone. They hire an individual that fits well with their values, significance, culture and climate. Your social media footprint gives employers an insight into your passions, interests, communications, community, work habits and life/work balance. The *digital you* helps an employer create a positive emotional connection. To assess your digital profile, consult the *Digital You Checklist* at the end of this chapter (pages 183-184).

Reciprocity and Teams

Throughout your life, you will be part of a team, whether as a youth on the soccer field, in a school club, a college fraternity, or as an adult on a community board or project team. You will also play both roles on a team: Teacher and student. What we also know is that reciprocity is critical to a team's success.

In Druskat's and Wolff's 2009 article "Building the Emotional Intelligence of Groups," three conditions are cited (listed below) that are essential to a group's effectiveness—and *reciprocity is needed to create each condition*. When these three conditions are absent, teams are still able to cooperate and participate with each other, but the team won't be as effective as it could be because members will choose to hold back rather than to fully engage.

1. Mutual trust among members (transparency)

2. A sense of group identity (a feeling among group members that they belong to a unique and worthwhile group)

3. A sense of group efficacy (a belief that the team can perform well, and group members are more effective working together rather than apart)

Teams that demonstrate reciprocity create emotionally intelligent norms in that the attitudes and behaviors become habits to support behaviors for building trust, group identity and group efficacy.

Group norms accomplish **three things**

1. **Create resources** for working with emotions (e.g., common vocabulary)

2. **Foster an affirmative environment** (e.g., a team that responds to challenges with a *can-do attitude*; a team that favors optimistic images over negative ones)

3. **Encourage proactive problem solving** (e.g., a team that takes control and finds a solution, even if the solution lies in another group's domain)

Creating a Climate of Team Reciprocity

- Teams that demonstrate **interpersonal understanding** sense when a member is not on the same emotional wavelength and are open to understanding the issue. Having a norm that encourages interpersonal understanding facilitates awareness of unspoken issues.

- **Perspective taking** is a technique teams use to solve problems or make decisions. This skill consciously removes emotion by collecting and combining perspectives in a mechanical way (affinity diagrams, brainstorming). A more effective approach to perspective taking is to ensure that team members see one another making the effort to grapple with perspectives, which provides the kind of trust that leads to greater participation among members.

- Establishing norms in the group for both **confrontation** and caring by regulating team members' emotions helps the team feel comfortable calling the foul when a team member crosses the line.

- Establishing norms that reinforce **caring** behavior can make all the difference in having group members acknowledge a person's feelings.

- *Interpersonal understanding, perspective taking, confrontation* and *caring*—these norms build trust and a sense of group identity among members.

A Final Technique *The Skill of FeedForward*

Marshall Goldsmith, mentioned earlier as the leading leadership coach, coined the phrase "FeedForward" after a discussion he had with Jon Katzenbach, author of *The Wisdom of Teams: Real Change Leaders and Peak Performance*. Typically, feedback "focuses on a past, on what has already occurred—not on the infinite variety of opportunities that can happen in the future. As such, feedback can be limited and static, as opposed to expansive and dynamic."

Goldsmith observed more than ten thousand individuals as they participated in a fascinating experiential exercise. In the exercise, participants were each asked to play two roles. In one role, they were asked to provide feedforward—that is, to give someone else suggestions for the future and help as much as they can. In the second role, they were asked to accept feedforward—that is, to listen to the suggestions for the future and learn as much as they can. The exercise typically lasted for 10-15 minutes, and the average participant had 6-7 dialogue sessions. In the exercise, participants were asked to:

- **Pick one behavior that they would like to change** Change in this behavior should make a significant, positive difference in their lives
- **Describe this behavior to randomly selected fellow participants** This is done in one-on-one dialogues; it can be done quite simply: *I want to be a better listener*
- **Ask for feedforward** Get two suggestions for the future that might help them achieve a positive change in their selected behavior (they are only allowed to give ideas for the future)
- **Listen attentively to the suggestions and take notes** Participants are not allowed to comment on, or critique, the suggestions, or even to make positive, judgmental statements such as, *That's a good idea*
- **Show gratitude** The participant then thanks the "giver" for their suggestions
- **Switch roles** The process repeats with the "giver" now asking the "receiver" what they would like to change
- **Provide feedforward** Give two suggestions aimed at helping the other person change

When the exercise was finished, Marshall asked participants to provide one word that best described their reaction to this experience. The words provided were almost always extremely positive, such as "great," "energizing," "useful" or "helpful." The most common word mentioned was "fun."

This activity is an excellent example of reciprocity—*teaching and being taught in action!*

Practice feedforward daily

Join the Smart2Smarter Community *to access*
the following activities and additional
RECIPROCITY *resources and assessments*
online at www.Smart2Smarter.com

Lead and Be Led book and website
Teach and Be Taught: The Capacity to Trust book and website
Lead and Be Led Derailers book
The Digital You Checklist book and website
Employability and Reciprocity website
Why Smart Leaders Fail website
Teach and Be Taught: 10 Hijacking Behaviors website
"T" Coaching Method website
Authentic Communication Coaching website

Activity   Lead and Be Led

Your emotions and actions impact those you lead. Research indicates that a 10% increase in the perception of a leader creating a positive emotional work climate results in a three-fold increase in performance output and customer satisfaction.

Complete

Highlight the laws that you naturally follow as a leader. In the left column are *The Ten Laws of Attracting Followers*, with the opposite provided for comparison and contrast in the right column. What do you demonstrate that attracts a positive future state? What do you need to give up or manage better to stop attracting a negative future state? Discuss your responses with a confidant, your team, boss or coach. Ask for suggestions to *amplify the positive* and minimize the negative laws of attraction.

Lead and Be Led	
Positive Energy That Inspires Self and Others	**Negative Energy That Derails Self and Others**
Want it, but don't need it! Express gratitude for your current successes. Allow more to flow into your life by cultivating a spirit of contentment and acceptance.	**Need it** Absolutely require what you want in order to be successful. Express it in a very demanding way.
Want with relaxation and ease Remember the difference between *lead* and *force*. Replace *hurry* with *patience*.	**Want with force and compulsion** Try to control and make everything happen your way.
Open yourself to something better Visualize the end result and lead others to figure out the "hows."	**Insist on specifics** Insist that what you want must manifest in a particular way and by a particular method.
Be happy without having it all You can be happy while still desiring some things to be better. Appreciate what is working now.	**Dwell on what's wrong, broken and lacking** Eliminate the creative flow by desiring in a pressured and grasping way.
Trust and be vulnerable Trust that wisdom from self and others is waiting to be discovered. Embrace vulnerability and humility.	**Allow fear and ego to rule** Refuse to relax, trust and be transparent because you think you must control everything yourself.
Know why you want it Ask yourself, *What purpose will this serve?* What emotional state do you desire and anticipate?	**Avoid conscious creation** No attempt to understand why you want something or to explain your motives to others.
Explore your reasons The more benefits and reasons you can imagine, the more likely it is that you will attract results.	**Maintain only one reason for wanting** No attempt to expand your mind or consider all the benefits to self and others.
Take small steps Any step forward brings you closer to your desired future state. Incremental actions lead to monumental results!	**Freeze yourself into inactivity** Think that big steps take too much energy and involve too much personal risk, so you do nothing and stay frozen and safe.
Exercise patience and consistent action Success is the progressive realization of an idea. Free yourself from linear time, and live in the now.	**Demand it now** Insist on the need to hurry and have it *now* because you can't be happy without it.
Believe that you and others are worth it You do deserve what you want. Identify and eliminate any self-limiting beliefs.	**Believe in your own stories of inferiority** Tell yourself you do not deserve good things in life. Enjoy the role of victim, martyr or scapegoat.

Activity   Teach and Be Taught *The Capacity to Trust*

Part One What and how we trust during interpersonal transactions will influence our capacity to trust. What you focus on first when interacting with others also impacts your capacity to trust. The Reina's, authors of *Trust and Betrayal in the Workplace*, present three kinds of "trust focus"—or—that impact interactions.

Directions

Review the three *Capacity to Trust* categories in the chart below. In the second column, put a (+) next to the characteristics that you do well to establish trust. In the third column, put a (+) next to the characteristics that you expect or need from others to establish trust. Add up the (+)'s in both columns.

	What I do well to establish trust	What I expect from others to establish trust
Contractual Trust (trust of *character*) occurs when a relationship starts or develops by:		
Managing expectations		
Establishing boundaries		
Delegating appropriately		
Encouraging mutually-serving intentions		
Keeping agreements		
Being consistent		
Communications Trust (trust of *disclosure*) occurs when one does not hesitate to share information by:		
Telling the truth		
Admitting mistakes		
Giving/receiving feedback		
Maintaining confidentiality		
Speaking with good purpose		
Competence Trust (trust of *capability*) occurs when each person acknowledges and appreciates talents by:		
Allowing people to make decisions		
Involving others and seeking input		
Helping people learn new skills		
Total		

Based on the model of Drs. Michelle and Dennis Reina, authors of *Trust and Betrayal in the Workplace*.

Reflect and Learn

How do you demonstrate trust?

- Which trust category do you demonstrate most often to develop a reciprocal relationship?
- Provide an example of when you demonstrated this *trust behavior* and how the relationship was enriched.
- In which trust category do you need to develop more *trust behavior* to have reciprocal relationships?
- Provide an example of when a lack of this *trust behavior* caused harm to a relationship.

What do you want from others to demonstrate trust?

- Which trust category do you need most from others to build a relationship of trust?
- Provide a behavioral example of when another person demonstrated a "needed" *trust behavior* and how your relationship was enriched.
- Which trust category is not needed as much from another person for you to build a trusting relationship?
- Provide an example of when this trust behavior was lacking, and your relationship was not harmed.

Join the Smart 2 Smarter Community and learn to *TRUST* SMARTER!

Part Two Questions to ask and answer to sustain reciprocal relationships built on trust:

Image	Do I look, sound and act like you want or need?
Expertise	Do I have the expertise that you want or need?
Commitment	Do I demonstrate unconditional commitment to our relationship?
Vulnerability	Do I believe that we can be vulnerable to take risks and grow through our relationship?
Emotional Connection	Do we create and store shared emotional experiences that bring out each other's personal best?

Activity   Lead and Be Led Derailers

The following eight leadership/followership behaviors were identified in my 2008 article, "Why Smart Leaders Fail."

Strength →	When Exaggerated or Hijacked →	Employee Impact
Achievement Orientation Leaders tend to have a high achievement drive and often think others don't need help in setting goals.		Engaged employees do want clarity in their performance goals and in how goals relate to the business.
Self-Reliance Leaders lean toward self-reliance. They believe others don't need supervision.		Engaged employees need some supervision and support to achieve their performance or career goals.
Intuition Leaders use intuition to make decisions.		Actually, engaged employees want to understand the structure and process of how a leader arrives at a decision.
Profit or Results Leaders are measured on achieving profits, gains or other results. People are resources to achieve that goal.		When employees do not understand how their efforts contribute to the profit, they feel used and engagement wanes.
Decision Style High-achieving leaders make decisions quickly and implement immediately, often without much discussion. *Do as I say!*		Engaged employees want to know their decision authority and range, and want guidance on how to implement decisions.
Critique First Quick to criticize first and speak their mind.		The engaged employee wants to be appreciated first and to share their perspective.
Self-Confidence Project high confidence in self.		Engaged employees develop self-confidence after being recognized for a series of successes.
Time Orientation Everything is a crisis, or nothing is urgent.		Engaged employees will experience burnout or boredom. When is it really a fire, and when is it better to implement fire prevention?

- What behaviors on the above list do you see as limiting this person's leadership effectiveness?
- What are you tolerating, and what is the consequence of this toleration?
- What would you like the leader to stop/start doing that would have the biggest impact for you?

Activity   The Digital You Checklist

Boris Epstein, CEO and Founder of BINC, a professional search firm, states employers will continue to use the *digital classroom* to learn about new hires. Boris presents a list of success strategies to use to present a positive emotional connection through your digital footprint. First ask:

1. How can you make your digital footprint more attractive?
2. How can your digital footprint demonstrate the ability to teach and be taught?

Challenge Have a friend or colleague review your digital footprint

LinkedIn

- Has genuine recommendations from teachers, peers, managers, colleagues, etc.
- Has a more complete profile, as well as a picture
- Is a member of groups related to their profession or expertise
- Has hobbies or interests outside of work
- Participates and highlights involvement in projects related to community service
- Updates their online profile every two months
- Links to their employer, website, blog or other projects of interest

Blog

- Has interesting things to say about their respective profession and industry
- Provides insight about life outside of work, including family, friends, hobbies, education
- Does not badmouth current or previous employer
- Provides links to current social networking profiles

- Includes a link to their current resume
- Updates new posts regularly
- Keeps content non-controversial

Facebook

- Respects the overlap between personal and professional lives
- Updates often and keeps content non-controversial
- Keeps pictures of family and friends to a minimum

Twitter

- Tweets often, 2-10 times a day
- Healthy follower/following ratio
- Doesn't just update, but responds to others and receives updates

Google

- Does not lead to anything controversial
- Leads to profession-related discussions and commentary on other social media sites
- Leads to their online blog, website or social media profiles
- Doesn't come up blank

Boris Epstein is the CEO and Founder of BINC, a Professional Search Firm that specializes in the software marketplace (www.askbinc.com).

Join the Smart2Smarter Community and learn to GIVE and RECEIVE SMARTER!

Final Thoughts

The SMARTER Way to Bring Humanity Into the Workplace

Congratulations! You now know the seven SMARTER skills every employer wants and every smart employee needs to obtain career success and significance. But here's the big question: *What is the "win" for the global workplace when employees display these SMARTER skills?* The answer is a system of humanity for both the individual and the workplace that increases business profits, performance results and career significance. So, what does it look like when this happens?

When I googled the definition of humanity, here are the terms I found: "Human nature," "human condition" and "humans."

> Without work, all life goes rotten. But when work is soulless, life stifles and dies.
> *–Albert Camus*

Human nature The psychological characteristics that all normal humans have in common; it is the concept that there is a set of inherent *distinguishing characteristics, including ways of thinking, feeling and acting.* This includes the emotional and social characteristics of compassion, altruism, or similar positive aspects of human nature along with aggression, fear, or similar negative aspects.

Human condition The totality of experience of existing as a human. This includes the *experiences of being human* in a social, cultural, and personal context.

Humans Humans are social by nature and are uniquely adept at utilizing systems of communication for self-expression, the exchange of ideas, and organization. Humans also create complex social structures composed of many cooperating and competing groups. Social interactions between humans have established a wide variety of values, social norms and rituals, which together form the basis of human society. Furthermore, *humans have a desire to understand and influence their environment.* This natural curiosity has led to the development of advanced tools and skills, which are passed down culturally.

Wikipedia, 2010. Retrieved from http://www.wikipedia.org

On further research, I found Sylvie Lapointe, a blogger from Ottawa, Canada, who referenced the book *GungHo* by Ken Blanchard and Sheldon Bowles. The authors' premise is that "people do not leave their spirit at the door of their workplace." They contend that when one leaves their spirit, essence, or humanity at the door, companies and employees lose. And *what* they lose is the emotional and social "smarts" that make one human.

In his book, *Humanity at Work: Encouraging Spirit, Achievement and Truth to Flourish in the Workplace*, Santo Costa "shows in thirty-six letter-essays how to carry that emotional balance across all your days—and how to be grateful for each one of them." He suggests "ways to turn anxiety and fear of change in the workplace to a climate of 'kindness, mercy, [and] empathy,' the kind of support we sometimes experience at home in the heart of our families." He states, "We don't really need to be two different selves for work and for home; we don't need to 'suit up' in steely emotional armor each morning for the day ahead."

In reviewing the above definitions, *humanity appears to be the essence of what it means to live SMARTER.* Throughout this book, you have learned that when employees feel good at work, they will likely make more efforts to please customers and be engaged; they will feel *in flow* and, as a result, will produce increased revenues. You have also learned that emotional connections are contagious; therefore, we all have a responsibility for creating and sustaining a positive climate of humanity. The ability to inspire positive feelings is a core component of humanity.

> Humanity in the workplace means that you are a social being who brings your strengths, your emotions and your passions into every day to achieve personal and communal success and significance.

Another core component of humanity is the ability to understand and adapt to our environment. The more tolerant and open the feedback, the more effective the adaptation and change. Humanity requires truly open and honest feedback within the workplace.

It also requires engaging people in their hearts and in their minds. To foster humanity in the workplace, you've got to inspire and engage employees more deeply and fully. Companies need to allow employees to bring their emotions to work, to encourage reciprocity and to reward evolving. Being human is intensely personal. For a system of humanity to occur in any organization, each individual must be free to think, feel and do what brings out their personal best.

Humanity Is Always Evolving

Unlike IQ, which is unchanging from childhood, social and emotional intelligence is always evolving. In fact, our global humanity requires this evolution. As we evolve, our SMARTER skills usually become more developed with age and maturity. The importance of creating systems to evolve our humanity is essential to success in the workplace. Utilizing the power and energy of one's emotions and social connections will increase experiences of *flow*, and promote creative problem solving and SMARTER decision making.

Humanity also requires good mastery of emotions. Some people are better at this than others, but everyone can learn how to more masterfully manage their emotional skills. Research into emotions has been greatly enhanced by brain-imaging technologies in the last decade. For the first time ever, scientists have been able to study the functioning of the brain on living subjects and to map the parts of the brain responsible for thinking and feeling.

As thinking human beings, we value our rationality and cognitive powers that set us apart from the animal kingdom. The neocortex (the center for rational thinking and decision making) is the newer, more highly developed part of the brain in humans. The emotional parts of the brain are located in the more ancient, central areas called the limbic system, which includes the amygdala, the area of the brain that's most active during an emotional hijacking.

We have learned that all emotions are, in essence, impulses to act. The very root of the word "emotion" is from the Latin verb *to move*. The direct connection between emotions and actions is obvious from watching animals or children. Only in civilized adults do we expect actions to be distanced from emotional reactions. However, even as highly intelligent and civilized adults, we can never disengage our emotional brain—it is always there, sending emotional signals to act and react, even when there is no logic to it.

Mastery of emotions requires mastery of the *interpretation of events*. Throughout this book, you have learned that our emotional responses are primal, hard-wired, and stored in the brain's amygdala. These hard-wired memories are caused by our interpretation of events—real or imagined. Mastery, as a skill, is to challenge the interpretation of events by managing how we behave, what we say and how we handle a situation. These SMARTER choices are expressed in our actions, such as the expression of tolerant communication, listening more than talking, or scheduling time for self-care. A workplace with a culture of humanity has an emotional and social radar system that rewards *acts of humanity* and does not tolerate *breaches in humanity*—whether these breaches are toward one's peers, boss or customers! That is what humanity looks like in the workplace.

SMARTER Skills and Humanity in the Workplace

When we want to move forward in our lives, we must know what to do. Creating a system of humanity in the workplace requires making choices, knowing what actions to take and recognizing and building on strengths. It is about learning, training and conditioning, but also about discovery, creation and ownership. It is defining, honoring, rewarding and celebrating the SMARTER behaviors that create this system of humanity at work.

There are several roads toward developing the SMARTER skills that lead to a system of humanity in the workplace. For example, you can focus on increasing positive feelings by engaging in more pleasant activities. Or you can prune (weed out) negative emotions about the past. Try making a concerted effort to challenge your thinking style and develop an optimistic attitude. A simple step, such as becoming more mindful of the "magic ratio," can increase the amount of positive events that happen daily in your own and others' lives.

Humanity is all about pursuing positive feelings and relationships. Positive emotions incorporate the past, the future and the present. Positive emotions about the *past* are increased by gratitude, forgiveness and freeing yourself of limiting core beliefs and assumptions. Positive emotions about the *future* are increased by learning to cultivate an optimistic attitude. Positive emotions about the *present* involve two very different things: *Pleasures* and *gratifications*. Pleasures can be increased by giving and receiving "acts of kindness." Gratifications, on the other hand, are more difficult to process. They are characterized by absorption, engagement and being *in flow*—"in the zone." Gratifications come about through the exercise of your strengths and values.

The Business Side of Humanity

Humanity at work also consists of using your strengths as frequently as possible to obtain career and workplace success and significance. For corporations—big or small—the degree that each worker can find meaning in his or her work will be reflected in the quality of commitment and excitement (or lack of it) that

Using your strengths in the service of something larger than yourself leads to a truly meaningful and good life.

is present in the workplace, and ultimately in the competitiveness of the business. There is actually a longing in most individuals to find true meaning, joy or enthusiasm. For true commitment to take place in any relationship, whether at work or at home, there must be an alignment of *human* ideals and values.

Companies that want their workers to contribute with their heads and hearts accept that emotions are part of being human. Humanity requires a paradigm shift in people management that also includes the managing and optimizing of positive feelings. The most successful change programs reveal that organizations connect with their people most directly through values—and that values, ultimately, are about beliefs and feelings. When an organization denies the validity of emotions in the workplace or seeks to permit only certain kinds of emotions, two things happen: 1) Managers first cut themselves off from their own emotional lives; in turn, they then cut off the ideas, solutions and new perspectives that other people can contribute, and 2) Humanity is stifled, and the organization and its community lose.

Humanity in the Workplace—Now It's Your Turn

SMARTER skills are your roadmap to bringing humanity into the workplace. As an employee, ask: *What can I do to demonstrate SMARTER actions in the workplace?* As a leader, ask: *How do I demonstrate, inspire and reward the SMARTER actions of humanity?* And, as a company, ask: *What values and norms will build and reinforce a system of humanity at our company?*

Humanity at work is not a destination, but a journey. Use the tools in this book, create your own stories of humanity, and spread the word through *human actions and communications.*

Make humanity contagious through positive feelings and global connections.

Choose a SMARTER skill to master, then move on to another, and another. Share this book with others. Pay it forward.

And please, share your *SMARTER wins* on the *Smart2Smarter Community* website. I welcome the opportunity to high-five your success!

An important concept in our country is Ubuntu—the essence of being human. Ubuntu speaks particularly about the fact that you can't exist as a human being in isolation. It speaks about our interconnectedness. You can't be human all by yourself. And when you have this quality (Ubuntu) you are known for your generosity.

—Archbishop Desmond Tutu
South African Spiritual Leader and Social Activist

For use of this book and its principles in a college course or workplace professional development or leadership program, contact Cynthia Kivland at Cynthia@Smart2Smarter.com for curriculum material and volume discounts.

SMARTER Activities & Tools

References & Resources

Chapter 1   Introduction

Bridges, W. (2000). *Job Shift: How to Prosper in a Workplace Without Jobs*. Larkspur, CA: William Bridges & Associates; Cambridge, MA: Perseus Books (1994).

Cherniss, C., & Goleman, D. (Eds.). (2001). *The Emotionally Intelligent Workplace: How to Select For, Measure, and Improve Emotional Intelligence in Individuals, Groups, and Organizations*. San Francisco, CA: Jossey-Bass.

Collins, J. (2001). *Good to Great: Why Some Companies Make the Leap...and Others Don't*. New York, NY: Harper Business.

Collins, J. C., & Porras, J. I. (1997). *Built to Last: Successful Habits of Visionary Companies*. New York, NY: Harper Business.

Gardner, H. (2004). *Frames of Mind: The Theory of Multiple Intelligences* (20th Anniv. ed.). New York, NY: Basic Books.

Goldsmith, M. (with Reiter, M.). (2007). *What Got You Here Won't Get You There: How Successful People Become Even More Successful!* New York, NY: Hyperion.

Goleman, D. (2006). *Emotional Intelligence: Why It Can Matter More Than IQ* (10th Anniv. ed.). New York, NY: Bantam Books.

Goleman, D. (2006). *Working with Emotional Intelligence*. New York, NY: Bantam Books.

Goleman, D. (2009). *Leadership That Gets Results* (HBR OnPoint Enhanced Edition) [Digital PDF]. Boston, MA: Harvard Business Review.

Grantham, C. (2000). *The Future of Work: The Promise of the New Digital Work Society.* New York, NY: McGraw-Hill.

Hesselbein, F., & Goldsmith, M. (Eds.). (2009). *The Organization of the Future 2: Visions, Strategies, and Insights on Managing in a New Era.* San Francisco, CA: Jossey-Bass.

Pink, D. H. (2006). *A Whole New Mind: Why Right-Brainers Will Rule the Future.* New York, NY: Riverhead Books.

Rifkin, J. (2004). *The End of Work: The Decline of the Global Labor Force and the Dawn of the Post-Market Era.* New York, NY: Tarcher.

Seligman, M. E. P. (2006). *Learned Optimism: How to Change Your Mind and Your Life.* New York, NY: Vintage Press; New York, NY: Knopf (1991).

Wechsler, D. (1940). Non-intellective factors in general intelligence. *Psychological Bulletin, 37*, 444-445.

Web Resources

Critiques of Daniel Goleman's Model of EI and of EI tests: http://www.eqi.org

Daniel Goleman (father of emotional intelligence): http://www.danielgoleman.com

Emotional Competency and Social Skills: http://www.emotionalcompetency.com

Emotional Intelligence, practical information: http://eqi.org

Emotional Intelligence, scientific information: http://www.unh.edu/emotional_intelligence

Emotional Intelligence Consortium, dedicated to research on emotions and emotional intelligence in the workplace: http://www.eiconsortium.org

Emotional Intelligence Institute: http://www.e-ii.org

Emotional Needs Audit (assessment and resources): http://www.enaproject.org

Emotionally Literate Schools: http://therulerapproach.org

Future of Work: http://www.thefutureofwork.net

Institute for Health and Human Potential (IHHP): http://www.ihhp.com

Six Seconds, a global organization teaching the skills of emotional intelligence: http://www.6seconds.org

SMARTER Employability Model by Cynthia Kivland: http://www.smart2smarter.com

TalentSmart®: http://www.talentsmart.com

Chapter 2   Iceberg

Barsade, S. G. (2002). The ripple effect: Emotional contagion in groups. *Administrative Science Quarterly*, *47*(4), 644-675.

Feist, G. J., & Barron, F. (1996, June). Emotional intelligence and academic intelligence in career and life success. Paper presented at the Annual Convention of the American Psychological Society, San Francisco, CA.

Gordon, J. (2008). *The No Complaining Rule: Positive Ways to Deal with Negativity at Work.* Hoboken, NJ: Wiley.

Handy, C. (2002). Elephants and Fleas: Is Your Organization Prepared for Change? *Leader to Leader, 24* (Spring).

McClelland, D. C. (1973). Testing for competence rather than intelligence. *American Psychologist*, *28*(1), 1-14.

Murray, H. A. (2008). *Explorations in Personality* (70th Anniv. ed.). New York, NY: Oxford University Press.

Rosenthal, R. (1977). The PONS Test: Measuring sensitivity to nonverbal cues. In P. McReynolds (Ed.), *Advances in Psychological Assessment*. San Francisco, CA: Jossey-Bass.

Sartre, J.-P. (1984). *Being and Nothingness: The Principal Text of Modern Existentialism* (H. Barnes, Trans.). New York, NY: Washington Square Press.

Sartre, J.-P. (2000). *The Transcendence of the Ego: An Existentialist Theory of Consciousness* (F. Williams & R. Kirkpatrick, Trans.). New York, NY: Hill and Wang Press; New York, NY: Noonday Press (1960).

Schulman, P. (1995). Explanatory style and achievement in school and work. In G. Buchanan & M. E. P. Seligman (Eds.), *Explanatory Style*. Hillsdale, NJ: Erlbaum.

Seligman, M. E. P. (2006). *Learned Optimism: How to Change Your Mind and Your Life.* New York, NY: Vintage Press; New York, NY: Knopf (1991).

Sternberg, R. J. (1997). *Successful Intelligence: How Practical and Creative Intelligence Determine Success in Life.* New York, NY: Plume; New York, NY: Simon & Schuster (1996).

Sternberg, R. J., & Williams, W. (1988). Group Intelligence: Why some groups are better than others. *Intelligence*, *12*(4), 351-377.

Web Resources

Amygdala information (the brain's impulse center):
http://www.mondovista.com/amygdala/index.html

Myers-Briggs Type Indicator®—Global research and Applications Personality Inventory: https://www.cpp.com/products/mbti/index.aspx

Occupational Personality Questionnaire (OPQ32)—Personality and work environment selection and development tool: http://www.shl.com/WhatWeDo/PersonalityAssessment/Pages/OPQQuestionnaire.aspx

The Positivity Ratio (change your life using the 3-to-1 ratio): http://www.positivityratio.com

Chapter 3 Personal Best: Focus on Me

Bradberry, T., & Greaves, J. (2009). *Emotional Intelligence 2.0*. San Diego, CA: TalentSmart®.

Cooper, R. K., & Sawaf, A. (1998). *Executive EQ: Emotional Intelligence in Leadership and Organizations*. New York, NY: Perigee.

Covey, S. R. (2004). *The Seven Habits of Highly Successful People: Powerful Lessons in Personal Change*. New York, NY: Free Press.

Goleman, D., & Kabat-Zinn, J. (2007). *Mindfulness @ Work: A Leading with Emotional Intelligence Conversation with Jon Kabat-Zinn*. [Audiobook, CD]. New York, NY: Macmillan Audio.

Hudson, F. M., & McClean, P. D. (2000). *Life Launch: A Passionate Guide to the Rest of Your Life* (3rd ed.). Santa Barbara, CA: Hudson Institute Press.

Klein, E., & Izzo, J. B. (1999). *Awakening Corporate Soul: Four Paths to Unleash the Power of People at Work* (2nd ed.). Canada: Fairwinds Press.

Maslow, A. H. (1987). *Motivation and Personality* (3rd ed.). New York, NY: HarperCollins.

Salovey, P., & Sluyter, D. J. (Eds). (1997). *Emotional Development and Emotional Intelligence: Educational Implications*. New York, NY: Basic Books.

Web Resources

StrengthsFinder Profile—learn your five top themes, in descending order (fee-based): http://www.strengthsfinder.com/113647/Homepage.aspx

Your Personal Mission Statement Builder guides you to discover your values and goals toward building a better life: http://www.franklincovey.com/msb

Chapter 4 Strengths: My BestFit Life

Bradberry, T., & Greaves, J. (2009). *Emotional Intelligence 2.0*. San Diego, CA: TalentSmart®.

Buckingham, M. (2005). *The One Thing You Need to Know...About Great Managing, Great Leading and Sustained Individual Success*. New York, NY: Free Press.

Buckingham, M., & Clifton, D. O. (2001). *Now, Discover Your Strengths*. New York, NY: Free Press.

Campbell, D. (1974). *If You Don't Know Where You're Going, You'll Probably End Up Somewhere Else*. Allen, TX: Thomas More.

Farren, C. (1997). *Who's Running Your Career? Creating Stable Work in Unstable Times*. Austin, TX: Bard Press.

Fisher, C. D., & Noble, C. S. (2000, August). Emotion and the illusory correlation between job satisfaction and job performance. Paper presented at the Second Conference on Emotions in Organizational Life, Toronto, Canada.

Goldsmith, M. (2010). *Mojo: How to Get It, How to Keep It, How to Get It Back if You Lose It*. New York, NY: Hyperion.

Hudson, F. M., & McClean, P. D. (2000). *Life Launch: A Passionate Guide to the Rest of Your Life* (3rd ed.). Santa Barbara, CA: Hudson Institute Press.

Kaye, B. (2001). *Up is Not the Only Way: A Guide to Developing Workforce Talent*. Boston, MA: Intercultural Press.

Kaye, B., & Jordan-Evans, S. (2008). *Love 'em or Lose 'em: Getting Good People to Stay* (4th ed.). San Francisco, CA: Berrett-Koehler.

Leider, R. J. (2004). *The Power of Purpose: Find Meaning, Live Longer, Better*. San Francisco, CA: Berrett-Koehler.

McGraw, P. C. (2001). *Self-Matters: Creating Your Life from the Inside Out*. New York, NY: Free Press.

Moses, B. (2003). *What Next? The Complete Guide to Taking Control of Your Working Life*. New York, NY: Dorling Kindersley.

Peterson, C., & Seligman, M. E. P. (2004). *Character Strengths and Virtues: A Handbook and Classification*. New York, NY: Oxford University Press.

Weisinger, H. (2000). *Emotional Intelligence at Work: The Untapped Edge for Success*. San Francisco, CA: Jossey-Bass.

Ziglar, Z. (1998). *Success for Dummies*. Foster City, CA: IDG Books Worldwide.

Web Resources

BestFit Career Star (available for download): http://www.smart2smarter.com

BestFit Discovery Tools by Cynthia Kivland (Personal Best Zone, Workplace Engagement Values, and the Career Health Inventory and Development Guide): http://www.smart2smarter.com

CPP, Inc. (publisher of the Myers-Briggs Type Indicator® (MBTI), Strong Interest and Skills Inventory®, the FIRO-B® and the Thomas Kilman Conflict Inventory® assessments): https://www.cpp.com

The following tools are great resources. Visit their website for more information:

AAI 360: http://www.aai-assessment.com

Career Anchors—Discovering Your Real Values: http://www.wiley.com

Career Liftoff Interest Inventory (CLII): http://www.careerliftoff.com

Career Value Card Sort: http://www.careertrainer.com

(The) Conflict Dynamics Profile: (training) http://www.smart2smarter.com, or (information) http://www.conflictdynamics.org

Creatrix: http://www.creatrix.com

Emotional Intelligence 2.0: http://www.talentsmart.com

Emotional Intelligence Skills Assessment 360 (EISA 360): (training) http://www.smart2smarter.com, or (information) http://www.pfeiffer.com

(The) Emotional Quotient Inventory 2.0 (EQ-i 2.0): (training) http://www.smart2smarter.com, or (information) http://www.mhs.com

Motivated Skills Card Sort: http://www.careertrainer.com

Resilient! 360©: http://www.resiliencei.com

SEI™: http://www.6seconds.org

StrengthsFinder: http://www.gallup.com

Well-Being Finder: http://www.gallup.com

Work Behavior Inventory (WBI): http://www.aai-assessment.com

Chapter 5   Mastery: Thrive or Survive

Backus, W. (1994). *Learning to Tell Myself the Truth*. Minneapolis, MN: Bethany House.

Byron, K. (with Mitchell, S.). (2002). *Loving What Is: Four Questions That Can Change Your Life*. New York, NY: Three Rivers Press.

Childre, D., & Cryer, B. (1998). *From Chaos to Coherence: Advancing Emotional and Organizational Intelligence Through Inner Quality Management®*. Burlington, MA: Butterworth-Heinemann.

Damasio, A. (1999). *The Feeling of What Happens: Body and Emotion in the Making of Consciousness*. Orlando, FL: Harcourt.

Daniels, M. (2006). *Awakening the Emotional Intelligence: Mastering the Heart*. Charleston, SC: BookSurge.

De Beauport, E. (with Diaz, A. S.). (2002). *The Three Faces of Mind: Think, Feel, and Act to Your Highest Potential* (2nd ed.). Wheaton, Il: Quest Books.

Ekman, P. (2007). *Emotions Revealed: Recognizing Faces and Feelings to Improve Communication and Emotional Life* (2nd ed.). New York, NY: Owl Books.

Ekman, P., & Friesen, W. V. (2003). *Unmasking the Face: A Guide to Recognizing Emotions from Facial Clues*. Upper Saddle River, NJ: Prentice Hall.

Ellis, A. (2005). *Feeling Better, Getting Better, Staying Better: Profound Self-Help Therapy for Your Emotions* (3rd ed.). Atascadero, CA: Impact.

Ellis, A., & Harper, R. A. (1975). *A Guide to Rational Living* (3rd ed.). Chatsworth, CA: Wilshire Books.

Freedman, J. (2007). *At the Heart of Leadership: How to Get Results with Emotional Intelligence*. San Francisco, CA: Six Seconds Emotional Intelligence Press.

Goleman, D., Goleman, T., & Epstein, M. (1996). *Relaxation & Mindfulness: Emotional Intelligence* [Audiobook, Cassette]. Sound Horizons.

Gottman, J. (with Silver, N.). (1994). *Why Marriages Succeed or Fail...And How You Can Make Yours Last*. New York, NY: Fireside.

Gottman, J. (with DeClaire, J.). (1997). Raising an Emotionally Intelligent Child: The Heart of Parenting. New York, NY: Fireside.

Harp, D. (with Feldman, N.). (1999). *The Three Minute Meditator: 30 Simple Ways to Unwind Your Mind While Enhancing Your Emotional Intelligence* (3rd ed.). New York, NY: MJF Books.

Jeffers, S. (2006). *Feel the Fear...And Do It Anyway: Dynamic Techniques for Turning Fear, Indecision, and Anger Into Power, Action, and Love.* (20th Anniv. ed.). New York, NY: Ballantine Books.

Karpman, S. (1968). Fairy tales and script drama analysis. *Transactional Analysis Bulletin, 7*(26), 39-43.

Manz, C. C. (2003). *Emotional Discipline: The Power to Choose How You Feel; 5 Life-Changing Steps to Feeling Better Every Day.* San Francisco, CA: Berrett-Koehler.

Mehrabian, A. (1980). *Silent Messages: Implicit Communication of Emotions and Attitudes.* Belmont, CA: Wadsworth.

Mehrabian, A. (2009). *Nonverbal communication.* Piscataway, NJ: Aldine Transaction.

Orloff, J. (2010). *Emotional Freedom: Liberate Yourself from Negative Emotions and Transform Your Life.* (2nd ed.). New York, NY: Three Rivers Press.

Salovey, P., & Sluyter, D. J. (Eds.). (1997). *Emotional Development and Emotional Intelligence: Educational Implications.* New York, NY: Basic Books.

Salovey, P., Brackett, M. A., & Mayer, J. D. (Eds.). (2004). *Emotional Intelligence: Key Readings on the Mayer and Salovey Model.* Port Chester, NY: Dude.

Smith, B. (2004). *Discover Your Blind Spots: How to Stop Repeating Everyday Business Mistakes.* Dallas, TX: Clear Direction.

Sundquist, B. (2005). *The Seven Faces of Anxiety: How to Recognize What's Going on When Anxiety Shows Up as Anger, Irritability or Worry* [Teleclass]. Offered at http://www.coachville.com

Treasurer, B. (2008). *Courage Goes to Work: How to Build Backbones, Boost Performance, and Get Results.* San Francisco, CA: Berrett-Koehler.

Web Resources

Amygdala information (the brain's impulse center):
http://www.mondovista.com/amygdala/index.html

Barbra Sundquist (mentor coach): www.becomeacertifiedcoach.com

Karpman Drama Triangle (the latest research): http://www.karpmandramatriangle.com

Six Seconds Network, a global organization supporting people to make positive choices: http://www.6seconds.org

The Three Minute Meditator—techniques to reduce stress, control fear and diminish anger: http://www.thethreeminutemeditator.com

The Work of Byron Katie® is a great way to work with issues before they become issues: http://www.thework.com/resources.asp

Chapter 6   Attraction

Andreas, S. (2002). *Transforming YourSelf: Becoming Who You Want to Be.* Moab, Utah:

Real People Press.

Bandura, A. (1997). *Self-Efficacy: The Exercise Of Control*. New York, NY: Worth.

Bandura, A., & Cervone, D. (1983). Self-evaluative and self-efficacy mechanisms governing the motivational effects of goal systems. *Journal of Personality and Social Psychology, 45*(5), 1017–1028.

Beck, J. S. (2008). *Questions and Answers about Cognitive Therapy*. Retrieved from (Beck Institute for Cognitive Therapy and Research) http://www.beckinstitute.org

Bennis, W. (2009). *On Becoming a Leader: The Leadership Classic* (20th Anniv. ed.). Philadelphia, PA: Basic Books.

Branden, N. (1995). *Six Pillars of Self-Esteem: The Definitive Work on Self-Esteem by the Leading Pioneer in the Field*. New York, NY: Bantam Books.

Branham, L. (2005). *The Seven Hidden Reasons Employees Leave: How to Recognize the Subtle Signs and Act Before It's Too Late*. New York, NY: AMACOM.

Brockner, J., & Elkind, M. (1985). Self-esteem and reactance: Further evidence of attitudinal and motivational consequences. *Journal of Experimental Social Psychology, 21*(4), 346-361.

Burns, D. D. (1999). *Feeling Good: The New Mood Therapy*. New York, NY: Avon Books.

Byrne, R. (2006). *The Secret*. New York, NY: Atria Books/Hillsboro, Oregon: Beyond Words.

Carson, R. D. (1990). *Taming Your Gremlin: A Guide to Enjoying Yourself*. New York, NY: HarperPerennial; Dallas, TX: The Family Resource (1983).

Coopersmith, S. (1981). *The Antecedents of Self-Esteem*. Palo Alto, CA: Consulting Psychologists Press; New York, NY: W. H. Freeman (1967).

Deci, E. L. & Ryan, R. M. (1995). Human autonomy: The basis for true self-esteem. In M. H. Kernis (Ed.), *Efficacy, Agency and Self-Esteem* (pp. 31-49). New York, NY: Plenum Press.

Domino, G. (1970). Identification of potentially creative persons from the Adjective Checklist. *Journal of Consulting and Clinical Psychology, 35*(1), 48-51.

Ellis, A., & Harper, R. A. (1975). *A Guide to Rational Living*. Chatsworth, CA: Wilshire Books.

Fredrickson, B. L. (2009). *Positivity: Groundbreaking Research Reveals How to Embrace the Hidden Strength of Positive Emotions, Overcome Negativity, and Thrive*. New York, NY: Crown.

Harackiewicz, J. M., & Larson, J. R., Jr. (1986). Managing motivation: The impact of supervisor feedback on subordinate task interest. *Journal of Personality and Social Psychology, 51*(3), 547-556.

Harter, S., & Jackson, B. K. (1992). Trait vs. nontrait conceptualizations of intrinsic/extrinsic motivational orientation. *Motivation and Emotion, 16*(3), 209-230.

Heatherton, T. F., & Ambady, N. (1993). Self-esteem, self-prediction, and living up to commitments. In R. F. Baumeister (Ed.), *Self-Esteem: The Puzzle of Low Self-Regard* (pp. 131–141). New York, NY: Plenum Press.

Hill, N. C., & Ritchie, J. B. (1977, December). The effect of self-esteem on leadership and achievement: A Paradigm and a Review. *Group & Organization Management, 2*(4), 491-503.

Leonard, T. J. (1998). *The Portable Coach: 28 Surefire Strategies for Business and Personal Success.* New York, NY: Scribner.

Losier, M. J. (2010). *Law of Attraction: The Science of Attracting More of What You Want and Less of What You Don't.* New York, NY: Wellness Central.

Lyubomirsky, S. (2007). *The How of Happiness: A Scientific Approach to Getting the Life You Want.* New York, NY: Penguin Press.

MacKinnon, D. W. (1965). Personality and the realization of creative potential. *American Psychologist, 20*(4), 273-281.

Mercer, M. W., & Troiani, M. V. (1998). *Spontaneous Optimism: Proven Strategies for Health, Prosperity and Happiness.* Barrington, IL: Castlegate.

Merton, R. K. (1968). *Social Theory and Social Structure.* New York, NY: Free Press.

More, M. (1996, Sept/Oct). Dynamic Optimism: Philosophy and Psychology for Shattering Limits. *Awareness.* Retrieved from http://www.awarenessmag.com

Mossholder, K. W., Bedeian, A.G., & Armenakis, A.A. (1981). Role perceptions, satisfaction, and performance: Moderating effects of self-esteem and organizational level. *Organizational Behavior and Human Decision Processes, 28*(2), 224-234.

Perry, M. J. (with Griggs, R. E.). (1996). *The Road to Optimism: Change Your Language–Change Your Life!* Fort Collins, CO: Tantalus Books.

Salovey, P., & Mayer, J. D. (1990). Emotional Intelligence. *Imagination, Cognition, and Personality, 9,* 185-211.

Seligman, M. E. P. (2006). *Learned Optimism: How to Change Your Mind and Your Life.* New York, NY: Vintage Press; New York, NY: Knopf (1991).

Strom, R. (1971). *Teachers and the Learning Process.* Upper Saddle River, NJ: Prentice-Hall.

Tolle, E. (2004). *The Power of Now: A Guide to Spiritual Enlightenment.* Novato, CA: New

World Library/Vancouver, B.C., Canada: Namaste.

Wiskup, M. (2007). *The It Factor: Be the One People Like, Listen to, and Remember.* New York, NY: AMACOM.

Web Resources

Authentic Happiness, dedicated to the practice of Positive Psychology, founded by Dr. Martin Seligman: http://www.authentichappiness.com

Coach training site founded by Thomas Leonard: http://www.coachville.com

International Positive Psychology Association (IPPA): http://www.ippanetwork.org

Law of Attraction Tools: http://lawofattractiontools.com

Positive Psychology Center—resources and research on positive psychology: http://www.ppc.sas.upenn.edu

The Secret (based on the book *The Secret*): http://www.thesecret.tv

Chapter 7   Resilience

Bevere, J. (2006). *Driven by Eternity: Making Your Life Count Today and Forever.* New York, NY: Warner Faith.

Block, P. (2009). *Community: The Structure of Belonging.* San Francisco, CA: Berrett-Koehler.

Bourne, E. (2003). *Coping With Anxiety: 10 Simple Ways to Relieve Anxiety, Fear and Worry.* Oakland, CA: New Harbinger.

Bridges, W. (2004). *Transitions: Making Sense of Life's Changes* (25th ed.). Cambridge, MA: Da Capo Press.

Britten, R. (2002). *Fearless Living: Live Without Excuses and Love Without Regret.* New York, NY: Perigee Books.

Brooks, R., & Goldstein, S. (2004). *The Power of Resilience: Achieving Balance, Confidence, and Personal Strength in Your Life.* New York, NY: McGraw-Hill.

Ellis, A., & Harper, R. A. (1975). *A Guide to Rational Living* (3rd ed.). Chatsworth, CA: Wilshire Books.

Gottman, J. (with Silver, N.). (1994). *Why Marriages Succeed or Fail...And How You Can Make Yours Last.* New York, NY: Fireside.

LeDoux, J. (1998). *The Emotional Brain: The Mysterious Underpinnings of Emotional Life.* New York, NY: Touchstone.

Maddi, S., & Khoshaba, D. (2005). *Resilience at Work: How to Succeed No Matter What Life Throws at You.* New York, NY: AMACOM.

Maurer, R. (1996). *Beyond the Wall of Resistance: Unconventional Strategies That Build Support for Change.* Austin, TX: Bard Books.

Maurer, R. (2009). *Introduction to Change Without Migraines*™ [E-book; Audio podcast]. Maurer and Associates™. Retrieved from http://www.beyondresistance.com

Moos, R. H., & Schaefer, J.A. (1986). Life transitions and crises: A conceptual overview. In R.H. Moos & J.A. Schaefer (Eds.), *Coping with Life Crises: An Integrated Approach* (pp. 28-33). New York, NY: Plenum.

Nash, L. (2000). *The Bounce Back Quotient: 52 Action Oriented Ideas for Bouncing Back From Any Change or Setback in Life.* St. Louis, MO: Prism.

Prend, A. D. (1997). *Transcending Loss: Understanding the Lifelong Impact of Grief and How to Make It Meaningful.* New York, NY: Berkley Books.

Reivich, K., & Shatté, A. (2003). *The Resilience Factor: 7 Keys to Finding Your Inner Strength and Overcoming Life's Hurdles.* New York, NY: Broadway Books.

Scheier, M. F., & Carver, C. S. (1985). Optimism, coping and health: Assessment and implications on generalized outcome expectancies. *Health Psychology, 4*(3), 219-247.

Scheier, M. F., & Carver, C. S. (1992). Effects of optimism on psychological and physical well-being: Theoretical overview and empirical update. *Cognitive Therapy and Research, 16,* 201-228.

Schlossberg, N. K. (with Robinson, S.P.). (1996). *Going to Plan B: How You Can Cope, Regroup, and Start Your Life on a New Path.* New York, NY: Fireside.

Schlossberg, N. K. (2007). *Overwhelmed: Coping with Life's Ups and Downs* (2nd ed.). New York, NY: M. Evans.

Schlossberg, N. K., Goodman, J., & Anderson, M. (2006). *Counseling Adults in Transition: Linking Practice with Theory.* New York, NY: Springer.

Schutz, W. C. (1989). *Joy: Twenty Years Later: Expanding Human Awareness.* Berkeley, CA: Ten Speed Press.

Seibert, A. (2005). *The Resiliency Advantage: Master Change, Thrive Under Pressure, and Bounce Back from Setbacks.* San Francisco, CA: Berrett-Koehler.

Seligman, M. E. P. (2004). *Authentic Happiness: Using the New Positive Psychology to Realize Your Potential for Lasting Fulfillment.* New York, NY: Free Press.

Seligman, M. E. P. (2006). *Learned Optimism: How to Change Your Mind and Your Life.* New York, NY: Vintage Press; New York, NY: Knopf (1991).

Seligman, M. E. P. (2007). *What You Can Change and What You Can't: The Complete Guide to Successful Self-Improvement.* New York, NY: Vintage Books.

Thompson, H. (2010). *The Stress Effect: Why Smart Leaders Make Dumb Decisions—And What to Do About It.* San Francisco, CA. Jossey-Bass.

Waldroop, J., & Butler, T. (2001). *The 12 Bad Habits That Hold Good People Back: Overcoming the Behavior Patterns That Keep You From Getting Ahead* [formerly published as *Maximum Success*]. New York, NY: Currency Books.

Web Resources

Amygdala information (the brain's impulse center): http://www.mondovista.com/amygdala/index.html

Change Management Without Resistance by expert Rick Maurer (books and tools): http://www.beyondresistance.com

Organizational Resilience, assessments and research: http://www.wfd.com/products/resilienceinfo.html

Perceived Stress Level, a free tool that measures the degree to which you are experiencing stress in your various life situations: http://www.roadtowellbeing.ca/stress.html

Resilience Institute, for integrated leadership training: http://www.resiliencei.com

Road to Well-Being, with resources on resilience: http://www.roadtowellbeing.ca

Self-Growth resources: http://www.selfgrowth.com

The Stress Effect, with bonus materials and ARSENAL™ Assessment: http://thestresseffect.com/tse_bonusmaterials.htm

Chapter 8   Tolerance

Barsade, S. G., Ward, A. J., Turner, J. D. F., & Sonnenfeld, J. A. (2000). To your heart's content: A mode of affective diversity in top management teams. *Administrative Science Quarterly, 45,* 802-836.

Chang, R. (2001). *The Passion Plan at Work: A Step-by-Step Guide to Building a Passion-Driven Organization.* San Francisco, CA: Jossey-Bass.

Dasborough, M. T., & Ashkanasy, N. M. (2002). Emotion and attribution of intentionality in leader–member relationships. *The Leadership Quarterly, 13*(5), 615–634.

De Waal, F. (2009). *The Age of Empathy: Nature's Lessons for a Kinder Society.* New York, NY: Harmony Books.

Friedman, T. L. (2007). *The World Is Flat: A Brief History of the Twenty-First Century* (Rev. ed.) [Release 3.0]. New York, NY: Picador.

Goleman, D. (2006). *Social Intelligence: The New Science of Human Relationships.* New York, NY: Bantam Books.

Goleman, D. (2006). *Working with Emotional Intelligence.* New York, NY: Bantam Books.

Gordon, M. (2009). *Roots of Empathy: Changing the World Child by Child.* New York, NY: The Experiment.

Hallowell, E. M. (1998). *Worry: Hope and Help for a Common Condition.* New York, NY: Ballantine Books.

Hallowell, E. M. (2006). *Crazy Busy: Overstretched, Overbooked, and About to Snap!* New York, NY: Ballantine Books.

Hallowell, E. M. (2009, March). *Overloaded Circuits: Why Smart People Underperform* (HBR OnPoint Enhanced Edition) [Digital PDF]. Boston, MA: Harvard Business Review; originally published January, 2005.

Hallowell, E. M., & Ratey, J. J. (2006). *Delivered from Distraction: Getting the Most out of Life with Attention Deficit Disorder.* New York, NY: Ballantine Books.

Horn, A. (2010). *Gifts of Leadership: Team Building Through Focus and Empathy.* Toronto, Canada: BPS Books; Toronto, Canada: Stoddart (1997).

Humphrey, R. H. (2004). Empathy and authentic leadership. Presented at the inaugural 2004 summit of the Gallup Leadership Institute, Omaha, NE.

Humphrey, R. H., & Berthiaume, R. D. (1993). Job characteristics and biases in subordinates' appraisals of managers. *Basic and Applied Social Psychology 14*(4), 401–420.

Kellett, J. B., Humphrey, R. H., & Sleeth, R. G. (2006). Empathy and the emergence of task and relations leaders. *The Leadership Quarterly, 17,* 146-162.

Lencioni, P. (2008). *The Three Big Questions for a Frantic Family: A Leadership Fable About Restoring Sanity to the Most Important Organization in Your Life.* San Francisco, CA: Jossey-Bass.

Luthans, F., Wahl, L. K., & Steinhaus, C. S. (1992, Winter). The importance of social support for employee commitment. *Organizational Development Journal,* 1–10.

Mackay, H. (1999). *Dig Your Well Before You're Thirsty: The Only Networking Book You'll Ever Need.* New York, NY: Currency.

Martin, L. (2004). *Briefcase Moms: 10 Proven Practices to Balance Working Mothers' Lives.* Vancouver, B.C., Canada: Cornerview Press.

McGarvie, B. J. (2006). *Fit In, Stand Out: Mastering the FISO FACTOR–The Key to Leadership Effectiveness in Business and Life.* New York, NY: McGraw-Hill.

Mehrabian, A. (1980). *Silent Messages: Implicit Communication of Emotions and Attitudes.* Belmont, CA: Wadsworth.

Orem, S. L., Binkert, J., & Clancy, A. L. (2007). *Appreciative Coaching: A Positive Process for Change.* San Francisco, CA: Jossey-Bass.

Pink, D. H. (2006). *A Whole New Mind: Why Right-Brainers Will Rule the Future.* New York, NY: Riverhead Books.

Rifkin, J. (2010). *The Empathic Civilization: The Race to Global Consciousness in a World in Crisis.* Cambridge, England: Polity Press; Los Angeles, CA: Tarcher (2009).

RoAne, S. (2000). *How To Work a Room: The Ultimate Guide to Savvy Socializing in Person and Online.* New York, NY: HarperCollins.

Thiederman, S. (2008). *Making Diversity Work: 7 Steps for Defeating Bias in the Workplace* (Rev. ed.). New York, NY: Kaplan.

Zander, R. S., & Zander, B. (2002). *The Art of Possibility: Transforming Professional and Personal Life.* New York, NY: Penguin Books.

Web Resources

Appreciative Inquiry Commons, a great site for research, articles and tools: http://appreciativeinquiry.case.edu

Emotion Literacy Advocates™ features tools and articles to master emotional literacy: http://emolit.org/learningtools.html

Foundation of Economic Trends—Jeremy Rifkin's expertise on global economic and social trends: http://www.foet.org

Roots of Empathy, a Canadian-based foundation dedicated to building empathy in children and adults: http://www.rootsofempathy.org

Social Networking in Plain English—a short video on the power and process of social networking: http://www.commoncraft.com/video-social-networking

Chapter 9   Evolve

Bolles, R. N. (2010). *What Color Is Your Parachute? A Practical Manual for Job-Hunters and Career-Changers* (Rev. ed.). Berkeley, CA: Ten Speed Press.

Branham, L., & Hirschfeld, M. (2010). *Re-Engage: How America's Best Places to Work Inspire Extra Effort in Extraordinary Times*. New York, NY: McGraw-Hill.

Bridges, W. (1998). *Creating You & Co.: Learn to Think Like the CEO of Your Own Career*. Cambridge, MA: Perseus Books.

Buckingham, M. (2005). *The One Thing You Need to Know…About Great Managing, Great Leading, and Sustained Individual Success*. New York, NY: Free Press.

Citrin, J. M., & Smith, R. A. (2005). *The Five Patterns of Extraordinary Careers: The Guide for Achieving Success and Satisfaction*. New York, NY: Crown Business.

Dean, B. (2004, October). Persistence. *Coaching Toward Happiness Newsletter, 2*(22). Retrieved from http://www.coachingtowardhappiness.com/AHC/vol2num22.htm

Deci, E. L. (1971). Effects of externally mediated rewards on intrinsic motivation. *Journal of Personality and Social Psychology, 18*, 105-115.

Dyer, W. W. (2005). *The Power of Intention: Change the Way You Look at Things and Things You Look at Will Change*. Carlsbad, CA: Hay House.

Eisenberger, R., Kuhlman, D. M., & Cotterell, N. (1992). Effects of social values, effort training, and goal structure on task persistence. *Journal of Research in Personality, 26*(3), 258-272.

Eisenberger, R., & Selbst, M. (1994). Does reward increase or decrease creativity? *Journal of Personality and Social Psychology, 66*, 1116-1127.

Frankel, A., & Snyder, M. L. (1978). Poor performance following unsolvable problems: Learned helplessness or egotism? *Journal of Personality and Social Psychology, 36*, 1415-1423.

Frodsham, J., & Gargiulo, B. (2005). *Make It Work: Navigate Your Career Without Leaving Your Organization*. Mountain View, CA: Davies-Black.

Goldsmith, M., Lyons, L., & Freas, A. (Eds.). (2000). *Coaching for Leadership: How the World's Greatest Coaches Help Leaders Learn*. San Francisco, CA: Jossey-Bass.

Goldsmith, M., Robertson, A., Greenberg, C. L., & Hu-Chan, M. (2003). *Global Leadership: The Next Generation*. Upper Saddle River, NJ: FT-Prentice Hall.

Harackiewicz, J. M. (1979). The effects of reward contingency and performance feedback on intrinsic motivation. *Journal of Personality and Social Psychology, 37*(8), 1352-1363.

Hawkins, D. R. (2002). *Power vs. Force: The Hidden Determinants of Human Behavior*. Carlsbad, CA: Hay House; Sedona, AZ: Veritas (1995).

Hesselbein, F., & Goldsmith, M. (Eds.). (2006). *The Leader of the Future 2: Visions, Strategies, and Practices for the New Era.* San Francisco, CA: Jossey-Bass.

Leider, R. J. (2005). *The Power of Purpose: Creating Meaning in Your Life and Work* (2nd ed.). San Francisco, CA: Berrett-Koehler.

Leonard, T. J., Talley, L., & Coach U, Inc. (1997). *The Distinctionary: Let Language Evolve You.* CoachVille, LLC (coachville.com). Retrieved from http://www.distinctionary.com

Levinson, S., & Greider, P. C. (2007). *Following Through: A Revolutionary New Model for Finishing Whatever You Start* (2nd ed.). Bloomington, IN: Unlimited Publishing; New York, NY: Kensington (1998).

McClelland, D. C. (1998, September). Identifying competencies with behavioral-event interviews. *Psychological Science, 9*(5), 331-339.

Peterson, C., & Seligman, M. E. P. (2004). *Character Strengths and Virtues: A Handbook and Classification.* New York, NY: Oxford University Press.

Pink, D. H. (2006). *A Whole New Mind: Why Right-Brainers Will Rule the Future.* New York, NY: Riverhead Books.

Rao, S. S. (2005). *Are You Ready to Succeed? Unconventional Strategies for Achieving Personal Mastery in Business and Life.* New York, NY: Hyperion.

Shankman, M. L., & Allen, S. J. (2008). *Emotionally Intelligent Leadership: A Guide for College Students.* San Francisco, CA: Jossey-Bass.

Sloane, P. (2010). *How to Be a Brilliant Thinker: Exercise Your Mind and Find Creative Solutions.* London, England: Kogan Page Press.

Starnes, D. M., & Zinser, O. (1983). The effect of problem difficulty, locus of control, and sex on task persistence. *Journal of General Psychology, 108,* 249-255.

Sternbergh, B., Weitzel, S. R., & Center for Creative Leadership. (2001). *Setting Your Development Goals: Start with Your Values.* Greensboro, NC: CCL Press.

Watkins, M. (2003). *The First 90 Days: Critical Success Strategies for New Leaders at All Levels.* Boston, MA: Harvard Business School Press.

Williams, R., & Williams, V. (1998). *Anger Kills: Seventeen Strategies for Controlling the Hostility That Can Harm Your Health.* New York, NY: HarperPaperbacks.

Web Resources

Center for Creative Leadership, a renowned leadership development center: http://www.ccl.org

Core Dynamics of Conflicting Energy (training courses):
http://www.innerhumandesign.com

CPP, Inc. (professional development and leadership resources): https://www.cpp.com

Destination Innovation—innovation tools and trends by Paul Sloane, a leading author and speaker on innovation: http://www.destination-innovation.com

Marshall Goldsmith Library—the world's leading coach offers articles and trends: http://marshallgoldsmithlibrary.com

MentorCoach®—a virtual university that exclusively trains helping professionals to become coaches: http://www.mentorcoach.com

Social Networking in Plain English—a short video on the power and process of social networking: http://www.commoncraft.com/video-social-networking

Workforce Coach Institute—a global training and coaching firm whose mission is to bring humanity into the workplace: http://www.workforcecoachinstitute.com

Chapter 10   Reciprocity

Alba, J. (2009). *I'm on LinkedIn: Now What???* Cupertino, CA: Happy About.

Anand, R. (2010). Emotional intelligence and its relationship with leadership practices. *International Journal of Business and Management, 5*(2), 65-76.

Arbinger Institute. (2010). *Leadership and Self-Deception: Getting Out of the Box* (2nd ed.). San Francisco, CA: Berrett-Koehler.

Ashkanasy, N. M., Hartel, C. E. J., & Zerbe, W. J. (Eds.). (2000). *Emotions in the Workplace: Research, Theory, and Practice.* Westport, CT: Quorum Books.

Bacharach, S. B. (2006). *Get Them on Your Side.* Avon, MA: Platinum Press.

Bass, B., & Riggio, R. E. (2006). *Transformational Leadership* (2nd ed.). Mahwah, NJ: Erlbaum.

Boyatzis, R. E. (1982). *The Competent Manager: A Model for Effective Performance.* New York, NY: Wiley.

Boyatzis, R. E., & Goleman, D. (2009). *Social Intelligence and the Biology of Leadership* [Digital PDF]. Boston, MA: Harvard Business Review.

Brandon, R., & Seldman, M. (2004). *Survival of the Savvy: High-Integrity Political Tactics for Career and Company Success.* New York, NY: Free Press.

Cassara, L. (2004). *From Selling to Serving: The Essence of Client Creation.* Chicago, IL: Dearborn Trade.

Cherniss, C., & Adler, M. (2004). *Promoting Emotional Intelligence in Organizations: Guidelines to Help you Design, Implement, and Evaluate Effective Programs.* Alexandria,

VA: ASTD Press.

Cherniss, C., & Goleman, D. (Eds.). (2001). *The Emotionally Intelligent Workplace: How to Select For, Measure, and Improve Emotional Intelligence in Individuals, Groups, and Organizations*. San Francisco, CA: Jossey-Bass.

Clouse, R. W., & Spurgeon, K. L. (1995). Corporate analysis of humor. *Psychology: A Journal of Human Behavior, 32*, 1-24.

Cooperrider, D. L., & Whitney, D. (2005). *Appreciative Inquiry: A Positive Revolution in Change*. San Francisco, CA: Berrett-Koehler.

Crowley K., & Elster, K. (2009). *Working for You Isn't Working for Me: The Ultimate Guide to Managing Your Boss*. New York, NY: Portfolio.

Diener, E., Helliwell, J. F., & Kahneman, D. (2010). *International Differences in Well-Being*. New York, NY: Oxford University Press.

Dotlich, D., & Cairo, P. C. (2003). *Why CEOs Fail: The 11 Behaviors That Can Derail Your Climb to the Top and How to Manage Them*. San Francisco, CA: Jossey-Bass.

Druskat, V. U., & Wolff, S. R. (2009, March). *Building the Emotional Intelligence of Groups* (HBR OnPoint Enhanced Edition) [Digital PDF]. Boston, MA: Harvard Business Review.

Easterbrook, J. A. (1959). The effect of emotion on cue utilization and the organization of behavior. *Psychological Review, 66*(3), 183-201.

Epstein, S. (1990). Cognitive-experiential self-theory. In L. Pervin (Ed.), *Handbook of Personality Theory and Research* (pp. 165-192). New York, NY: Guilford Press.

Feldman, D. A. (1999). *The Handbook of Emotionally Intelligent Leadership: Inspiring Others to Achieve Results*. Paonia, CO: Leadership Performance Solutions Press.

Finkelstein, S. (2004). *Why Smart Executives Fail: And What You Can Learn from Their Mistakes*. New York, NY: Portfolio Trade.

Friedman, T. L. (2007). *The World Is Flat: A Brief History of the Twenty-first Century* (Rev. ed.) [Release 3.0]. New York, NY: Picador.

Frigda, N. H. (1988). The laws of emotion. *American Psychologist, 43*(5), 349–358.

Gardner, W. L., & Avolio, B. J. (1998). The charismatic relationship: A dramaturgical perspective. *Academy of Management Review, 23*(1), 32-58.

George, J. M. (1995). Leader positive mood and group performance: the case of customer service. *Journal of Applied Psychology, 25*(9), 778-794.

George, J. M. (2000). Emotions and leadership: The role of emotional intelligence. *Human Relations, 53*(8), 1027-1055. Retrieved from http://hum.sagepub.com/content/53/8/1027.abstract

Gerstner, C. R. & Day, D. V. (1997). Meta-analytic review of leader–member exchange theory: Correlates and construct issues. *Journal of Applied Psychology, 82*, 827–844.

Glanz, B. A. (1996). *Care Packages for the Workplace: Dozens of Little Things You Can Do to Regenerate Spirit at Work.* New York, NY: McGraw-Hill.

Goldsmith, M., Lyons, L., & Freas, A. (Eds.). (2000). *Coaching for Leadership: How the World's Greatest Coaches Help Leaders Learn.* San Francisco, CA: Jossey-Bass.

Goleman, D. (2006). *Social Intelligence: The New Science of Human Relationships.* New York, NY: Bantam Books.

Goleman, D., Boyatzis, R., & McKee, A. (2002). *Primal Leadership: Realizing the Power of Emotional Intelligence.* Boston, MA: Harvard Business School Press.

Gottman, J. (with Silver, N.). (1994). *Why Marriages Succeed or Fail...And How You Can Make Yours Last.* New York, NY: Fireside.

Graen, G. B., & Uhl-Bien, M. (1995). Relationship-based approach to leadership: Development of leader–member exchange (LMX) theory over 25 years: Applying a multi-level multi-domain perspective. *The Leadership Quarterly, 6*(2), 219–247.

Hochschild, A. R. (2003). The Managed Heart: Commercialization of Human Feeling (2oth Anniv. ed.). Berkeley: University of California Press.

Hunter, J. C. (1998). *The Servant: A Simple Story About the True Essence of Leadership.* Roseville, CA: Prima.

Isen, A. M., Daubman, K. A., & Nowiki, G. P. (1987). Positive affect facilitates creative problem solving. *Journal of Personal and Social Psychology, 52*(6), 1122-1131.

Katz, L., & Epstein, S. (1991). Constructive thinking and coping with laboratory induced stress. *Journal of Personal and Social Psychology, 61*, 789-800.

Katzenbach, J. R., & Smith, D. K. (2003). *The Wisdom of Teams: Creating the High-Performance Organization.* New York, NY: HarperBusiness; Boston, MA: Harvard Business School Press (1993).

Kawasaki, G. (2008). *Reality Check: The Irreverent Guide to Outsmarting, Outmanaging, and Outmarketing Your Competition.* New York, NY: Portfolio Press.

Kellerman, B. (2004). *Bad Leadership: What It Is, How It Happens, Why It Matters.* Boston, MA: Harvard Business School Press.

Keltner, D., Marsh, J., & Smith, J. A. (Eds.). (2010). *The Compassionate Instinct: The Science of Human Goodness.* New York, NY: W.W. Norton.

Kivland, C. M., & Nass, L. (2003). Emotional Intelligence in an Outcome-Based Environment:

Career Applications for Leadership, Team and Performance Success. *Career Planning and Adult Development Journal.*

Kleiner, A. (2003). *Who Really Matters: The Core Group Theory of Power, Privilege, and Success.* New York, NY: Currency.

Lee, B. (1998). *The Power Principle: Influence with Honor.* New York, NY: Fireside.

Lencioni, P. (1998). *The Five Temptations of a CEO: A Leadership Fable* (10th Anniv. ed.). San Francisco, CA: Jossey-Bass.

Lencioni, P. (2007). *The Three Signs of a Miserable Job: A Fable for Managers (and their employees).* San Francisco, CA: Jossey-Bass.

Lencioni, P. (2008). *The Five Dysfunctions of a Team: A Leadership Fable.* San Francisco, CA: Jossey-Bass.

Lipman-Blumen, J. (2006). *The Allure of Toxic Leaders: Why We Follow Destructive Bosses and Corrupt Politicians—And How We Can Survive Them.* New York, NY: Oxford University Press.

Mandler, G. (1975). *Mind and Emotion.* New York, NY: Wiley.

Martin, C., Dawson, P., & Guare, R. (2007). *Smarts: Are We Hardwired for Success?* New York, NY: AMACOM.

Mayer, J. D., & Salovey, P. (1997). What is emotional intelligence? In P. Salovey & D. Sluyter (Eds.). *Emotional Development and Emotional Intelligence: Implications for Educators* (pp. 3-31). New York, NY: Basic Books.

Morgan, H., Harkins, P., & Goldsmith, M. (Eds.). (2005). *The Art and Practice of Leadership Coaching: 50 Top Executive Coaches Reveal Their Secrets.* Hoboken, NJ: Wiley.

Orem, S. L., Binkert, J., & Clancy, A. L. (2007). *Appreciative Coaching: A Positive Process for Change.* San Francisco, CA: Jossey-Bass.

Patterson, K., Grenny, J., McMillan, R., & Switzler, A. (2002). *Crucial Conversations: Tools for Talking When Stakes Are High.* New York, NY: McGraw Hill.

Patterson, K., Grenny, J., McMillan, R., & Switzler, A. (2005). *Crucial Confrontations: Tools for Resolving Broken Promises, Violated Expectations and Bad Behavior.* New York, NY: McGraw-Hill.

Ping, D., & Clippard, A. (2005). *Quick-to-Listen Leaders: Where Life-Changing Ministry Begins.* Loveland, CO: Group.

Rafaeli, A., & Sutton, R. I. (1989). The expression of emotion in organizational life. In L.L. Cummings & B. M. Staw (Eds.), *Research in Organizational Behavior, 11,* 1-43.

Rath, T., & Clifton, D. O. (2009). *How Full Is Your Bucket: Positive Strategies for Work and Life*. New York, NY: Gallup Press.

Reina, D., & Reina, M. (2006). *Trust and Betrayal in the Workplace: Building Effective Relationships in Your Organization* (2nd ed.). San Francisco, CA: Berrett-Koehler.

RoAne, S. (2000). *How To Work a Room: The Ultimate Guide to Savvy Socializing in Person and Online*. New York, NY: HarperCollins.

Salovey, P., & Mayer, J. D. (1990). Emotional Intelligence. *Imagination, Cognition, and Personality, 9*(3), 185-211.

Salovey, P., Mayer, J. D., & Brackett, M. A. (Eds.). (2004). *Emotional Intelligence: Key Readings on the Mayer and Salovey Model*. Port Chester, NY: Dude.

Schneider, B., & Bowen, D. E. (1995). *Winning the Service Game*. Boston, MA: Harvard Business School Press.

Simon, H. A. (1982). Comments. In M. S. Clark and S. T. Fiske (Eds.), *Affect and Cognition* (pp. 333–342). Hillsdale, NJ: Erlbaum.

Spencer, L. M., & Spencer, S. M. (1993). *Competence at Work: Models for Superior Performance*. New York, NY: Wiley.

Wiskup, M. (2010). *Don't Be That Boss: How Great Communicators Get the Most Out of Their Employees and Careers*. Hoboken, NJ: Wiley.

Web Resources

Boris Epstein, CEO and Founder of BINC, a Professional Search Firm specializing in the software marketplace: http://www.askbinc.com

Cassara Clinic®—The Client Creator™ Process (emotional blueprint to attract clients): http://www.cassaraclinic.com

CPI Leadership Report (for leadership development and selection): https://www.cpp.com

Crucial Conversations, an excellent website for tools, books and training on engaging in crucial conversations: http://www.vitalsmarts.com

FeedForward Coaching Tool—Marshall Goldsmith's webcast and instructions on using this method: http://www.marshallgoldsmithfeedforward.com/html/FeedForward-Tool.htm

Gallup Organization, a research and polling organization on workforce trends and resources: http://www.gallup.com

Hay Group, for Emotional and Social Intelligence Inventory: http://www.haygroup.com

Leadership, and resolving problems created by self-deception: http://www.arbinger.com

Multifactor Leadership Questionnaire (Bernard M. Bass & Bruce J. Avolio)—the benchmark assessment for transformational leadership: http://www.mindgarden.com/products/mlq.htm

Positive Bucket (based on the book *How Full is Your Bucket*):
http://strengths.gallup.com

Positive Impact Test (Gallup's Organization Strengths website):
http://strengths.gallup.com

SHL Leadership Report, a Leadership Development Report based on the Occupational Personality Questionnaire and Core Leadership Competency (visit site for sample report):
http://www.smart2smarter.com

Why Smart Leaders Fail, by Cynthia Kivland: http://www.smart2smarter.com (Reciprocity)

Digital Reciprocity

100+ Smart Ways to Use LinkedIn:
http://www.linkedintelligence.com/smart-ways-to-use-linkedin

Social Media Footprint:
http://mashable.com/2009/04/08/social-media-recruitment

Videos

First, watch this (Twitter in Plain English):
http://www.youtube.com/watch?v=ddO9idmax0o

Second, watch this (Twitter Search in Plain English):
http://www.youtube.com/watch?v=jGbLWQYJ6iM

Social Bookmarking in Plain English:
http://www.commoncraft.com/bookmarking-plain-english

Social Networking in Plain English—a short video on the power and process of social networking: http://www.commoncraft.com/video-social-networking

Final Thoughts   The SMARTER Way to Bring Humanity Into the Workplace

Blanchard, K., & Bowles, S. (1998). *Gung Ho! Turn On the People in Any Organization.* New York, NY: William Morrow.

Costa, S. (2008). *Humanity at Work: Encouraging Spirit, Achievement and Truth to Flourish in the Workplace.* Chapel Hill, NC: Chapel Hill Press.

Takamine, K. (2002). *Servant-Leadership in the Real World: Re-Discovering Our Humanity in the Workplace*. Frederick, MD: PublishAmerica.

Web Resources

Humanity First: http://humanityfirst.org

Sylvie Lapointe—Organizational consultant and blogger, and owner of L2 Emergence: http://l2emergence.com/index.html

Index

About the Author

Cynthia Kivland M.Ed., Board Certified Coach, Master Career Counselor, and president of Smart2Smarter, a coaching and training firm. Cynthia has dedicated her practice to working with clients, leaders and teams to remove the obstacles that stand in the way of them being their personal best. She believes that it takes a new kind of "smarts" to achieve both career success and significance in the global economy. Cynthia holds advanced degrees, and is a Master Certified Counselor, Career Development Facilitator Instructor, Certified Talent and Leadership Coach, and Certified Online Course Instructor and Developer. She is also a member of Emonet, an international group of scholars and practitioners dedicated to knowledge and research about emotions in the workplace. As an international expert on emotional and social intelligence, Cynthia is sought after as a speaker, trainer and coach to help smart people become SMARTER.

www.Smart2Smarter.com

smart*2* SMARTER

47585992R00138

Made in the USA
Charleston, SC
10 October 2015